Around and About

Memoirs of a South African Newspaperman

——— MICHAEL GREEN ———

davidphilip

First published in 2004 in southern Africa by
David Philip Publishers, an imprint of New Africa Books (Pty) Ltd
99 Garfield Road, Claremont 7700, South Africa
www.newafricabooks.co.za

© in text: Michael Green
© in published work: New Africa Books (Pty) Ltd

ISBN 0 86486 660 7

Cover and text design: Fresh Identity
Project manager: Karen van Eden
Editor: Jennifer Stastny

Typeset in 11 pt (Times) by Fresh Identity
Printed and bound by MSP Print

Cover picture by newspaper cartoonist Jack Leyden.

CONTENTS

Foreword

In the glory that was Greece and the grandeur that was Rome, life expectancy was about 25; that is to say, on average every baby born could expect to live for 25 years. Lack of sanitation, ignorance about proper health care, and a good deal of violent behaviour accounted for the early deaths, especially of infants. If one got past childhood, the prospects of a reasonable life span were, of course, somewhat improved. But even the great and powerful did not usually survive for long. Alexander the Great, conqueror of the world as it was known at that time, was 33 when he died in 323 BC after eating and drinking too much at a banquet. Cleopatra, queen of Egypt, was 39 when she committed suicide by clasping the asp to her bosom. The Roman emperor Nero was 31 when he, too, committed suicide; his method was to cut his throat.

The pattern of early deaths continued into less violent times. One has only to consider the greatest figures in music and literature: Mozart was 35 when he died in 1791. Schubert was 31, Chopin 39, Mendelssohn 38, Schumann 46, and we are now into the mid-nineteenth century. Keats died of tuberculosis at the age of 26. Robert Burns was 37 when he had one drink too many with the boys, fell asleep by the roadside and died of rheumatic fever. Byron was 36 when he died of something called marsh fever while he was involved in a liberation war in Greece. Beethoven, deaf as a doorpost, lived to 57 and was regarded as venerable.

Today, in the developed economies of Europe, North America, Japan and Australasia, average life expectancy is approaching the 80 mark. Infant mortality is very low and modern medicine cures a great many illnesses that used to be fatal; heart disease for example. Each of us has four grandparents. My four are all buried in the Woltemade cemetery in Cape Town, and not one of them reached the age of 60. The last died in 1937. The illnesses that killed them are curable today. Many of their own children lived into their eighties and nineties.

Philosophical musings like these are, I suspect, very much the habit of those for whom the years are advancing. You don't worry much about life expectancy when you're 20 years old. At 70-plus it's a different story. At one of the social gatherings I attend regularly, the conversation often takes a familiar pattern. 'I hear that Jackson's losing his sight.' 'Wilson died last Sunday; thrombie.' One of the more mournful characters says that if you're over the age of 70 and you wake up without any aches and pains you know that you're dead. A former colleague of mine, much older than me, said in a recent letter: 'There is absolutely nothing to commend old age.'

Well, there is memory. One should look forward in life, but there is enjoyment in looking back, too – and there may be instruction as well. It is easy to romanticise things past, and to forget about the ugly and inconvenient and unpleasant aspects of everyday life in an earlier era. We switch on the lights and turn on the tap without thinking what it was like, not so very long ago, without these amenities. I think that the flush lavatory, with water-borne sewage, is the greatest invention of the modern era; the work of a Victorian gentleman named Thomas Crapper, whose name enriched the English language, albeit impolitely.

So I do not underestimate the virtues of the present. But at the same time, one can look fondly back to many of the experiences and values of the past. This is why I have tried to set down some of my recollections from a life that has not been adventurous or even particularly exciting but has, I think, been interesting and varied.

I have been a journalist in South Africa for more than 55 years. In retirement I continue to write for two publications, about wine and music and general affairs. My career as a full-time newspaperman covered 45 years. For twenty of those years, I was an editor, of three different papers – one morning, one afternoon and one Sunday. For another ten years, I was a deputy editor.

Those were rough times in which to run a newspaper, with editors continually harassed by a government that disliked any criticism and introduced a battery of menacing laws in an attempt to stifle its critics. Even the normal problem of trying to meet the needs of readers was magnified by the diverse, uneven and sometimes hostile nature of South African society. Some people thought that we, the English-language press, were too soft on the Nationalist government and pointed approvingly to papers that had been closed down (to which, of course, we replied that it was better to have some voice than none). Others thought we were communists, agitators, troublemakers. And amid all this tugging and pulling one had to try to fulfil the basic duty of any newspaper, which was and is to tell the truth as fully and fairly as possible. One also had to try to keep the newspaper solvent. Politically independent newspapers do not survive if they make consistent losses.

But of course there were also plenty of good times, and I have tried to describe some of these in this collection of memories. It is a story of the old South Africa, not the new. I retired in 1992, two years before the first democratic elections. I believe that with all its difficulties and dangers and risks, the new South Africa is infinitely preferable to the old one, and that also goes for people like myself who are conventionally regarded as having been 'privileged' (as I started work at the age of seventeen, I don't think I was especially privileged).

But not everything in the old South Africa was bad, and I hope that those who read these pages will agree with that statement. The personae are mainly white people, but remember, this is the South Africa of half a century ago, when the black population was less than half the size it is now and when contact between various groups was restricted by history, geography, prejudice, fear and other factors, including laws imposed by a race-obsessed government.

This book is not an autobiography. I am not important enough or interesting enough for that. It is a memoir. I have tried to write as a competent reporter should, about other people, not about myself. There are some details about my own background and the circumstances of my newspaper career. But the interesting people are the others.

I have written this account almost entirely from memory. In retirement, I do not have recourse to newspaper files and editorial libraries. But it is as accurate as I can make it.

The title of this book, *Around and About*, was suggested by my old friend David Philip, who thought, correctly in my view, that it reflected the discursive and informal nature of the contents.

Michael Green
Durban
2004

ONE

The colonial town

Astrology is defined in the Oxford dictionary as being the art of judging the reputed occult influence of stars, planets, etc. on human affairs. It is an ancient art that originated in Mesopotamia about five thousand years ago and was absorbed into many advanced cultures of the past, such as those of Greece, Rome, India and China. Today the sceptics probably far outnumber the believers, as they have most likely done since Nicolaus Copernicus demonstrated in 1530 that the Sun, not the Earth, was the centre of our planetary system.

Nevertheless, it is because of the demands of astrology that I know the exact time of my birth, 10.15 am on a Friday morning a long time ago, in Sister Snow's nursing home in Fort Street, Bulawayo, Southern Rhodesia. About 55 years after this not particularly memorable day at Sister Snow's, my life had taken some unexpected turns. A friend of mine was a professional astrologer; for an appropriate fee she would consider the stars and chart your destiny. She offered me a detailed forecast as a birthday gift, and I accepted; dull would be he of soul who could resist the temptation to look at what the stars foretell.

She told me that a vital piece of data for her calculations was the precise hour of my birth, so, somewhat shame-faced, I obtained the information from my mother. When my friend produced her report on my prospects, it took the form of a circular chart covered with cryptic figures and a lengthy written analysis headed Sun Taurus, Moon Libra and Cancer Ascendant (Pluto in First House). The report contained plenty of the pleasant generalities usually associated with fortune-telling (not a phrase favoured by astrologers) and predicted, inter alia, that I would have a reasonably successful and happy life.

Perhaps all this sounds rather trivial. Let me tell you about Patric Walker. If the name seems familiar it is because he is – or was – probably the best-known newspaper astrologer in Britain. For a long time the *Daily News*, the Durban newspaper of which I was editor for fifteen years, published his column daily. I used to read it occasionally, amused to think that some people would take all this seriously.

Then the column failed to appear for two or three days. What drew my attention to the omission was an instant flood of letters from enraged readers. In a long newspaper career, I can think of no topic that drew so big a correspondence in so short a time.

I asked the paper's arts editor, Sjoerd Meijer, why the column had not appeared. It was sent by airmail from London, he said, (these were pre-computer days) and there had been a hiccup in the deliveries. Please don't let it happen again, I entreated him. A couple of years later, there was a similar lapse in the delivery service. Meijer and his colleagues went to the old newspaper files and clipped out what Patric Walker's stars had foretold five years before. These items went into the paper for several days and there wasn't a word of complaint.

The Bulawayo in which I was born was a quaint little colonial society. Cecil John Rhodes, after whom the country had been named, had been dead for only 28 years and many of the older white people still referred respectfully to 'Mr Rhodes'. On Rhodes's birthday, 5 July, the Rhodes and Founders public holiday in the old Rhodesia, most men wore a sprig of blue plumbago in their lapels; the plumbago was Rhodes's favourite flower.

Bulawayo had a white population of about 10 000 and a black population of perhaps three times that number. No doubt there were interracial tensions but I as a child was totally unaware of them. My dearest friend was Henry, surname forgotten, who came from Inyazura in the eastern part of the country and worked for my parents for nearly fifteen years.

My father did an office job in the Rhodesia Railways headquarters in Bulawayo, owned a house, ran a car, played golf at weekends, drank whisky and belonged to the local Masonic lodge. My mother did not work; her time was occupied with golf, bridge, tea parties and looking after my younger brother and myself. All this on a modest income. An uneven society, for sure, but a land of milk and honey for the lucky ones.

I went to the Milton junior and senior schools, named not after the author of *Paradise Lost* but after Sir William Milton, administrator of Southern Rhodesia in the early colonial days, from 1898 to 1914. Milton was run on the lines of an English public school: Latin, Greek, rugby, cricket, housemasters, hymns at assembly, and prefects who were allowed to cane fags. As a concession to the hot climate, the school uniform was blue shirts and khaki shorts. No blazers were required, but school ties and long stockings were compulsory. On Sundays we sweated our way to church in long grey flannels, blazers, white shirts, ties and straw hats.

One of the boys at Milton before my time was a chubby-faced lad named Hendrik Frensch Verwoerd, of whom more anon.

Needless to say, the pupils were all white children. Nevertheless, the standard of education given to what was then a fairly small black population was surprisingly high, thanks largely to the efforts of the churches. Mr Robert Mugabe and his political friends may have odd ideas about how to run a country and an economy, but they nearly all speak remarkably good and articulate English, as South African radio and television listeners must have noticed. The legacy of a good educational system.

I sang in the Anglican church choir. The choirmaster was one of our schoolteachers, a bald man named Pop Downing, who had the gift of perfect pitch (Mozart had it too) and liked showing it off in a harmless way. 'Right, Mr Organist,' he would call from the choir stalls to the organ loft above. 'Let's start with A flat. Baaaaaaa.' The organist would play the note. Our choirmaster was right every time.

One of the clergymen whom we encountered was a severe and unsmiling man who preached eloquent, powerful and cheerless sermons. Years later, when I was living in Cape Town, I saw his name in the newspapers. By then he was in charge of a mission station and had been convicted of molesting children.

A decade or two later, I was working in Bloemfontein and, in the course of some research, came across contemporary accounts of the misfortunes of the first bishop of Bloemfontein, in the late nineteenth century. He, too, became overly fond of children and had to beat a hasty retreat over the Free State border, into the Cape Colony, to avoid prosecution. Today, in the early 21st century, revelations about this kind of behaviour, in various parts of the world, have become depressingly frequent. The French, in their pleasantly cynical way, describe homosexuality as the English clergyman's disease.

Bulawayo was nothing if not secure, to use one of the buzzwords of the modern era. Because of the town's flat terrain and short distances, the bicycle was a much-favoured means of transport. Every child rode one to school and every school was equipped with large bicycle sheds. We debated at length the merits of Hercules, Raleigh and Humber bicycles, and any boy who had a racing-style bike, with backbreakingly low handlebars, was the envy of all.

Every Friday evening, I would ride by bike a couple of kilometres to meetings of the Wolf Cubs. It was dark, I was ten years old, and I didn't have a care in the world. Some cyclists had a headlight powered by a dynamo fitted to the rear wheel. I could not indulge in such luxuries. My light was a candle in a square corned-beef tin from which the top had been removed. This was attached to the handlebar. The flickering flame, protected by the surrounding tin, was adequate warning to other road users that a juvenile cyclist was abroad.

Because my father was a railways employee, he had substantial concessions on train travel. Every year we would go by train to Cape Town, which was home to both my parents, for a four-week seaside holiday with our car, a Chevrolet, on an open truck at the back of the train, protected by a tarpaulin. The fast train took three days and two nights to cover the 3 000 kilometres between Bulawayo and Cape Town, and I became an expert on the stations en route: places like Figtree, Francistown, Fourteen Streams, Warrenton, Touwsrivier, De Doorns and Konstabel are stamped indelibly on my memory. Many of these stations were no more than low sandy platforms populated by poorly clothed black children offering wooden giraffes, elephants, crocodiles for sale to the passengers.

The train was hauled by a steam engine, two in the mountains of the Western Cape, and on a long curve one could lean out of the window and have a splendid view of a spectacle that today is almost forgotten: a huge Garratt locomotive at full steam pulling twenty passenger coaches at about 70 kilometres an hour.

The romance of steam was a very real thing, sullied only by the smoke grit that came through the windows, blackening sheets, pillows and fingernails. After three days, we all needed a bath. Trains in those days did not have showers, and we had to make do with what my mother called a cat's lick in the fold-down washbasin in the compartment.

The true glory of train travel was the dining saloon: long menus, low windows, ceiling fans, heavy embossed cutlery, leather upholstery and immaculate stewards (one would not have dared to call them waiters). These have now been replaced, alas, by canteen-style food and service, except of course on the Blue Train. But in those far-off days every long-distance passenger train was like the Blue Train.

TWO ——

The old Cape

C ape Town was, and still is, a kind of ancestral home to me, though I have not lived there for more than 40 years. My roots in South Africa go fairly deep. My father's father, John Harold Green, came here in 1878. His family had lived for a long time in Lambeth, London, on the south bank of the Thames. I learned something about them through the efforts of a cousin of mine, Francis Crawford. Francis grew up and worked for a time in east Africa; his father, Sir Frederick Crawford, was married to my father's sister and was one of the last colonial governors of Uganda.

Francis has lived most of his life in the United States and many years ago took the unusual step (for my family) of embracing the Mormon faith, the Church of Jesus Christ of Latter-day Saints. Apparently, Mormons believe that the ultimate path to Heaven is eased if one compiles a record of one's ancestors, hence a great Mormon interest in genealogy. Francis sought my help in connection with some family members and eventually rewarded me by sending me a family tree dating back to the early eighteenth century, with births, deaths, baptisms and marriages as recorded in church registers.

John Harold Green, my grandfather, was born in Lambeth in 1861 and came to South Africa in 1878, in the company of his slightly older brother, to join the Natal Mounted Police as a trooper. He served in the Anglo-

Zulu War of 1879 and had part of one finger removed by a Zulu assegai. As the Zulus hung on to their spears and did not throw them, this must have involved some close combat. In later years, he would show the damaged hand to his young children and explain mournfully that when he came to South Africa he was so poor and hungry that one day he just chewed his finger off.

After the war, he joined the Cape Town Fire Brigade and then moved to Walvis Bay, then spelled Walfisch Bay, which was a British enclave in German South-West Africa. He was one of the first white settlers in that desolate area and ran a trading store and fishing boats. He married the daughter of a trader and hunter, an Irishman named Gunning, and produced five children. The oldest, Angus Percy Green, known throughout his life as Apie, was born in 1894 and seems to have been the first white child born at Walvis Bay. He was awarded the Military Cross in World War I, captained the Villagers rugby team in Cape Town and became a well-known businessman.

Life at Walvis Bay was disrupted by the outbreak of World War I in 1914. Threatened by a German military advance on the village, the handful of local whites was removed by a British warship to Cape Town, where most of them remained for good.

My father was born in 1903 in Mossel Bay, where his mother had gone for the confinement. Mossel Bay was also the home of my grandfather's brother, Robert Shedden Green, his fellow trooper in the Natal Mounted Police. He was a veteran of the famous battle of Rorke's Drift, where a British garrison of about 150 men held a Zulu impi of 3 000 at bay and were later rewarded with eleven Victoria Crosses, a record for one engagement. Robert Shedden Green was wounded by a stray bullet fired by an inaccurate Zulu warrior. After the war, he settled at Mossel Bay, ran a shop there and became well known in the town as 'our Rorke's Drift man'.

In 1956, while on a visit to Mossel Bay, I met his widow, who was very old. Imagine meeting the widow of a man who fought at Rorke's Drift! His daughter was alive until recently, and his grandson, Dr Glen Shedden Green, an engineer, lives in Sydney, Australia. Dr Glen Shedden Green was a founding member of the South African nuclear research team based at Pelindaba, near Pretoria, but during a decade of work there he developed serious misgivings about the programme and about the then government, and he migrated to Australia in 1971.

My father, one of five children, spent many years in Rhodesia. His brother went to Johannesburg. Two of his sisters went to east Africa and married people who became prominent: Sir Frederick Crawford, the Ugandan governor; and Lieutenant-Colonel Gerald Ainslie, a lawyer in Kenya. A third sister spent most of her life in England. They all died at the Cape, with the exception of one who died quite young and is buried in Uganda. Homing pigeons.

My mother's father, Henry Weston Allkin, was a Lancashireman who came to Cape Town in the 1880s. He worked in a bicycle shop at Wynberg, eventually bought the shop and then graduated to cars, becoming a pioneer of the infant South African motor industry. He was the first importer of Dodge cars from the United States and Fiat cars from Italy, and today I have a silver cigarette box presented to him in the 1920s by the Fiat company in Turin.

He owned racehorses and had some success on the racetrack. His house in Bushwood Road, Mowbray, is still standing, but the extensive site that was occupied by his stables has long since been subdivided for further houses.

My quite idyllic youth in the fledgling Rhodesia ended when I was thirteen years old and our family moved to Cape Town. My father was a victim of Parkinson's Disease, an extraordinary affliction that seems to be rather rare nowadays but was fairly common half a century ago. It is defined as a chronic disorder of the central nervous system, leading to physical slowness, tremors, paralysis and muscular rigidity.

The most common cause 60 or 70 years ago was, I understand, a particular type of encephalitis, which itself is an inflammation of the brain caused by a virus. Towards the end of World War I, in 1918, an exceptionally virulent form of influenza swept around the world, a disaster that is almost forgotten today. This Spanish Flu, as it was called, ranks with the Black Death, the dreaded plague of the Middle Ages, as the most destructive epidemic in history – until the arrival of AIDS in the 1980s. In 1918 and 1919, an estimated 30 million people died of the

Spanish Flu in every part of the world, far more than were killed in the war, and it is reckoned that more than 50 times that number were ill at some time or another. In India, 12 500 000 people are said to have been killed by the influenza, and more than half a million died in the United States.

South Africa did not escape, though the fatalities here were relatively few. Here and elsewhere, some of those who recovered from the influenza later became ill with an apparently mild form of encephalitis, a fever with some facial paralysis that was cured within a week or two. In some cases, alas, the virus lurked dormant for years before emerging as Parkinson's Disease. Thus a fairly large number of people of my father's generation, born about the turn of the century, became Parkinson's sufferers. Sailor Malan, the World War II air ace who later led the Torch Commando in street protests against the Nationalist government in South Africa, was one; Sister Kenney, a celebrated figure in Australian nursing, was another; Henry Herrmann, well known in Cape Town as a property auctioneer, was yet another. The novelist Arthur Koestler and the famous American photographer Margaret Bourke-White were also victims of Parkinson's.

My father contracted encephalitis in 1919, when he was a boy of sixteen, and soon recovered. About fifteen years later, the signs of Parkinson's appeared. By the time he was 40, he could not continue working, which is why he left Bulawayo for Cape Town. He lived for another 36 years. His physical handicaps – an almost paralysed left arm and left leg, badly slurred speech and restricted use of his right arm and leg – gradually worsened, and in the last few years he was mobile only in a wheelchair. His mental functions remained unimpaired. So did his sense of humour.

There are always blessings; one has only to count them. My father's illness might have been viewed by outsiders as a tragedy, a sadness or a burden. To us it was a fact of life. I remember as a young man receiving commiserations from a Cape Town city councillor, Sydney East, who had just learned from a mutual friend about my father's disabilities. 'It must be tough for you,' he said sympathetically. I was indignant. 'It's nothing of the sort,' I replied.

Nor was it. With his patience and humour and commonsense, my father set an example for all of us. Everybody liked him. Most people, I think, admired him. Children loved him, especially his four grandchildren. I think he was a crucial factor in shaping the characters of my own two children. It helps to learn to care about people at an early age. All being well, it becomes a habit ingrained for a lifetime. Whatever deficiencies my children may or may not have, no one would, I think, accuse them of being uncaring.

My parents had sufficient capital and income to buy a smallholding at Hout Bay, with a comfortable house and a beautiful garden in which my father grew, for sale, dahlias and hydrangeas, violets and freesias, strawberries and mushrooms. He had a staff of one, a Xhosa man who learnt, over the years, to prune hydrangeas expertly, divide dahlia bulbs to get the maximum of new plants, lay irrigation pipes (the property was served with water by a mountain stream), tend to Muscovy ducks (which for some obscure reason he always called Donald ducks) and perform the hundred and one other tasks necessary in a place like this.

My brother and I were sent to private schools, not the most expensive ones, but good ones. I went to Christian Brothers' College at Green Point, which closed down about 70 years after its establishment. In our matric class of 1946, about fifteen of the 27 boys passed first-class. This was the Joint Matriculation Board examination, which was considerably more difficult than the Senior Certificate exam written at most schools. My contemporaries at CBC were a rather motley crowd, I think. One of them, Stuart Saunders, became principal of the University of Cape Town; another, John Whitmore, became famous for his surfboards. Bob Steyn became a lawyer, a journalist and eventually the registrar of the South African Media Council. Harvey Ward became a journalist and then a controversial political broadcaster in Ian Smith's Rhodesia. David Bloomberg became the mayor of Cape Town. Robin Thorne achieved instant fame by clean bowling Len Hutton for five runs when the MCC played Border at East London on their 1948–49 tour of South Africa.

In those days, Hout Bay was a community of small farmers, retired people, artists, fishermen and a few affluent individuals who drove to town in smart cars. The rest of us took what must have been the slowest bus in the Cape Peninsula, an ancient Railways Road Service vehicle that took about an hour and a quarter for the journey, travelling up the Hout Bay valley, through Constantia to Wynberg, then all the way along Main Road into Cape Town. One of the two drivers on this route was a man named Trautmann, a member of a long-established Hout Bay family whose name is remembered in Trautmann's Cottages, the little holiday resort at the foot of Chapman's Peak.

The slow bus had its compensations. I read copiously as it crawled to and from Hout Bay, mainly books from the South African Public Library in the Cape Town Gardens. It was, in a sense, an education.

Among the better-known citizens of Hout Bay was Cecil James Sibbett, who was born in Ireland in 1881, came to Cape Town in 1897, founded an advertising agency, and for a year was assistant political secretary to Cecil John Rhodes, an experience that appears to have been the high point of his long life. He died aged 86. Sibbett was best known as the founder of the National Thrift Organisation, of which he was chairman for 40 years, but the Rhodes connection was the one he valued. Mount Rhodes was the name he chose for his big property on the western slopes of the Hout Bay valley. That is still its name, but the place is now an upmarket housing estate. In Sibbett's day, the property was conspicuous for a splendid plantation of silver trees, and some of them are still there today.

Another prominent local was Dr S H Skaife. Stacey Skaife was one of South Africa's most distinguished biologists, an authority on, among other things, bees and ants. He had a wide audience because he was a skilled radio broadcaster. He was also, improbably, a writer of Afrikaans crime stories. He and his wife lived in a house high above the old Hout Bay Hotel golf course. They had tame, or partly tame, peacocks, and guests had to be careful; if you turned your back on a peacock it was quite likely to give you a sharp nip on the backside.

The Skaifes' neighbour was Andrew Porter, who was a dentist in Cape Town for many years. His wife was a member of the Sedgwick family, who have been connected with the Cape wine and liquor industry for more than a century. His son, also Andrew Porter, became a distinguished music critic in London. Other members of his family are well known in the motor industry in Cape Town.

Harold van Hoogstraaten, later a member of parliament, was chairman of the ratepayers' association.

Another resident was Cyril Hall, then a judge of the Cape Supreme Court and later a judge of appeal. Hall was known in the legal profession as 'Foxy', a reference to his somewhat vulpine appearance. He was a curious case. He was born in an English country vicarage, came to South Africa as a child, married the daughter of an Afrikaans Nationalist senator, and became a staunch supporter of the Nationalist Party at a time when it was hardly respectable for an English speaker to adopt such a position.

As a young newspaper reporter, I ran foul of Mr Justice Hall when he put into practice his belief in the principles of apartheid. He travelled very occasionally on the Hout Bay bus. He did not know me but I knew who he was. Those days, the early 1950s, saw the beginnings of the policy of racial segregation, and on the Hout Bay bus the front section was reserved for white people by means of a moveable 'Whites Only' sign clipped to the overhead luggage racks. Coloured and black people sat at the back.

On one occasion, the 5.30 pm bus became crowded when it reached Wynberg and the Coloured passengers spilled out of their mini-homeland at the back and stood in the passageway at the front. Judge Hall, who was sitting on the aisle, became restive and told the bus conductor that 'these people' should not be there. The conductor, a spirited young white man, said that the Coloured passengers also wanted to get home and that the next bus was at 11.00 pm. The judge asked the conductor for his name and staff number, which were given. And few days later I learned that the conductor had been transferred from the relative comfort of the Hout Bay route to the job of loading freight at Lynedoch station near Stellenbosch.

I wrote a report for the *Cape Argus* newspaper about this, calling the complainant The Man in the Grey Hat and not identifying him beyond saying that he was an important person. I think that these days a newspaper would say exactly who was involved, but we were more careful in those days in what we said about Supreme Court judges. The report caused considerable debate in Cape Town, and of course the subject of it knew soon enough that I was the author.

We never exchanged one word, but a little time later I reported a Supreme Court case that followed a clash between the police and Sailor Malan's Torch Commando outside the Houses of Parliament. The presiding judge was Mr Justice Hall. The press bench was very close to the judicial bench, and every now and then he would glance at me with less than total affection.

The feeling in Cape Town, incidentally, was very much on the side of the bus conductor and the passengers he was trying to protect. So much for the political canard that ordinary white South Africans all supported apartheid and that none of them opposed it.

Hout Bay's artistic community included the sculptor Ivan Mitford-Barberton, who created the bronze leopard that still stands on a rock at the southern end of the Hout Bay beach, and Terence McCaw, a landscape painter of rare charm and distinction.

Like most rural communities, Hout Bay had its share of eccentrics. One was an elderly man named Boonzaaier, uncle of the artist Gregoire Boonzaaier. He used to walk a couple of kilometres to our property, Longacre (in the Hout Bay Valley, about five kilometres from the sea), to play draughts with my father, an activity that did not always appeal to the latter.

A man named Brink, a retired schoolmaster, was another frequent and unannounced visitor. He would come to collect sacks of acorns from our oak trees, which he used to feed his pigs. In return, he would leave numerous anti-communist pamphlets, which my father found as unexciting as the draughts.

In our extensive garden there was a small cottage that was, for a time, occupied by Uncle Cecil, my mother's brother. Uncle Cecil was rotund and jolly and gay, though nobody used that term then. In those days a gay bachelor meant a man about town, not a homosexual. Uncle Cecil was well-spoken and well-dressed. He had been educated at St Andrew's College at Grahamstown, after which his father, perceiving that this son was not an intellectual giant, had fixed him up with a job in the Shell Company, the sort of thing that should lead to a comfortable and unchallenging minor managership 30 years later. But his father, my grandfather, died three years later, leaving Uncle Cecil a fair sum. He promptly resigned his job, sailed off to the United States, lived it up in New York, becoming friendly with a multimillionaire named Wrigley, who made chewing gum, and returned to South Africa after eighteen months more or less penniless.

Fortunately for him, his father had had the foresight to tie up most of his inheritance in an untouchable trust, providing him with a modest income that kept him going until the end of his life at the age of 80. He chopped and changed jobs with startling frequency, working as an insurance salesman, ship's steward, barman, bookseller, poultry farmer and, eventually, rich old lady's companion, but he always remained financially afloat.

Uncle Cecil used to take me to concerts. He had played the double bass in his school orchestra, and he considered himself something of a jazz pianist, having taken lessons at the Felix de Cola school of music in Cape Town. He was a terrible player. His method was to strike a few recognisable chords of his favourite piece, *September in the Rain*, and then bang away aimlessly in what he described as 'rhapsodisation'. At concerts, he would adopt an extremely critical attitude to any pianist who performed, no matter how distinguished he or she might be. As some international celebrity gave a magisterial performance of Brahms or Beethoven or Schumann, Uncle Cecil would hiss loudly, 'Mistakes, mistakes.' Those sitting near him looked bemused, amused, or just cross.

Uncle Cecil had a friend named George who was also a bachelor and who in the fullness of time surprised everybody by getting married. George was a real pianist; he had studied music and had aspirations to be a concert musician. Alas, he was continually distracted by other matters – he appeared to be fairly wealthy and travelled a good deal – but at the age of about 45, he decided to take up the piano seriously again. He moved a piano into our cottage in the garden and drove over every day, and often in the evening, from Rondebosch, where he lived, to practise in the peace and solitude of the Hout Bay valley. The sound was not obtrusive, but we could hear him, practising with painstaking slowness as recommended by every piano teacher in the world.

He spent months working on Chopin's *Etude (Study) in C sharp minor, Op 10, No. 4*, an exceptionally difficult and complex piece that is intended to be played with great rapidity (the composer marked it 'presto'). At the end of this period, it was no better or faster than it was when he started. I had played this study, hesitantly and badly (and too slowly), from time to time, but George's efforts made the music intimately familiar to us all. My father averred that our gardener used to sing the tune as he pruned and mowed and cleaned; surely the first Xhosa gardener to sing Chopin on his rounds. After some months, George seemed to become bored with the whole business. He took his piano away and we heard no more of the Chopin *Etude*. Meanwhile, at our piano in the house, Uncle Cecil was still thundering away in the evenings with *September in the Rain*, rhapsodised.

My father's favourite acquaintance was unquestionably a man named David, a member of the (so-called, if you like) Coloured community. He was a cheerful fellow who did odd jobs and owned a battered old Ford, held together in part with wire and string. He would call when the *snoek* were running in Hout Bay, and my father would – with considerable nimbleness, considering his physical disabilities – climb into the passenger seat, assisted by shoves and grunts from David. With my father holding on for dear life they would rattle off at high speed (David was seldom sober), returning in triumph an hour or so later with *snoek* that had cost very little. After these exertions, David would be invited into the sitting room of our house and given a tumbler full of Kimberley Club sherry. He would knock it off at one gulp and depart.

Crayfish were usually a shilling (twenty cents) each at the Hout Bay harbour. Almost every Sunday afternoon, a dozen of my young friends, men and women, would visit Longacre. After tea and tenniquoits on the lawn (some of the amorous antics persuaded me to rename it 'tennicoitus') my mother would serve a crayfish mayonnaise buffet for perhaps fifteen people. We were not rich. It was an affordable luxury then.

After beer and supper, we would gather around the piano and sing favourite items from the musicals of the time, me at the keyboard, with the words on the musical score in front of me, for the singers. *Oklahoma*, *Annie Get Your Gun*, *South Pacific* and, a little later, *My Fair Lady* and *The Sound of Music*. Am I alone in thinking that tunes aren't what they used to be? After half a century, I can well remember dozens of melodies from those old shows, and I still play them today, from music that has become a little tattered round the edges. But I cannot remember a single tune from *Moulin Rouge* and *Chicago*, to mention two big musicals that I have seen as films in recent years.

And do people sing at home today? I doubt it. Television seems to have put an end to self-entertainment at home, which is a pity. There really is no substitute for doing something yourself, no matter how badly, whether it's playing tennis, playing a musical instrument or just singing.

Among the youthful visitors to my parental home at Hout Bay were Aubrey Sussens, later to become the godfather of the public relations industry in South Africa; Pat Tebbutt, later a Supreme Court judge; Alan Scholefield, who became a well-known novelist; Maxwell Leigh, Brian Barrow and Glynn Croudace, Cape Town journalists and authors; William Papas, who became an internationally known artist and cartoonist; and many others who later made an impact in the world.

THREE

The beginnings of apartheid

Having matriculated at the age of sixteen, I spent some months learning shorthand and typing, then a prerequisite for a job as a journalist, and in 1947 joined the *Cape Argus* in Cape Town as a cadet reporter, aged seventeen years and three months. Much too young, really. In later years, I preferred to hire job applicants with university degrees for the obvious reason that they were better educated and more mature. Nevertheless, many journalists of my generation started work young and emerged none the worse for it, among them editors such as Harvey Tyson of *The Star* in Johannesburg, the late Tertius Myburgh of the *Sunday Times*, Andrew Drysdale of the *Cape Argus*, and Rex Gibson, last editor of the now defunct *Rand Daily Mail*.

Note that these are all English-language journalists. The Afrikaans papers insisted on university degrees, and many of their journalists used their jobs as stepping stones to higher things, usually in politics. Among my youthful contemporaries, for example, Hennie Smit and Louis Stofberg became members of parliament, and various others became important people in the public service, the South African Broadcasting Corporation and the judiciary. *Die Burger* in Cape Town, the establishment Afrikaans paper, was the principal processor. The most celebrated example was Dr D F Malan, who progressed from being editor of *Die Burger* to being prime minister. Dr H F Verwoerd was editor of *Die*

Transvaler, in Johannesburg, before he moved up to become prime minister. Dr A P Treurnicht, the cabinet minister who left the Nats to form the ultra right-wing Conservative Party, was editor of *Hoofstad* in Pretoria.

These people were polemicists rather than reporters, and their papers showed it. They were more interested in espousing causes than in conveying the news, and this is one of the reasons why, at that time, the English-language papers outsold their Afrikaans counterparts (it is a different story today). In the early 1950s Horace Flather, editor of *The Star*, who was originally an English immigrant, gave evidence before a government-appointed commission of inquiry into the press. This commission laboured for ten years, at great cost to the taxpayer, and brought forth a mouse of a report that resulted in no practical action. The general feeling at the time was that the whole exercise was an attempt to intimidate the English press, which then, and for the following 35 years, was a thorn in the side, or a pain in the backside, of the Nationalists.

At one point, the chairman of the commission, Mr Justice Helm van Zyl, asked Flather if he could speak Afrikaans (knowing full well that he could not). Flather replied that he couldn't. 'But Mr Flather,' said the commissioner in contrived tones of pain and concern, 'what would you do if you were placed in charge of an Afrikaans paper?'

'I'd double its circulation in six months,' replied Flather.

There was an element of truth in that breezy response.

When I joined the *Cape Argus*, General Jan Christiaan Smuts was the prime minister, the second World War had ended in victory, and the British royal family had visited South Africa a few months before. It is probably difficult for South Africans of the republican era to imagine the enthusiasm generated by the royal visit. The visitors arrived in Cape Town on the battleship *HMS Vanguard* one hot February morning, and tens of thousands of us crowded the streets to catch a glimpse of King George VI in white naval uniform, the smiling Queen Elizabeth (later greatly revered as the centurion Queen Mother), and the two princesses with conspicuously creamy English complexions. They travelled around the country by train for two months, and the later Queen Elizabeth II celebrated her 21st birthday in South Africa and made a speech that was broadcast in many parts of the world.

For white English-speaking supporters of Smuts's United Party government, it was a time of wellbeing, security and complacency. The rumblings of Dr Malan's Herstigte Nasionale Party about Afrikaner grievances and the *swartgevaar*, the black danger, were no more than clouds on the horizon. The much wider issue of black aspirations and eventual black political dominance did not loom large. Smuts himself was well aware of the problems ahead, and even more so was his principal lieutenant, Jan Hofmeyr, but it was the Nationalists who exploited the issue to win fearful white votes.

On 26 May 1948, all smiles disappeared from the faces of Smuts supporters. The general, a legendary figure then aged 78, had made a sad miscalculation of his electoral support. He had not organised before the election a constituency delimitation that would have revealed his weaknesses and allowed him to tighten his defences. He had relied on the total support of wartime ex-servicemen, overlooking the fact that many of them had grievances of their own: delays in demobilisation, difficulties in finding jobs, food shortages.

To everybody's surprise, not least the victors', the Nationalists squeaked in with a majority of five seats in the 150-seat House of Assembly. They owed their victory to one word: apartheid. The word was to become a symbol of political and social evil, and a millstone around South Africa's neck for the next 40 years and more.

It was not a new concept. The word apartheid had been bandied about by Nationalist politicians for a decade before that election, and it was also used in earnest discussion in Afrikaans academic circles. There it was stressed that the word meant differentiation, not discrimination; separate identity, not repression.

Such subtleties were conspicuously absent from the election campaign. Nobody was left in any doubt that apartheid meant, in one of the cruder political phrases, *die kaffer op sy plek en die koelie uit die land*; the kaffir in his place and the coolie out of the country. In fact, for many years the Nationalist government tried to persuade South African Indians to emigrate to India, offering them ludicrously inadequate inducements to do so. Almost nobody went, and one of South Africa's most valuable communities remained intact, to prosper to some degree in spite of apartheid, and eventually to see this evil policy abandoned.

The Nationalists played shamelessly on the fears and prejudices of white voters, especially those in rural areas. They succeeded in winning the 1948 election but they had a large minority of the total number of votes cast. In round figures, the United Party polled 524 000 votes; the Nationalists 402 000; N C Havenga's Afrikaner Party, who were allies of the Nats and subsequently joined them, 42 000; and other non-Nat bits and pieces, Labour Party, independents and so forth, 98 000.

The Nationalists won because of the unequal constituency system permitted in the Electoral Act to protect voters in sparsely populated areas. The South Africa that was brought into being in 1910 was still largely a farming country, and the electoral laws specified that country constituencies could have 30 percent fewer voters than heavily populated urban areas. The possible inequities are obvious; a vote in Beaufort West would be worth much more, in real terms, than a vote in Sea Point or Houghton. Whether the modern system of proportional representation is any better is open to question. Many people, myself included, like the idea of MPs being answerable to their voters, not their parties.

The Nationalists of the 1940s were experts at presenting their case at pre-election delimitation commissions. A commission of this kind, presided over by a Supreme Court judge, was supposed to be a quasi-judicial body that, after hearing representations from various interested parties, drew the boundaries of the constituencies for the coming election.

The commission was, of course, appointed by the government of the day, and in practice the government made sure that the commission members, or most of them, were not unsympathetic. This the Smuts government neglected to do and, moreover, the United Party took less trouble in advancing their arguments before the commission than did their Nationalist opponents waiting in the wings.

The result was a 1948 delimitation that favoured the opposition rather than the government, a mistake that the Nats were never to repeat once they had gained power.

I remember reporting on part of the proceedings of the delimitation in 1952, before the general election the following year. How the participants and observers kept straight faces I do not know. Solemn arguments about the common interests of pineapple farmers, and the differences between them and sheep graziers, were debated at great length, when everybody knew that politicians proposing these issues simply wanted to see their supporters deployed for the maximum electoral advantage.

It was, I think, in Bloemfontein that the constituencies were redrawn in such a way that the two Nat seats and two United Party seats were transposed into four Nat seats. And in Kimberley, some weird lines were drawn on the map to ensure that remote pockets of Nat supporters would be able to swing the issue their way in big urban seats.

After Dr Malan's Nationalists came to power in 1948, a good many of their waking hours were spent on scheming how to increase, by fair means or foul, their tiny majority in parliament. National interests took a back seat to Nationalist interests, a pattern of behaviour that was to persist for the next 40 years, to the great detriment of the country as a whole.

The Smuts government had initiated an immigration scheme that brought 20 600 settlers from Britain to South Africa in 1947 and 25 000 in 1948. They had to pay their own transport costs but they travelled in Union Castle ships in terms of a special contract between that company and the South African government.

Malan's new government believed, probably correctly, that most of these immigrants would vote against them. The Nats were saddled with what the newspapers called their Black War Record; many of them had openly supported Nazi Germany in World War II and most of them had opposed South Africa's involvement in the war on the side of Britain and America.

So the Nationalists blew cold on the immigration scheme. They ended the Union Castle contract and extended the period for obtaining South African citizenship from two years' residence to five. To be fair, the poor image in Europe of the new government did not encourage immigration. In any event, the number of immigrants dropped to 9 600 in 1949 and to 5 000 in 1950.

The long-term effect has been incalculable. If the Nats had been defeated in the 1953 election and a more reasonable and moderate government installed, there can be little doubt that all South Africans would have been saved a great deal of pain and suffering. The ultimate political ascendancy of black people was as predictable then as it was 40 years later, but the transition would have been much easier under a more sensible and sensitive government. But the Nats – in a minority not only of the entire population but even of the white voters – did what suited their narrow interests best, and were to continue in that vein for the next four decades.

The voting age was lowered from 21 to eighteen so that the rapidly growing number of young white Afrikaners could support the government. Six MPs from the mandated territory of South-West Africa (now Namibia) were brought into the South African parliament to bolster the government's small majority. This move did nothing for the interests of the country in terms of its relationship with the international community. Delimitation commissions were carefully chosen and shepherded into making the right decisions (for the ruling party).

And in the most cynical action of all, the government embarked on a long and bitter campaign to remove Coloured men from the common voters' roll in the Cape, where they had had full electoral rights since Union in 1910.

The irony was that, in pre-war days, many Coloured voters had supported Nationalist candidates, white people whom they knew and liked, especially in the farming communities of the Western Cape. But the Nats knew that no person of colour was going to swallow their fancy talk about the separate but equal aspects of apartheid. They knew that the Coloured voters might well cost them parliamentary seats in the Cape. So the Coloured voters had to go, on to a separate roll, voting for their own MPs, regardless of the bitterness and resentment caused in the process.

It was not easy for the government. The Coloured voting rights were protected in two entrenched clauses in the South Africa Act that had created the Union in 1910 (the other clause referred to the two official languages), and they could only be changed by a two-thirds majority of both Houses of Parliament. General J B M Hertzog, South Africa's third prime minister and the founding father of the modern National Party, had himself declared, in an earlier era, that to change the Coloured vote would be a betrayal of a sacred trust.

This did not deter his successors, who were not too pernickety about the methods they used. Malan could not obtain the necessary two-thirds majority when he introduced the Separate Representation of Voters Bill in parliament in 1951, and the Appellate Division of the Supreme Court ruled the legislation invalid. Then followed the High Court of Parliament Act, which purported to transfer authority over Acts of Parliament from the Appellate Division to a parliamentary 'court'. The High Court of Parliament (boycotted by the opposition) actually met, and in one of the most unseemly episodes in our political history various Nationalist nonentities jestingly referred to each other as 'regter' (judge).

The Appeal Court was again unimpressed and threw the legislation out. An attempt by the government to enlarge the Appeal Court also failed (the purpose this time was to get more friendly faces on the bench), as did a second attempt to obtain an authentic two-thirds majority in parliament.

Finally the government found a way, by enlarging the senate and thus obtaining the two-thirds parliamentary majority. Legal, but not moral, in the view of most people. All this took five years of bitter wrangling, and the effect was to alienate the Coloured people, who not surprisingly took a dim view of the whole business.

All this happened long ago but it is worth recalling, I think, because it was the real beginning of the apartheid policy that did such immense harm to South Africa over such a long period, with its miserable array of unjust laws: the Group Areas Act, the Immorality Act, the constant attacks on freedom of speech and freedom of assembly and indeed on individual liberties at every level.

It is also worth recalling because this oppressive programme activated the most vigorous opposition from very large numbers of white people in various sectors: the English-language universities, churches, newspapers, women's organisations, ordinary people at all levels. They were harassed and threatened and attacked by the politicians and the police, but they did not hesitate to stand up against obvious injustice, and I fear that today they are not given the credit due to them.

After five years of the most cynical political manipulation, the Nationalists still could not achieve an absolute majority of the votes cast.

In the 1953 general election, the United Party and its Labour Party allies polled, again in round figures, a total of 601 000 votes against the Nats' 599 000. There were still plenty of white voters who thought it was only a matter of time before the Nationalists were thrown out. I remember my colleagues taking bets in 1958 that the United Party, by then under the leadership of Sir De Villiers Graaff, would win the election of that year. Alas, this was a turning point. The Nats won convincingly, with an overall majority of about 150 000 votes and a massive parliamentary majority, 103 seats out of 156.

For years, people of my generation used to speculate about what might have happened if the United Party had scraped in with a small parliamentary majority in 1948 instead of losing by a few seats. Would it have made any difference to the long, slowly unfolding drama of South African political history?

Well, in the first place, the United Party would have set about restoring its political fortunes. Jan Hofmeyr may have been a visionary, and Smuts may have had his eyes fixed more firmly on Westminster and Washington than on Wakkerstroom and Westdene, but these men were not politically naïve. That immigration scheme would have been stepped up, bringing into the country tens of thousands of newcomers who would certainly not have supported the narrow, sectional policies of the Nationalists. The delimitation of constituencies would have received urgent attention. The Coloured voters of the Cape would have remained where they were.

Given this set of circumstances, the United Party would probably have won the election in 1953 and again in 1958. And would that have made a difference to the history of South Africa? Yes, I think so. Eventual black rule was as inevitable as the rising of the sun in the morning, but what happened before that would have been greatly changed. Hofmeyr and his friends aside, the United Party was by no means a group of liberals. Most of its members were white conservatives, even by 1948 standards. But they had a pragmatism and a better sense of justice than the Nats, largely because they were a much more diffuse party covering a much wider spectrum of opinion.

A degree of separation of different racial communities had been the South African norm for 300 years, and the United Party would not have gone around bravely breaking the barriers. But certainly, it would equally not have committed the ultimate folly of entrenching segregation at every level in the laws of the land. The United Party had too much common sense, and too much simple humanity, to have done this.

I remember reporting in the 1950s the proceedings of the government-appointed Road Transportation Board, which had powers to control public transport. The government had given notice that it intended to introduce apartheid on Cape Town's buses, which had never before been subjected to this treatment. The mayor of Cape Town, P J Wolmarans, led a municipal deputation to the Road Transportation Board to oppose the change.

Wolmarans was an Afrikaans-speaking man, a member of the United Party, no liberal but a decent and sensible person. He was rather inarticulate and he kept on repeating to the board, 'We don't want this. We've never had it in Cape Town. We don't want it.'

To which the Pretoria civil servant who headed the board would reply, politely and coldly, 'Mr Mayor, you must understand, it's the government's policy.'

I don't think this scene could have been enacted under a United Party government. The United Party would have been more relaxed about racial matters, more tolerant, less doctrinaire. It would certainly have been more responsive to criticism from the world at large. Its members were much more wordly and sophisticated than the Nationalists; J G Strijdom, for example, made his first trip outside the borders of South Africa only a few weeks before he became prime minister in 1954.

The United Party could not have stemmed the rising tide of black aspirations, but it could have made the adjustment easier, and it would not have alienated the Coloured and Indian people of South Africa as the Nats did. All South Africans would have been spared much pain and much shame. The final result would have been the same. The route and the timing would have been different.

FOUR

Potentates

In the course of my working life, I met eight of South Africa's eleven prime ministers and executive presidents, the omissions being Generals Botha and Hertzog, who were, as they say, a little before my time; and President Mbeki, who was after my time. Generally speaking, these encounters were infrequent and brief, and often in the company of a group. With one possible exception, none of these gentlemen is ever likely to have remembered me. But then I am writing about them, not they about me.

If ever there was a towering figure in the politics of his time, it was Jan Smuts, who was treated with respect and awe by friend and enemy to the day he died at the age of 80. The only comparable figure in South African history is Nelson Mandela. Smuts created his own mystique. Apart from being possessed of a massive intellect, he had covered a wide terrain of experience and authority in his long life, and he was by nature a somewhat remote and distant individual. You could never imagine Smuts being one of the boys.

I was a cub reporter on the *Cape Argus* – almost an infant reporter, one might say – when, a couple of weeks before Christmas 1947, I was sent to the prime minister's residence at Groote Schuur, Rondebosch, in the company of Neville Clayton, the paper's chief photographer. Every Christmas, the gardeners at Groote Schuur picked hundreds, maybe thousands, of blue hydrangeas from the banks of these flowers at the estate, to be sent to hospitals and children's homes throughout the Cape Peninsula. Neville Clayton's mission was to take, by prior arrangement, a photograph of General Smuts and one of his grandchildren among the flowers. My task was to write the caption, making sure I had the names right.

After a brief wait on the *stoep* of the beautiful old house, the general appeared, not quite dressed for an informal occasion: grey suit with waistcoat. He gave us an unsmiling nod. A little girl came out of a side door. Smuts grabbed her hand and marched the twenty metres or so to the nearest hydrangeas, where he sat on a chair that had been placed there for him. 'Kom, kom,' he said impatiently, as Clayton fiddled with his bulky Speed Graphic camera.

Neville Clayton was a very skilful photographer and not a man to be intimidated. 'Put the little girl on your lap, general,' he called out cheerfully. This was done awkwardly and with an ill grace. 'And smile, general, come on now, smile; please.'

The general tried unsuccessfully to rearrange his features into a smile. The result was a grimace, after which he stomped back at some speed into the sanctuary of his home while I asked the grandchild her name and age. The encounter had been less than epic, but it was memorable.

Six months later, Smuts was no longer prime minister. He was still a commanding figure. After the 1948 election, he was due to fly to England to accept the chancellorship of Cambridge University. Now out of office, he was not entitled to use official transport, but his successor, D F Malan, put an air force plane at his disposal. At Cambridge, where he had been a brilliant student 60 years before, he made an enormous impression, and it was clear that he was still a favourite among the British people, who had come to know him as one of their leaders in two world wars. Until Nelson Mandela's accession to power, Smuts was in many ways the only South African ever to have been a truly international figure.

As a young parliamentary reporter, I attended two or three press conferences that Smuts gave as leader of the opposition, and from the press gallery I often heard him speak in the House of Assembly. He spoke mainly in English, in the rather high-pitched Malmesbury accent that he had acquired in his boyhood and had never lost. The Malmesbury district, about 70 kilometres north of Cape Town, used to be celebrated for this *brei*, as it is called, and one of the stories of my youth went thus: English-speaking man, on the dance floor with Afrikaans girl: 'Are you from Malmesbury? I notice that you roll your r's.' 'Oh no, man, it's just my high-heeled shoes.'

Smuts's electoral defeat seemed to make little difference to his standing among white South Africans. On his first visit to Cape Town after the election, he stayed at the Civil Service Club (destroyed by fire in the 1970s) and Church Square was packed with a huge crowd waiting to welcome him. Three hundred thousand people turned out on the streets of Johannesburg for his 80th birthday celebrations in May 1950, only three months before he died.

In case my first impression of him gives the idea that he was a grumpy old man, I should perhaps add that Sir Keith Hancock's official biography of Smuts contains a photograph taken of the general the day before he died. He is wearing a cloth cap, he has two grandchildren on his lap, and he is all smiles.

Daniel Francois Malan had, in his old age anyway, a psychological advantage over any interviewer: he didn't smile much, if at all, and his glasses were so thick that you couldn't see his eyes properly and had little clue as to what he was thinking.

There is a famous photograph of Malan speaking in public immediately after the 1948 election. 'South Africa belongs to us once more,' he said, felt hat jammed on his head, thick glasses glinting above heavy jowls, and not a flicker of a smile or any other emotion. He might have been conducting a funeral service (he was a former minister in the Dutch Reformed Church).

He was 74 when he became prime minister and 80 when he retired. His ancestral home was a farm named, grimly, *Allesverloren*, (all is lost) in the Malmesbury district, and as a child he attended Sunday-school classes conducted by Jan Christiaan Smuts, four years his senior.

Allesverloren is still in the hands of the Malan family and is now one of the Cape's most distinguished wine estates, well known for its cabernet sauvignon, shiraz and port. What the old doctor would have made of all this is open to debate; he wasn't exactly a drinking man.

Nor was he a betting man. My colleague, James Clarke, of *The Star* in Johannesburg, has an amusing recollection of trying to interview Dr Malan in a hotel suite at Umhlanga Rocks in the early 1950s. Clarke had only recently arrived from England and knew little or nothing about certain Afrikaner sensibilities. It was early July, when Durban has its famous horse race, and by way of breaking the ice he asked the prime minister cheerfully, 'What do you fancy for the Durban July?'

Dr Malan walked out of the room, and Mrs Malan explained gently, 'Our religion frowns on gambling.'

N C 'Klasie' Havenga, Malan's deputy and a much more worldly man in many ways, was present, and he had the last word on this subject. As a crestfallen Clarke waited for Malan to return, Havenga said quietly, 'I've got my money on so-and-so; it's going to romp home.'

Dr Malan's pursuits were political, and ecclesiastic, and that was it. His interest in sport was zero. There was a story, perhaps apocryphal, that at the end of their three-month tour of South Africa, the 1949 All Black rugby players were ushered into the prime minister's office for a brief meeting. He welcomed them solemnly and expressed the hope that they would have a pleasant and successful stay in South Africa. In fact, they were on their way back to New Zealand the next day.

Dr Malan's grim visage and single-minded devotion to his apartheid policy gave rise to this type of story. At one point, the government's Department of Information decided that it would improve the prime minister's image if he were seen as a jollier type of person. In the course of a flattering pen portrait of him, intended for media distribution here and abroad, it said: 'It is sometimes thought that the prime minister does not have much sense of humour. This is not true. In 1932, he made a joke.'

There was some elaboration about the nature of the joke, but the damage was done, and Bob Connolly, cartoonist of the *Rand Daily Mail*, did a memorable drawing of Dr Malan's mouth being stretched wide into an artificial grin by two giant hands marked 'Department of Information'.

Round about 1952, Dr Malan made another joke. My old friend Aubrey Sussens, then of the *Cape Times*, and I were among some intrepid English-language reporters who journeyed to Piketberg, north of Cape

Town, for a meeting to be held there by the prime minister, in the heart of his own constituency.

In those days, if you were from the *Engelse Pers* it was wise, at Nat meetings, to keep your head down and your trap shut. Some Afrikaner critics of the government had no such inhibitions. *Bloedsappe*, they were called, blood saps; the SAP was the old South African Party, which had become the United Party, and many Afrikaners followed Smuts through thick and thin, even after 1948.

One such clan was attending Malan's meeting at Piketberg. They were all related, they were noisy and unruly at the back of the hall, and their family home was a farm in the Worcester area called Rondegat, or round hole, presumably because it had a round dam. They shouted out questions repeatedly and aggressively and there were sporadic punch-ups.

Malan was imperturbable. He had a way of pausing in mid-sentence during interjections and then resuming grammatically and logically as if nothing had occurred. On this occasion, he ran true to form. He knew exactly who his hecklers were but he ignored them, carrying on calmly after each outburst.

Eventually, however, they got under even his skin. And after a period of prolonged shouting and scuffling he peered myopically into the middle distance, wagged a finger in the general direction at the back of the hall, and said, *'En vir jou, my vriend, kan ek net sê jy's a square peg in a rondegat* (And for you, my friend, all I can say is, you're a square peg in a round hole).'

Johannes Gerhardus Strijdom succeeded Malan in 1954 but was prime minister for only four years before he succumbed to illness. He was a menacing character in public and a polite and unassuming one in private. He was, in a way, the last of the naked racists. Verwoerd and his successors tried to give some kind of philosophical gloss to their apartheid policies. Strijdom called it *baasskap* (being boss) and never tried to back away from that term. His reward was to be called the Lion of the North by his admirers (his political base was the then Northern Transvaal) and to be vilified by his many critics.

I heard him speak – harangue might be a better word – many times, but I interviewed him only twice, and then briefly. On each occasion, I approached him with some apprehension but was pleasantly surprised by his courteous attitude. Newspaper reporters sometimes have to be pushy, and on the second occasion I had to try to grab the prime minister on the steps of the Cape Town City Hall, where he had arrived to open a conference, in an attempt to obtain his comment on some important international development. A small army of minor officials and bodyguards barred my way, but Strijdom saw that I was trying to reach him, waved aside his minders and listened to my request with great concentration. He thought carefully, formulated his response to my question, made sure that there was no misunderstanding, shook hands and then made his way back to vexed officialdom. A good example for some bigwigs to follow.

Strijdom was married twice, the first time to the actress Marda Vanne, who was not really the marrying type. They were divorced very soon, in the days when divorce was a serious stigma in the conservative Afrikaans community. The Afrikaans newspapers were loyal to a fault; they never made any mention of the fact that the prime minister had been divorced. His second wife, Susanna de Klerk, was the sister of a right-wing Nat cabinet minister of the time, Jan de Klerk. She was also the aunt of a later and much more celebrated politician, former State President F W de Klerk.

Times change. When I was a young music student, a girl named Estelle Strijdom was a student pianist with the same tutor. She was the daughter of the prime minister. Her subsequent career suggests strongly that she long ago abandoned the ideas of the Lion of the North.

If genius and insanity are obverse sides of the same coin, then Hendrik Frensch Verwoerd must have come close to that definition. He was an educated man of powerful intellect. And his political notions were so obsessional and so intolerant as to verge on the maniacal. He was the grand apartheid man, the messiah whose mission was to preserve the white man in Africa. Today, his views are generally regarded as repulsive, wildly racist, quaint and even comical. But such was the force of his personality that in his own lifetime, he imposed his will on friend and foe alike.

I met Verwoerd only two or three times, and never alone. He was not the kind of person who granted interviews to newspapers that opposed him. One occasion I remember well was a tea party-cum-press conference on the back verandah of Groote Schuur after Harold Macmillan, the British prime minister, had made his famous winds of change speech to the South African Parliament in 1960. Macmillan was at his most urbane and aristocratic, giving amusing replies in drawling tones to the questions put to him. Verwoerd wore a fixed smile throughout the proceedings. Macmillan had just given his speech to parliament, and though he replied politely, Verwoerd regarded it as, to use a phrase that became trite, external interference in the domestic affairs of a sovereign country.

I don't think anybody actually liked Verwoerd, except, presumably, members of his own family. He was said to bully his own cabinet ministers, and he certainly bullied anybody else who did not agree with him. He was a cold fish, a hectoring, lecturing public speaker with a high-pitched voice and no apparent sense of humour. He tried to give a kind of moral respectability to apartheid by emphasising the 'separate but equal' angle, but I don't think anybody was deceived, especially not the black and brown people against whom the policy was aimed.

Some black leaders accepted office and rewards under the Bantustan policy that created artificial mini-states such as Transkei and Ciskei. At best, they were motivated by frustration and the inability to make progress in other ways. At worst, they were motivated by self-aggrandisement and self-enrichment. It didn't take long for the whole edifice to collapse once real change was in the air.

Verwoerd was born in Amsterdam, Holland, in 1901. His foreign origin was, like Strijdom's divorce, never mentioned by the Afrikaans papers or the government's propaganda machinery. Part of his childhood was spent in the former Rhodesia, where his father worked for the Dutch Reformed Church. For a time, Hendrik Verwoerd attended the same school in Bulawayo, Milton, as I did many years later; I suppose he is the school's most famous, or notorious, old boy.

By the time he was 26, Verwoerd was professor of applied psychology at Stellenbosch University. He became prominent in groups working to relieve the social plight of poor whites, and then he became editor of *Die Transvaler*, the Nationalist paper published in Johannesburg. Under his editorship it must have been one of the most boring papers ever printed, but the job was a stepping stone to politics, the cabinet in 1950 and the premiership in 1958.

His life ended when a parliamentary messenger, Dimitrio Tsafendas, plunged a knife into his chest at his seat in the House of Assembly on 6 September 1966. What would have happened to South Africa if he had not been murdered? The point can be debated in various ways. I think it is arguable that black political emancipation might have arrived more rapidly had Verwoerd lived to continue on his star-fixed course. His government had succeeded in suppressing internally the opposition coming from the African National Congress and its allies; the imprisonment of Nelson Mandela and Abraham Fischer and many of their colleagues dates back to the Verwoerd era. But these were short-term gains for the white supremacists. The opposition of a hostile world would probably have been intensified earlier. And within South Africa, the armed struggle, as it is called, might have assumed greater proportions than it eventually did, diminishing prospects for a conciliatory state at the end of the road. In the end, other, more reasonable Nationalists faced the facts of life and came to terms with the majority of the people. I don't think Verwoerd would ever have done that.

His descendants take a different view of life. His grandson and the grandson's wife are now both prominent in politics – as members of the ANC.

In my opinion, the only funny thing about John Vorster was his name: Balthazar Johannes Vorster, always known as John. Balthazar was one of the three wise men, the magi, who visited the baby Jesus in his crib at Bethlehem – and Balthazar was the one from Ethiopia, a black man. A grim irony, considering that Balthazar Johannes Vorster spent most of his time keeping the black man in his place and doing so with an array of brutally repressive laws worthy of the worst dictatorships of modern times.

Vorster had been minister of justice and of police before he succeeded Verwoerd as prime minister, and he had been grimly efficient in suppressing opposition. Detention without trial was his special contribution to the South African legal system, and many people suffered under it. He was in no sense a pleasant man, though the government's propaganda machine did its best by exploiting his liking for golf. I think it was Helen Suzman who said at the time that the propagandists had done their best to change Vorster from a hard-faced jailer into a jolly golfer. It was Vorster's laws that led to the death in detention of people like the Black Consciousness leader, Steve Biko. The police were given horrifying powers and used them in the manner of the Gestapo in Nazi Germany. At the inquest after Steve Biko's death, the distinguished lawyer, Sydney Kentridge, asked a senior police officer what statutes had guided him in his treatment of the prisoner. 'We don't work under statutes,' was the reply. So much for human rights.

These Nats were incapable of even trying to understand anybody else's point of view. An acquaintance of mine worked for Vorster for a time, trying to give his policies some kind of respectable interpretation for the world at large. He eventually gave up in despair, but before he did so he asked Vorster one day, with reference to some piece of discriminatory legislation, 'What would you think if you were a black man?' Vorster growled in Afrikaans, 'It doesn't apply. I'm not a black man.'

The public relations people had a hard job in trying to portray the prime minister in a sympathetic light. The truth was that he was not an agreeable person. 'Smile, please, Mr Prime Minister,' a photographer once said at a formal posing session. 'I am smiling,' replied Vorster without the slightest alteration of his facial muscles.

Vorster was savagely criticised by the English-language press, universities, churches and plenty of politicians, notably the redoubtable Helen Suzman. He held back from direct attacks on these critics, probably because he feared massive adverse reaction in the wider world. But he made the lives of his critics very difficult with laws that banned so many statements and disclosures that a newspaper editor had to be an amateur lawyer to survive.

I smile inwardly when I hear the ignorant or malicious modern comment that the newspapers of those days were cuddling up to the government, or were at least comfortable with it. It was very uncomfortable indeed, with editors frequently being visited by policemen investigating alleged infringements of this law or that, and being threatened daily by politicians (and incurring the enmity of many white businessmen who regarded people like myself as troublemakers and agitators).

Occasionally, Vorster would invite newspaper editors to a 'briefing' that was mainly useless, giving us information that we already knew and then asking us to regard it as confidential. He would see the Afrikaans editors and the English ones separately, reserving his spleen for the latter. We would meet at a conference room at parliament in Cape Town, and Vorster would get the proceedings off to a great start by saying in his most grim mood, 'Gentlemen, we might as well get one thing clear at the outset: you don't like me and I don't like you.'

Absolutely correct.

Vorster's downfall was a Department of Information scandal, which forced his resignation from the premiership in 1978. He continued for a short time as a non-executive, mainly ceremonial state president. The scandal involved the secret expenditure of many millions of rands of public money in an attempt to win friends and influence people in South Africa, Europe and the United States. The very fact that taxpayers' money, to the tune of about R35-million, could be used to finance an apparently independent commercial newspaper, *The Citizen*, indicates how far the Nat government had gone in assuming that it could do as it liked.

Vorster's successor, P W Botha, is still alive and living near George, the constituency that he represented in parliament for many years. Like many of his critics, I had a kind of grudging respect for him. He was a political survivor, and he did try to ease what was called 'petty apartheid' by the repeal of legislation such as the Mixed Marriages Act and the pass laws. He also made an effort to bring people of colour into the parliament in Cape Town, something that had not happened for 40 years. His tricameral parliament, in which the Coloured and Indian communities were represented, was fatally flawed and was opposed by most English-language newspapers, including mine, the *Daily News* in Durban, but excluding the Johannesburg *Sunday Times*, then under the editorship of Tertius Myburgh. It was flawed because, among other reasons, it did not address the political aspirations of the black African majority, and it failed. But it did show a pragmatism that would have been quite unbelievable in the days of Verwoerd.

P W Botha was, and probably still is, an irascible and dogmatic man, not given to sweet reasonableness when confronted with points of view other than his own. As with Vorster, my meetings with him were confined to group gatherings of English-language editors for more of those famous confidential briefings. He wasn't as hostile as Vorster, but he didn't exude charm. On the whole, he got a pretty reasonable press from editors who were aware that he was making some kind of struggling, albeit reluctant, progress against the sins and follies of the past. That didn't improve his temper as far as we were concerned. He knew my name and the fact that I came from Natal, 'English' Natal. As we all shook hands at the end of a meeting, he would look at me and say, 'Just remember, you're a South African too, hey.' It was very annoying at the time. Now it's just an amusing memory.

There are many stories about P W Botha's short temper. My favourite, which is apparently true, concerns a meeting in Pietermaritzburg that Botha attended with Owen Horwood, then minister of finance and head of the Nats in Natal. Horwood had been principal of Natal University and was not popular with the students. Oddly enough, he had been quite popular at an earlier stage, when he was a professor of economics and chairman of the university's cricket club (he himself had been a good cricketer). I think he was one of those people who are too self-important and heavy-handed when advanced to higher authority.

It had been revealed in the press, after he left the university and became a cabinet minister, that Horwood's sole academic qualification was a BCom degree, the Bachelor of Commerce being about the most basic grade you could obtain from a university. This caused some mirth, especially among the students who disliked Horwood. And there were plenty of them outside the Pietermaritzburg City Hall when P W Botha and Horwood walked from their car to the entrance of the hall.

'BCom, BCom, BCom,' the students chanted derisively at Horwood. Botha completely misunderstood the situation. He produced his famous wagging forefinger and shouted back at the students, 'I'm perfectly calm. You be calm.'

Like Vorster before him, Botha was forced out of office in 1989 when it became clear, even to his followers, that his policies were leading the country nowhere and that time was running out. F W de Klerk, his successor, is still very much part of our public scene and his past role is familiar to everybody. His speech to parliament on 2 February 1990, when he announced the unbanning of the ANC and other organisations and the release of political prisoners, is one of the great watersheds in the history of South Africa.

De Klerk was later awarded the Nobel Peace Prize jointly with Nelson Mandela, but I'm not sure that he has been given all the credit he deserves. To Nelson Mandela must go the major recognition for the peaceful political and social revolution in South Africa, and this is accepted worldwide. Nevertheless, it was F W de Klerk who set the machinery in motion. With the help of the army and the police, he and the Nats could have held on to power for perhaps another decade, but the consequences would have been awful. He had the vision to see that, and to take political action that ran counter to his entire life's experience. He deserves a salute for that.

Some time before the election that brought Nelson Mandela to power, De Klerk had lunch in Cape Town with half a dozen of us English-language newspaper editors. It was a pleasant occasion. He was buoyant, humorous and seemed not at all downcast about what he must have anticipated: his eventual removal from the highest office in the land. We discussed the political developments, and at one stage he said with a little smile: 'I suppose you fellows reckon you were right all the time.'

Today's new young politicians and journalists accuse us of having played ball with the Nats during their long reign. The leader of the Nats, F W de Klerk, knew better.

There is nothing I can say about Nelson Mandela that has not been said a thousand times before. Like all mortals, he has some shortcomings, but he is a wonderful human being. To have spent 27 years in jail for your legitimate political beliefs and to have emerged so free of resentment, bitterness or spite is almost superhuman. South African has been fortunate to have such a man taking the reins at such a crucial juncture in our history.

Mandela came to power after I retired from newspapers and I have met him only once; my daughter, Pippa, who is well known in the newspaper and broadcasting world, knows him much better. My sole meeting with Nelson Mandela was when he attended a lunch given by newspaper editors about two years before he became state president. At that time, he did not have the perquisites of office, and workers at the Daimler-Benz factory had contributed their time to build him a free red Mercedes car that was formally presented to him, with the appropriate publicity.

Mandela spoke to us about his hopes and plans, and at one stage emphasised that his people did not have the creature comforts we enjoyed. He said figuratively, 'I do not have a safe job, a warm, dry house, pension and medical benefits, such as you have.'

One of our impious editors interjected: 'Yes, but you have a better car than I have.' General amusement, in which Mandela joined, like the big man he is.

There is one more potentate in southern Africa with whom I had brief acquaintance. Robert Mugabe.

In 1982, six Argus Company editors travelled to Harare to see for ourselves how Zimbabwe was faring after two years of independence. We had been there towards the end of Ian Smith's lengthy rule – he was prime minister of Rhodesia for sixteen years – and we were interested in making a comparison, now that the new government had had two years to settle down after the initial jubilation and celebration.

We were rather impressed at what appeared to be peace and goodwill in the capital city (this was before the killing of thousands of anti-government black people in another part of the country, Matabeleland, the work of soldiers acting on Mugabe's orders). In Harare, the black officials who had replaced white people seemed polite and efficient, the white people seemed relatively at ease in spite of the president's 'socialist' ideals, and the most conspicuous sign of change was the high-speed convoy of police cars and a large black Mercedes that raced in and out of town, sirens screaming, from the suburbs every day. This was President Mugabe going to and from his office. Bob Mugabe and the Wailers, the locals called it, after a famous reggae group called Bob Marley and the Wailers. There was humour, but no particular malice in the description, any more than there was in the story that the British troops who gave protection during the change to independence said they thought that Mugabe was a Yorkshireman, because if you spelled his name backwards it was 'E-ba-gum'.

Through our Zimbabwe editorial representative, Robin Drew, we asked for and were swiftly granted an interview with the president. We met him in a government office in a pleasantly informal atmosphere. Mugabe was accompanied by one official, presumably some kind of secretary. No bodyguards, no security officers, no entourage. Robin Drew asked him if he minded if the proceedings were recorded on tape. No problem. Sitting behind a desk, the president asked us if we would like to ask questions or whether he should first give a rundown on the situation in Zimbabwe. We said we preferred that he should speak first, whereupon he spoke calmly, lucidly, reasonably for perhaps 20 minutes, without reference to a note of any kind.

The next day, Robin Drew gave us a typescript of the tape recording. Mugabe's remarks, made off the cuff, were word perfect; no hesitation, no searching for a phrase, no repetition, even the commas and full stops were silently in place. We agreed among ourselves that it was an impressive performance and an indication of an unusually well-organised and well-ordered mind. Of his intelligence we had no doubt.

His disarming manner did contain a hint of things to come. Here are some of his exact words, as taped: 'Our view is that the resources we have in the country belong to the people as a whole. We see in that philosophy a morality which enables us to live together, to be equals, as owners of our God-given natural resources. To us, really, capitalism is anathema. We don't believe in it. We believe in socialism. But, having said that, I should also add that we recognise the reality of the capitalist system in this country. We have inherited it and we cannot ignore it. We cannot transform it overnight.'

After we had asked the president plenty of questions, he chatted to us and asked interestedly about matters in South Africa. What was originally set down as a 30-minute interview went on for nearly an hour and a half, and ended with photographs and hand-shaking all round. I have an amusing photograph of Robert Mugabe, much shorter than me, clasping my hand in both of his and looking up, laughing.

What went wrong? What happened to change this apparently sophisticated, pragmatic, reasonable man into a person so extreme that many people came to regard him at best as a tyrant, and at worst as a monster? I don't know. Some people say that old age and illness have upset the balance of his mind. Others say he is a political opportunist who will do anything to retain power, even in his dotage. Another theory is that the sweet reasonableness of an earlier era was simply a false front to conceal the true man, a ruthless ideologue waiting for his time to assail anybody in his way.

Whatever the reasons, the fact is Robert Mugabe has virtually destroyed the once-prosperous Zimbabwe. One may feel sorry for the white farmers who, after generations of effort (involving many black employees), have been dispossessed of their land. One should feel even sorrier for the black population in general, who are starving because food production has dropped dramatically.

And it is difficult not to feel unease at the fact that, in spite of everything, Robert Mugabe remains very popular in Africa and, indeed, in South Africa.

FIVE

The entertainers

I had my first experience of the theatre when I was about seven or eight years old and my parents took me to some kind of musical revue on the stage of one of the three cinemas in Bulawayo.

The principal performer was a little grey-haired woman named Lady Hicks. She was the wife of a celebrated English actor named Sir Seymour Hicks. He had a cigarette brand named after him, Sir Seymour it was called, and every town had billboards of Sir Seymour, handsome, smiling, hair combed back, puffing away on one of his cigarettes. Everybody smoked in those days, a fashion endorsed by two successive British sovereigns, Edward VIII and George VI. The fact that King George, father of Queen Elizabeth, died of lung cancer at the age of 56 didn't deter anyone. I have at home a book that contains some photographs of the most famous of all Springbok rugby flyhalfs, Bennie Osler (1901–1962). There he is, in blazer and flannels, dapper and powerful, a coiled watch-spring of a man – and always with a cigarette in his hand. It is hardly conceivable today.

Lady Hicks, wearing a black evening dress, played the piano in a strumming kind of way and sang wistful little songs:

'I love you dearly, dearly, and I know that you love me
You are my honey, honeysuckle, I am the bee.'
(Albert H Fitz)

A few years later, at school at Christian Brothers' College at Green Point, Cape Town, I was in the same class as a boy who became a famous actor, Nigel Hawthorne. His father was a doctor at Camps Bay. Nigel and I were good friends and played in the same school rugby team. He was a well-built lad and I (and, as far as I know, my other school friends) had no inkling of the homosexuality that became his lifestyle, in a discreet and apparently non-promiscuous way.

He was a student at the University of Cape Town for a couple of years and took small parts in one or two minor Cape Town theatre productions. Then he left for England to seek fame or fortune. In 1953, my newspaper job took me to London for a year. I phoned Nigel Hawthorne and we had a drink together. He was poor, battling but not unhappy, employed in some small roles at the Comedy Theatre in London's West End.

I never saw him again, but I rejoiced when, about 35 years later, he became famous, first on television, then in films, and was knighted by the queen. He died of cancer in 2001.

My own experience of acting was brief, inglorious and comical. At the age of twelve I was a fat boy and, taking the part of Portia in a school reading of *The Merchant of Venice*, I brought the house down with the line, 'My little body is aweary of this great world.' Three or four years later, I participated in a school production of *Julius Caesar*, as one of the conspirators who assassinate Caesar. In my enthusiasm, I lunged with my rubber dagger at the wrong man, who said loudly and indignantly, 'You can't kill me, I'm Brutus.' This, amid ribald acclamation from the audience, brought my acting career to a close.

I did, however, develop an involvement with the theatre on the other side of the footlights. As a young reporter with Cape Town's *Cape Argus* newspaper in the late 1940s, I began reviewing plays for the paper, starting with the most modest amateur productions and gradually working my way to the status of official theatre critic. Like most journalists, I learned on the job and eventually acquired sufficient knowledge and confidence to express what I believed were reasonable opinions.

Cape Town had a really busy theatrical life in the 1950s and 1960s. The National Theatre Organisation, formed shortly after World War II to promote culture in small towns as well as big cities, staged some outstanding plays in Cape Town. Leonard Schach, a major figure in the history of South African theatre, produced some of them; I recall brilliant productions of Ben Jonson's *Volpone* and Tennessee Williams's *Cat on a Hot Tin Roof*. Schach emigrated to Britain in the 1970s, unable to stomach South Africa's Nationalist government any longer.

Many prominent stage people visited the Cape in the first two decades after World War II. Maurice Chevalier came and charmed everyone with what I suspect was a carefully retained French accent. Another Frenchman, Marcel Marceau, the world's most famous mime, gave some unforgettable performances in the old Alhambra Theatre, creating a wide array of characters without saying one word. In one scene, he portrayed a man trying on two masks – a comic mask and a tragic mask. He covered his face with his hands and removed them to reveal an inane grin, the comic mask. Another swift movement of hands to face, a moment's pause, and then the hands were dropped to show a racked, anguished face.

Within seconds, the audience actually believed that he was covering his face with masks, so convincing was the illusion. The masks were changed with ever-increasing rapidity – and then he could not remove the grinning mask. He pulled and tugged at his face with mounting desperation, and the weird, static grin began to look more and more sinister as he did so. You could sense the tension in the theatre. And then the mask came away, to reveal Marceau's own face, weary and drawn after the ordeal. All done with hands, mobile features and a wonderful imagination. I have seen many great solo performers in the theatre and I think I would rate Marcel Marceau the most fascinating of them all.

There was an amusing postlude to this particular show. A party was held backstage in Marceau's honour and I was fortunate enough to be invited. A local bigwig wanted to impress the maestro by speaking to him in French, of which he knew not one word. He was incautious enough to seek advice from a mischievous French speaker at the party. 'How,' he inquired, 'do I thank Mr Marceau in French for this wonderful evening?' 'Quite simple,' came the reply. 'You say, *merci beaucoup pour une soiree epouvantable.*' The big shot bustled over to the artist and delivered the phrase. Marcel Marceau bowed gracefully and said, 'Enchante', enchanted, one of those extravagant French expressions used to indicate great appreciation. His admirer left, and Marceau turned to those of us near him and said: 'Ee has jus sanked me for a tairrible evening.'

Danny Kaye came to Cape Town at the height of his fame and beguiled large audiences with his rather innocent humour. At one point, I recall, he persuaded the audience to hold up lighted matches, creating a fairyland atmosphere in the darkened theatre. I don't suppose anybody carries matches these days. This was a long time ago.

Danny Kaye was proud of the fact that his shows were clean and free of any obscene or suggestive content. His publicists said you could take anybody to a Danny Kaye show, from a child aged six to a little old lady aged 90, and they were right. Off-stage, however, the star was not always so careful. On a Sunday off, he was taken on a fishing trip in False Bay, on a big motorboat owned by Vic Cohen, a well-known attorney from Simonstown. Cohen was friendly with the Stodel brothers who ran African Consolidated Theatres and he often arranged excursions for performers brought to South Africa by that organisation. The boat was big – it could carry 30 or 40 people – but not so big that you were unaware of the very rough seas that seem to be the norm south of Simonstown in the Cape Point area. Danny Kaye soon began to look very sad indeed. He left his fishing rod clamped on the deck and said he would go down to the large cabin below and have a rest. While he was there, some pranksters hauled in his line, tied a heavy iron bar to it and threw it overboard, causing the ratchet to fly into action. 'A fish, Danny,' they cried. 'You've got a fish.'

Danny Kaye came leaping up the steps from the cabin, giving his head a sickening thump on an overhead beam in the process. He grabbed his rod and fought the 'fish' for a long time. Eventually, he brought his catch to the side of the boat and saw that it was a piece of iron. By now, an uneasy silence had descended on the spectators. The silence was soon broken. Danny Kaye broke into a stream of foul language that unnerved even the old hands. He used words they didn't know existed, and he used them mainly to refer to those around him. It was a chilly ride back to Simonstown, meteorologically and spiritually.

Emlyn Williams, a quietly spoken Welshman, was another great solo performer. He was a playwright who had won wide fame and fortune with an excellent psychological thriller called *Night Must Fall*, and he was an actor of high distinction. He had become celebrated in Britain and the United States for his one-man Charles Dickens recitals, and this was the show he brought to Cape Town.

Charles Dickens himself had enormous success when, in the 1850s and '60s, he toured Britain and the United States with readings from his own books. Emlyn Williams recaptured this earlier scene perfectly. A big false beard and Victorian clothing gave him an uncanny resemblance to the great novelist, and his only stage props were a leather-bound book and a small table. He would begin each scene by reading from the book, soon to put it aside on the table and continue from memory, acting the part of each character with great virtuosity. In an excerpt from *A Tale of Two Cities,* he would cite the references to Madame Defarge sitting at the base of the guillotine, knitting, and enact the scene, with chilling effect. Another memorable moment was provided by the railway signalman in a Dickens ghost story, reeling back in horror as a spectral figure shouts, 'Look out, look out.'

Sir Lewis Casson and Dame Sybil Thorndike were a husband-and-wife team who had been around a long time and were part of theatre history. In 1924, Dame Sybil created the title part on the London stage in Bernard Shaw's *Saint Joan*, one of the greatest plays in the English language (Sir Lewis also had an important role as De Stogumber, the bloodthirsty chaplain who is shattered by seeing the burning of Joan at the stake). Shaw had had the reputation of being a cynical, destructive, clever writer, but *Saint Joan,* written in simple modern contemporary language, revealed the depth and humanity of his personality. Both Dame Sybil and Sir Lewis were celebrated Shakespearean actors, and in the twilight years of their careers they gave play readings. It sounds a bit dull, but their dramatic skills were immense, as Cape Town audiences discovered when the couple read excerpts from Shakespeare and the poems of Robert Browning, such as his dramatic monologue, *My Last Duchess.*

After one show, I attended a supper at a Cape Town restaurant in honour of Sir Lewis and Dame Sybil. About 30 people attended, and at the table Dame Sybil was placed next to Uys Krige, the South African poet and writer. Sitting near me, some distance away, was Uys's wife, a formidable Afrikaans actress named Lydia Lindeque.

Uys and Lydia were an exceptionally gifted couple, although they were perennially impecunious; art and culture are wonderful, but they are not usually money-spinners. At that stage, they did not own a car, and after the meal I gave them a lift back to their modest cottage in Newlands. Lydia had recently acted in Robinson Jeffers's modern American version of *Medea*, the classical Greek tragedy by Euripides. Dame Sybil was famous for her performance in the standard English version by Gilbert Murray. Sitting in the back of the car, Uys asked Lydia whether she had discussed the play with Dame Sybil.

'Ag yes man, Uys,' she said, 'but she likes that ol'-fashion English stuff by Gilbert Murray. Typical.' Both Uys and Lydia spoke English with marked South African accents, but they loved the English language.

Uys tut-tutted sympathetically and said, 'Lydia, give us a bit of the Jeffers *Medea* which you did recently.'

'Ag, Chrise, Uys. I can't recite it now.'

'Come, Lydia, come. You know, that part where Medea makes threats.'

'Oh, orraight. "I have my dark art that fools call witchcraft. Not for nothing I have worshipped the wild grey goddess that walks in the dark, the wise one, the terrible one, the sweet huntress, flower of the night…".'

So we chugged along De Waal Drive in my small car, with Lydia's big voice reverberating in the confined space while Uys clucked admiringly in the back seat. Wonderful people who were great pioneers of the English and Afrikaans theatre in South Africa. They don't make them like that any more.

In many ways, one of the most remarkable people to have graced South African footlights was Yvonne Bryceland, an actress who came from nowhere, so to speak, and became an international star. I knew Yvonne well for many years. At about 30, she worked in the editorial library of the *Cape Argus*, was married to a property salesman named Danny Bryceland, an immigrant from Britain, and was the mother of three young children. She came from a Catholic family of modest financial background – her elderly mother used to serve tea in the Newlands rugby grandstand on Saturday afternoons – but had considerable abilities. Her brother, Bruce Heilbuth, became a distinguished journalist on the *Cape Argus*, was an amateur opera singer of some merit, and was one of the most lovable people I have ever known.

Life with husband Danny was not altogether easy. He was a cheerful soul when drinking with the lads at the Café Royal in Church Street, but he was apparently extremely jealous and suspicious as far as his attractive and vivacious wife was concerned. Yvonne was a devout Roman Catholic, and as far as I know, she would never have strayed from the marriage bonds. She was not one to play around, as the phrase goes. Nevertheless, Danny's obsessional behaviour turned to violence against her and, after many anxious consultations with a Catholic priest, she eventually divorced him, a process that went against her deeply held beliefs.

It was a sad story because Yvonne was a naturally happy soul. While all this was happening she gained light relief, I assume, by acting in knockabout amateur farces in the Barn Theatre at Constantia, which was established by David Bloomberg, a Cape Town attorney who later became mayor. Bloomberg, the son of a former mayor, Abe Bloomberg, was interested in the theatre, and his wife, Toby Fine, was a well-known ballet dancer.

These amateur theatricals, which included some radio shows, agreed with Yvonne's ebullient personality (she was always prepared to assist in the complicated practical jokes we played on each other at the office). Then, after appearing in some more serious productions by the Cape Performing Arts Board, she met the playwright and director Athol Fugard, a Port Elizabeth man who became world-famous. He offered her a part in one of his plays. No knockabout comedy, this. Fugard was an intensely serious writer who was determined to expose the cruelties and follies of the apartheid policy, which was then in its relative infancy. His plays were powerful, sombre and compelling, and they soon found an international audience, being produced in London and New York. And Yvonne Bryceland, the girl upstairs in the office, became internationally known, revealing a hitherto unsuspected ability to portray the tired, the poor, the huddled masses of this world. I saw her only once in one of these roles, and I was amazed at the strength and poignancy of her acting.

Yvonne eventually found domestic happiness in her marriage to Brian Astbury, a photographer and stage director who was prominent in Cape Town's cultural life. Alas, she died of cancer in 1992, at the age of 65. She will be well remembered by a host of theatre-lovers in South Africa. To me, she is a brilliant example – I can think of several others – of high achievement from improbable beginnings.

There were, of course, many other South Africans who succeeded in the hard world of the international theatre and film industry. One was Moira Lister, who became a leading lady in British films in the 1950s and '60s; two of her better-known films were *John and Julie* and *The Yellow Rolls Royce*. And there was the brief and remarkable career of Laurence Harvey, who was born in Lithuania in 1928 and grew up in Johannesburg as Larushka Skikne. He worked his way up from small parts in British films to become a top Hollywood star, appearing in more than twenty films before his death at the age of 45.

Marda Vanne was a South African actress who became a prominent figure on the London stage. I remember her as a dignified, rather austere personality whose outward demeanour gave no hint of a quite unusual history. She was the daughter of Sir Willem van Hulsteyn, who was born in Holland in 1865, came to South Africa at the age of fifteen and became a leading lawyer in Johannesburg. At the time of the Anglo-Boer War, he was an adviser to the arch-imperialist Lord Milner. He was also a member of the South African Parliament for many years and was knighted for services to the British Empire on the coronation of King Edward VII in 1902.

This pillar of the old establishment produced an attractive daughter named Margaretha, who became an actress under the name of Marda Vanne. In due course she married, and her husband was the epitome of tough, uncompromising Afrikaner nationalism, none other than the redoubtable J G Strijdom, who was prime minister of South Africa from 1954 to 1958. Strijdom's aggressive political attitude did not concede much to black people, brown people, foreigners (he made his first trip to Europe a month before he became prime minister) or white people who were not Afrikaner nationalists. But he was interested in the theatre and he was polite and considerate in private; and he married the daughter of a knight of the British Empire.

The marriage was very brief, but it is unlikely that Johannes Gerhardus Strijdom was to blame. Marda Vanne was a lady who was happier domestically in the company of a woman rather than a man, and she eventually formed a long-standing association with a distinguished British actress named Gwen ffrangcon-Davies. They lived in England, and after the second World War the two of them visited South Africa many times and gave great pleasure to big audiences in a wide variety of theatre productions. Marda Vanne died in London in 1970, aged 73. Gwen ffrangcon-Davies died in 1992 at the age of 101.

In the Cape Town of the mid-twentieth century, the big glamorous shows, local and international, were staged in the Alhambra Theatre, one of those elaborate cinema buildings with a romantic historical theme – Durban's Playhouse is another example. Several big American musicals – *Oklahoma* was one of them – were presented there, plus ballet and some major Shakespearean productions involving actors from Britain. The foundation of the city's vibrant theatre life rested, however, on two small venues, the Hofmeyr Theatre in the city centre and the Little Theatre in the Gardens.

The Hofmeyr was run by Brian Brooke, who was born in the then Eastern Transvaal in 1911 and studied engineering at the University of Witwatersrand. Through sheer love of the theatre, he forsook engineering when he was in his mid-twenties and chose the financial uncertainty of the stage. He studied acting and production in England, where he met the woman who became his wife, an actress named Petrina Fry. After serving in Europe in World War II, he rented the Hofmeyr Theatre and established South Africa's first permanent professional theatre company.

For years, Brooke presented at least one play a month – often two – at the Hofmeyr Theatre, and over a period of nine years he ran up a score of more than 150 plays before moving to Johannesburg to establish the Brooke Theatre there. The plays were generally of good quality and were often recent imports from the London stage; in those days the anti-apartheid cultural boycott had not yet been imposed. There were a fair number of light comedies (Brian Brooke loved acting in these) but there were also up-to-date and provocative plays by people like John Osborne, Harold Pinter and Brendan Behan.

The language in some of these was rather vivid (remember, this was the 1950s). The Hofmeyr Theatre was owned by the Dutch Reformed Church and the building was in fact adjacent to the Groote Kerk in Adderley Street, and I sometimes wondered what the church elders would have said if they could hear the profanities being uttered within earshot of their holy ground. They probably turned a deaf ear and took the rent.

The Little Theatre, at the top of Cape Town Gardens, not far from the Mount Nelson Hotel, has had a much longer history than the Hofmeyr. It was founded in 1931 by the University of Cape Town's first professor of music, Professor W H Bell, and many of the actors in the early productions were members of the staff of the University's College of Music, including one who was later my piano tutor for many years, Minnie Seabridge. The theatre itself was a converted disused university chemistry lab. Seventy years later, it was still going strong, with something like 500 productions under its belt, not only plays but opera and ballet as well. For about 40 of those years, its director was Donald Inskip, who came to South Africa in 1932 and eventually became the university's deputy principal.

It is difficult to overestimate the importance of the Little Theatre's contribution to cultural and intellectual activity in South Africa. Generations of young Capetonians have been introduced to the great panoply of European culture through performances at the Little Theatre. As a young newspaper critic, I was involved with the Little Theatre for perhaps a dozen years in the 1950s and '60s, and I can still remember vividly many of the shows that enriched my life then: Shakespeare's *Romeo and Juliet,* produced by Rosalie van der Gucht, one of the great figures in the history of South African theatre; Christopher Fry's *The Lady's Not For Burning,* produced by Leonard Schach (Fry was a brilliant poet and playwright whose work seems to be sadly neglected these days); T S Eliot's *Murder in the Cathedral* and *The Cocktail Party;* Samuel Beckett's *Waiting for Godot;* Sheridan's *The Critic;* Albert Camus's *Caligula;* Giradoux's *Tiger at the Gates;* Bertolt Brecht's *The Good Woman of Setzuan;* John van Druten's *Bell Book and Candle;* *Antigone,* by Sophocles; *The Trojan Women,* by Euripides; *Five Finger*

Exercise, by Peter Shaffer, another brilliant playwright who seems to have fallen into obscurity these days.

And there was a long string of outstanding opera productions by Gregorio Fiasconaro, who came to South Africa as an Italian prisoner during World War II, stayed and made an enormous contribution to the development of music here. Those operas included Mozart's *Marriage of Figaro* and *Don Giovanni*; Puccini's *Gianni Schicchi* and *Turandot;* several delightful short operas by Gian-Carlo Menotti, another creative spirit who seems out of favour these days; Bartok's *Bluebeard's Castle;* and even an opera called *Dark Sonnet* by the formidable head of the university's College of Music, Erik Chisholm.

A large number of gifted actors, actresses and singers appeared in these productions. Names that come to mind are Cecilia Sonnenberg, the wife of a prominent businessman; René Ahrenson; Alec Bell and Gavin Haughton (the two tramps in *Waiting for Godot)*; Gretel Mills; Bill Flynn; Eveline Garratt; Percy Sieff; and the singers Gregorio Fiasconaro, Ernest Dennis, Desiree Talbot, Noreen Berry.

And what, you may ask, of the black actors, singers, producers and writers? The truth is that, at that time, there was a very limited exposure of black talent in the conventional city venues, certainly in Cape Town. No doubt there was a good deal of more informal activity in the townships occupied, by government decree or by tradition, by black and brown people, but only a small amount surfaced in the theatres patronised by the white folks. In Cape Town, the Eoan Group did valiant and highly rewarding pioneering work among the Coloured community, mainly in the musical sphere. Eoan comes from the word *eos,* Greek for 'dawn', and the name was most appropriate. The group was founded in 1933 by Helen Southern-Holt, an affluent white Cape Town resident and a largely unsung heroine of cultural development in South Africa. Many distinguished singers emerged from the Eoan Group, including May Abrahamse, Ruth Goodwin, Josef Gabriels, Didi Sydow, Richard Manuel and Gwen Michaels. As a young critic, I attended several of the Eoan Group's operatic productions and was invariably impressed by the high standard.

In a different category was a large-scale musical called *King Kong.* The title character was an African boxer and the cast was mainly black, with some very good dancers and singers among them. It was staged in Cape Town in about 1962, at the civic theatre at Camps Bay. The National Party government – yet to reach the worst excesses of apartheid – took a grudgingly permissive view of a black show being staged in a white suburb before a racially mixed audience. The musical director of *King Kong* was Stanley 'Spike' Glasser, whom I knew reasonably well. He was a 'serious' composer of distinction, and was at the time a member of the teaching staff of the university's College of Music. As a student, he had played centre in the Wits University rugby team, the only composer I know of who was also an accomplished rugby player.

The government may have taken a reasonably relaxed view of *King Kong* but Glasser, alas, fell foul of its obnoxious racial laws. One evening, a prying policeman shone his torch into cars parked near the Rhodes Memorial, and in one of them he found Spike and a woman member of the *King Kong* cast, Maud Damons, in a compromising situation. In those bad days, government's laws included the Immorality Act, which prohibited any kind of intimate relationship between black and white people; an immoral law, if ever there was one. The result was that Glasser and his friend both hastily departed for Europe. As far as I know, their friendship ended soon after that. Glasser became a music lecturer at a British university and remained in the country permanently.

Back in Cape Town, his wife, Mona, divorced him and in the fullness of time remarried another old friend of mine, Zach de Beer, whom I first knew when he was a medical student. De Beer became a businessman and politician, leader of the parliamentary opposition for a time, and a director of Anglo American. Both he and Mona are now dead.

Looking back over many years, I would rate *King Kong* as one of the high points of indigenous South African theatre. I have not seen many of the local productions that proliferated from the 1980s and '90s onward, but obviously Welcome Msomi's Zulu version of *Macbeth, Mmbatha,* must rank high. Another imposing piece has been Mzilikazi Khumalo's Zulu opera, *Princess Magogo,* about the mother of Dr Mangosuthu Buthelezi, the Zulu leader who has for many years been a South African cabinet minister.

Princess Magogo was the daughter of Zulu King Dinizulu, who in the nineteenth century was imprisoned by the British on the Atlantic island of St Helena. Magogo, sung in the opera by one of South Africa's major singers, the mezzo-soprano Sibongile Khumalo, chronicled the plight of her people under British colonial rule, a story filled with pathos and emotion.

In September 2002, an ambitious big musical was given its world premiere in Durban: *Far From the Madding Crowd*, a dramatisation of Thomas Hardy's famous novel. The authors are two brothers, Raymond and John Ellis, the first responsible for the music and the second for dialogue and lyrics. I suppose it says something for our values that they are probably far less known than their father, the late Graham Ellis, a charming and successful businessman who was much involved in horse racing and owned a Durban July winner.

Far From the Madding Crowd turned out to be a vivid and colourful representation of late Victorian England, well acted and well sung, with good atmospheric music, but it had the serious defect of lacking one big song that the audience could hum to themselves on the way home. After more than 50 years, it is easy to remember 'People Will Say We're In Love' from *Oklahoma* and 'Some Enchanted Evening' from *South Pacific,* and I can well recall the main tune from *King Kong*, but *Far From the Madding Crowd* is a blank in my musical memory. If the brothers Ellis can come up with a big winner (as their father did in racing) they might yet make a big impact in the wider world with their musical.

My own highly subjective review of theatre over the years would be incomplete without reference to one of the most remarkable people I have ever known: Professor Elizabeth Sneddon of Durban. She is a retired professor of speech and drama at the University of Natal and a theatrical director of distinction, and when she puts thoughts to paper – as she often does – she writes in the grand and expansive manner of an earlier age. Consider this excerpt from her annual report for the National Creative Arts Youth Festival, of which she is chairperson:

'The Festival is based on recognition of the fact that what distinguishes the living from the dead is the power to move 1) Physically, 2) Emotionally, 3) Intellectually.

We have five choices:

1. Be a hermit. Live in a cave by one's self with no knowledge of standards of living or of science. Hermits will probably die of malaria, tuberculosis, bilharzia or an attack from a predator whose power to kill is greater than theirs.

2. Be a victim of a group, sect or cult which claims to have direct access to the ear of God. For a tenth of your income the members will intercede for you and you will be 'saved' in 'the after life'.

3. Be a victim of a nation. Give the state 40 percent of your income and you will be protected by the political leadership. Armies, navies, air forces will be built and when the leaders say 'march' you march, or you will be executed as a traitor.

4. Acquire great wealth in the form of money or oil or land and you will have the leisure to be free because you will be able to buy the services and skills of others.

5. Be free. Develop the personal integrity for your choice of action, so that you can be utterly trusted to live in a community and to act as though you not only loved yourself in terms of health and fitness but all other living entities – human beings, animals and plants – equally.'

Interesting ideas? Yes. Even more interesting, perhaps, is the fact that Professor Sneddon was 95 years old when she wrote those words. I have known her well for 25 years, and she is the most remarkable elderly person I have encountered. Perhaps I should say mature person; she might object to being described as elderly. She has no false modesty about her abilities at an age when most people have lost their marbles. 'What you must understand,' she is fond of telling her close friends, 'is that I am twenty years younger than my calendar age.'

What is the secret of this astonishing defiance of the ageing process? The right genes, obviously. Elizabeth Sneddon comes from strong Scottish stock (though she was born and bred in Durban) and several members of her family lived to advanced years. She has never married; whether this is a factor I cannot say. Unremitting intellectual activity has probably been the crucial reason. As a university professor, Elizabeth

Sneddon guided, bullied and inspired thousands of students. She was not popular with everybody, but she has certainly been vastly influential in instilling cultural and intellectual values that have remained with her students all their lives. She has a theatre in Durban named after her, and the Sneddon Theatre at the university follows her example: it is well run, enterprising, innovative and up to date in its outlook and presentations.

Professor Sneddon has been retired from the university for more than 30 years, but she is as busy as ever, running her youth festival from her office on the Durban Berea with the help of a small staff, firing off letters daily, persuading business people to financially support her efforts to spread knowledge of music, dance, drama and literature among schoolchildren throughout the country. She is slightly built, well dressed, good looking, a living example of what the Romans called *mens sana in corpore sano*, a sound mind in a sound body.

She herself attributes her hyperactive longevity to her lifelong habit of taking a couple of teaspoons of honey every day, pointing out that honey recovered from ancient Egyptian sites proved perfectly edible after three thousand years of storage. Honey, according to Elizabeth Sneddon, improves the mind and the memory.

I don't think her life story is as simple as that, but I take some honey occasionally … when I remember to do so.

SIX

The sportsmen

Sport plays so dominant a role in South African society that even non-sporting people – actors and artists, writers and musicians – generally show quite an intelligent interest in rugby or soccer (one or the other), cricket, tennis, athletics and even boxing.

Newspaper journalists meet many sports players. It is in the nature of the job; they do not necessarily have to be sports writers that pontificate on, criticise or worship the idols of the playing fields. I did very little sports reporting in my long career, just part-time jobs, but I have always been interested in sport. And sportspeople often provide good material for the non-specialist newspaper journalist by way of insights into epic encounters on the field and, sometimes, because of achievements and idiosyncrasies off the field.

The first celebrated sportsman I met as a young reporter in Cape Town was a man named Barry Heatlie. The name doesn't mean anything to you? In his heyday, he was the most celebrated rugby player in South Africa. His heyday was, of course, a long time ago. In the late 1940s, Mr Heatlie, as we all called him, was a regular visitor to the editorial offices of the *Cape Argus*, an elderly man who had time on his hands and wanted to chat about rugby to anybody who would listen. He was usually palmed off on me because I was one of the most junior people in the office, but I didn't mind. He was an interesting old gentleman, in his ponderous way, and I can see him in my mind's eye now: a tall hulk of a once-powerful physique, neatly dressed in a grey pin-stripe suit, always wearing an Old Diocesan (Bishops' old boys) tie, always complaining that nobody these days could execute the grubber kick correctly, the one that goes along the ground.

This dear old soul was captain of the South African rugby team in 1896 when South Africa beat a touring English team in a match at Newlands. They weren't called Springboks then – that name came when Paul Roos led the first South African touring team to Britain in 1906 – but they had already played England six times, in 1891 and 1896, and this was their first victory. Barry Heatlie, born in 1872 at Worcester in the Cape, was a formidable forward and an excellent leader (he played for Western Province in 26 Currie Cup matches and was never on the losing side). He went to school at, of course, Diocesan College in Rondebosch, and before the Newlands match he supplied his team with jerseys from the school's rugby club. They were green jerseys and they established the pattern of Springbok colours in the years to come.

It was an historic triumph for Heatlie and his team, and the reporter from the *Cape Times* noted that there was such excitement after the match that it was some time before the exhausted players could make their way to the station to catch the train home. How poignant. How appealing. How different from the lifestyle of today's pampered sportsmen.

In the *Cape Argus* office, Mr Heatlie would sometimes talk about these grand old days, but he was usually more concerned about the inability of my colleague Dirk de Villiers to place his grubber kicks correctly. De Villiers, a fellow reporter, played centre for Western Province and kicked a drop goal that won the Currie Cup for Province against the former Transvaal in 1947. He often had to endure Mr Heatlie's comments about his shortcomings, but he took them in good part.

Barry Heatlie lived in Argentina for twenty years, working in the sugar industry, and he did much to spread the popularity of rugby in that country. He played rugby there until he was 49, and on his return to South Africa in 1925 he remained involved with the game. He died after being hit by a car in Cape Town in 1951.

Incidentally, his contemporaries knew him as 'Fairy' Heatlie, a good example of the sardonic humour sometimes shown by rugby players. His other nickname was Ox, which reminds me inevitably of the unkind definition of a Springbok rugby player: someone who is as strong as an ox and twice as intelligent.

My colleague, Dirk de Villiers, was a star for Western Province and played in the Springbok trials before a team was chosen to play the All Blacks in South Africa in 1949. Many knowledgeable people thought he should have been picked, but he wasn't, and I don't think his heart was really in it. He was much more interested in the theatre and art than he was in rugby, and his ambition was to become a playwright. He gave up rugby quite early and eventually settled in London, where he worked as a journalist. He has been there for nearly 50 years, and our close friendship of more than half a century has survived the distance.

His father was, like Barry Heatlie, one of the old Springboks. His name was Dirk Isaac de Villiers and I knew him quite well in his later years. He played for South Africa in 1910, in three Tests against the British Isles. He was a delightful elderly gentleman, a lawyer by profession, and he didn't talk much about his sporting prowess although I do remember him telling me that, when his team kicked off at the start of an important match, their champion, Duggie Morkel, would place the ball on the centre spot and kick it neatly between his opponents' posts. 'It didn't count for points, of course,' he said, 'but it certainly made the opposition nervous.'

Dirk Isaac, who studied law at Cambridge University and won a rugby blue, was also a first-rate cricketer and for a long time held the Free State batting record of 200 in a provincial match. He could probably have become a Springbok cricketer – he was chosen for the 'probables' against the 'possibles' in a trial match – but withdrew from contention because of family commitments. Those were the days when cricket and rugby men were amateurs, playing for the love of the game, not for money.

To complete the picture of an all-rounder, this De Villiers was an accomplished violinist. Incidentally, he was a brother of Reverend Marthinus Lourens de Villiers, the Dutch Reformed Church minister who wrote the music for *Die Stem*, one of South Africa's national anthems.

Another member of that 1910 Springbok team was Clive van Ryneveld of Cape Town, whom I met a few times in about 1950. He was the father of an old friend of mine, another and even more famous Clive van Ryneveld, who played rugby for England and captained the South African cricket team in the 1950s. The younger Clive van Ryneveld is very well known. Him and his brother, Tony, were both Rhodes Scholars at Oxford University. Apart from his sporting ability, Clive had a brief political career as a member of parliament for the Progressive Party and then became a businessman.

As a cricketer, Van Ryneveld was an outstanding batsman, tall with an upright stance, and a good leg-break bowler. I remember him once saying, in conversation, that tail-end batsmen had much more difficulty facing spin bowling than fast bowling. An interesting point. I suppose that an inadequate batsman has to think and move his feet against slow bowling, whereas he always has a chance of snicking a four off a fast bowler. I don't know if the theory holds true today. It seems to me that, in modern cricket, the arrival of a weaker batsman is the signal for the fast men to be given the ball so that they can hurl their thunderbolts at their hapless opponents. In this age of statistics, I wonder if there are any figures to show which method is more successful towards the end of an innings – guile or brute force.

Another rugby old-timer I encountered as a young reporter was Paul Roos, captain of the 1906 Springbok team that toured Britain, winning two Test matches, drawing one and losing one, to Scotland. When I spoke to him, it was in a political context. This elderly, retired school principal, with the big flowing moustache that he had had since his playing days, had been persuaded to stand for the Nationalist Party in 1948 and was duly elected member of parliament for Stellenbosch.

He was not really suited to the bitter political hurly-burly of those days; he belonged to another, gentler and better-behaved era. He died only five months after his election to parliament, and I cannot believe that he would ever have subscribed to the cruelties and crudities of the apartheid policy as it evolved under his party. In parliament he was often treated with good-humoured derision, an attitude that he countered with immense natural dignity and charm. Over the months, the scoffers gradually fell silent and he was treated with the respect he deserved. All the same, he was a relic of another age, often tut-tutting at the boisterous and acrimonious debate going on around him. As Scott Haigh, parliamentary correspondent for the *Cape Argus*, observed drily in one of his articles, too many bumpers spoiled the day's play.

While at school in the former Rhodesia in the 1930s and '40s, I was friendly with a lad who became one of those sports stars who appear from nowhere and, just as quickly, disappear from the public eye. His name was Des van Jaarsveldt and he was a big and speedy Number 8 rugby forward who played for Rhodesia in the days when it participated in the South African Currie Cup competition.

The boy from Bulawayo was a good player, no question about it, but everybody – including, I suspect, Des van Jaarsveldt himself – was surprised when, having never played an international match, he was chosen to captain South Africa in a Test against Scotland in Port Elizabeth in 1960. The Springboks won the game 18-10 – Scotland were not regarded as strong opposition at that time – and the captain performed creditably enough, scoring a try. But he was never chosen for the Springboks again, and most rugby followers today would have difficulty in remembering his name. A brief moment of glory.

It was said, at the time, that the Springbok selectors discovered only after they had chosen him that he could not speak a word of Afrikaans – his forebears came from Holland, not South Africa – and they lost no time in replacing him with an authentic, home-grown Afrikaner. Those were the days when the word racism was often taken to mean anti-Afrikaans or anti-English feeling, quite different from the modern usage (or over-usage).

When I was a reporter in the Argus Company's London office in 1953, I encountered two of the greatest athletes ever to perform in South Africa: Arthur Newton and Wally Hayward. Memories are short, fame is ephemeral, and perhaps these names do not mean much today. They were both long-distance runners. In 1953, Wally Hayward came to England to make an attempt on the world 100-mile road-running record and to participate in the celebrated London-Brighton race. He was conspicuously successful in both, but before that happened he spent some weeks in

London, training and acclimatising to English conditions. He stayed with Arthur Newton at the latter's modest house in Ruislip, West London, and I travelled there by train several times to report on his progress.

At the time, Arthur Newton was a reserved, but friendly, grey-haired man aged 70 (he died six years later). Only when I looked him up in newspaper files and references did I realise what an extraordinary runner he himself had been.

Born in England, he came to South Africa as a young man and taught at Hilton College, near Pietermaritzburg. He later became a farmer and started his running career when he was almost 40, after serving in World War I. In 1921, soldiers returning to Natal instituted the annual Comrades marathon between Durban and Pietermaritzburg, and in 1922 Newton ran the 86 kilometres in eight hours and 40 minutes, defeating 87 other runners. He won the Comrades again in 1923, 1924, 1925 and 1927, working his time down to six hours and 24 minutes. He went to Britain in 1928 and set a new 100-mile road record. Later that year, he went to the United States and ran from the Atlantic to the Pacific, a distance of 5 500 kilometres.

By 1938, Newton had broken all world records for marathon distances up to 100 miles, or 160 kilometres. This was the man who gave me tea and biscuits while chatting about Wally Hayward's prospects. He was still running two years after I met him, and by then had clocked up 100 000 miles (160 000 kilometres). He wrote three books about running and he gave me an autographed copy of one of them.

Wally Hayward himself, the man of the moment in 1953, was not exactly a spring chicken. He was 43, a stocky, barrel-chested man with close-cropped hair and a quiet, almost taciturn demeanour. He ran the 100 miles from Bath to London and broke the existing record by the proverbial mile. Then he took part, with dozens of other runners, in the 50 mile (80 kilometre) London-Brighton race. In the company of a photographer, I took the easy way over the route, by car. It was a lovely spring day, one to call to mind Robert Browning's words, 'God's in his heaven – All's right with the world.'

The race had a comical ending. Wally Hayward won by such a wide margin, and so long before his expected finishing time, that a Brighton mayoral reception committee that was supposed to welcome him arrived too late. By the time the mayor got to a podium decorated with bunting, Wally Hayward was having a hot shower in nearby changing rooms allocated for that purpose. The mayor was embarrassed, but not Wally Hayward, who was used to running without much recognition and didn't expect an official reception anyway.

Wally Hayward, who won several Comrades marathons, had a spell in limbo when he was declared a professional after well-wishers paid his fare to England in 1953. He returned to the formal running fold in due course, and ran the Comrades again at the age of 79.

My own sporting career was totally undistinguished. After leaving school, I played rugby for a few years for the Villagers club at Claremont, Cape Town, and eventually progressed as far as the third team. That doesn't sound very elevated, but the club did at that time have eleven teams playing in various leagues, and some of the people I played with did end up in the Villagers first team and a few even in the Western Province team.

I wasn't a dedicated player – one fairly relaxed practice game a week was sufficient for me – and I had even less natural aptitude for cricket. But cricket I loved, as do many rather hopeless players. The *Cape Argus* had a team that played occasionally, and it was not difficult to secure a place in it. Oddly enough, the team had a powerful core of ex-provincial and first-league players. Two brothers, Ken and Des Dimbleby, were both Western Province players. Ken was a news reporter and Des a sports reporter, and they were the sons of a long-serving editor of the Port Elizabeth paper, *The Herald*. Percy Kirkman, who later became sports editor, had, I think, played for Griqualand West. Pat Tebbutt, later well known as a High Court judge and as a sports commentator on the radio, had been good enough to play for the University of Cape Town's first team.

Our most celebrated cricketer on the editorial staff was Owen Wynne, who played six Test matches for South Africa in 1948 and 1949, against England and Australia, as an opening batsman. He was a quiet, self-effacing man with a quaint, rather elfin face and he never quite made the headlines as an international cricketer. He was a calm and courageous player of fast bowling, but good spinners often tied him in knots. I think his Test batting average was about 25, not too bad, but not too good either. I always liked him and I was sad to read, many years later, that he had been lost at sea, of all extraordinary things, while sailing on a yacht somewhere south of Cape Town.

The Dimbleby brothers were among many good sports players to emerge from a Port Elizabeth newspaper background. When I was a young editor, of *The Friend* in Bloemfontein, one of my acquaintances was the editor of the Eastern Province *Herald*, Andrew McLean 'Mac' Pollock, whose father had been a Presbyterian minister in Bloemfontein. Mac Pollock had two sons, Peter and Graeme, who became two of the country's most famous cricketers, and Peter a sports reporter for a time. And, of course, his grandson is Shaun Pollock, who became captain of the South African team. Mac Pollock literally dropped dead at the entrance to his office in Port Elizabeth in 1969, aged 56, and still editor of the paper.

My limited and modest cricket experience was far removed from the tumult and shouting of the Test-match arena. For years, I played every Sunday afternoon in the summer for the Kelvin Grove team, Kelvin Grove being the colloquial name for what is formally called the Western Province Sports Club, a very large social club at Newlands with extensive tennis and bowls facilities. We played our cricket on a ground so small that it was called the postage stamp. Most of the time, you had only to touch the ball for it to go for four, a gratifying situation for batsmen of my standard. We played nearly all our games at home because we preferred our facilities and did not mind hosting our opponents at the tea break and the prolonged drinks sessions that followed each game.

Our captain was Murray Bisset, a member of an old Cape family and a gentleman to his fingertips. He seemed incapable of being rude or heated, and he was courteous to the extreme. Nonetheless, he was a quiet and effective disciplinarian. Our cricket whites had to be immaculate, and our on-field behaviour likewise. Bisset chose the team every week, a one-man selection panel, and anybody who failed to meet his standards simply wasn't invited to play again.

He was an expert at judging the strength of the opposition, after making discreet inquiries. If our opponents looked unusually good, he would quietly include a couple of provincial or first-league players to give our performance some muscle. That didn't happen too often, and the core of the team, myself included, remained unchanged for years. It was cricket in the best traditions of the ancient game, and my guess is that all who played in those years, the 1950s and '60s, will have happy and sentimental memories of Sunday afternoons on the postage stamp at Newlands.

Cricket, above all other games, has the capacity to generate romance, humour, eloquence and nostalgia. Every true cricket-lover will understand exactly the sentiments expressed by the poet Francis Thompson a century ago, when he wrote about a visit to Lords in London and recalled his heroes of an earlier time:

'A ghostly batsman plays to the bowling of a ghost,
And I look through my tears on a soundless-clapping host
As the run-stealers flicker to and fro,
To and fro;–
O my Hornby and my Barlow long ago.'

SEVEN

The Friend

I became editor of *The Friend*, Bloemfontein, on 1 January 1964, having been acting editor for the previous three months. I was 33 years old, the youngest editor of any daily newspaper in the country, and proud of my new job, for *The Friend*, more than a hundred years old, had an ancient and honourable tradition.

The circumstances of my accession to editorship were unusual. Just over a year earlier, I had been transferred to Bloemfontein from the *Cape Argus*, Cape Town's afternoon paper, to become deputy editor of *The Friend*, a morning paper. The latter was a much smaller paper than the *Argus* – it had a daily circulation of about 10 000, compared with the *Cape Argus*'s 70 000 – but the transfer was a promotion and an opportunity for me.

The editor of *The Friend* was William Sword Robertson, fifteen years my senior, a delightful man who had spent just about all his working life on this title. In the normal course of events, I could have expected to spend several years working under him. But things turned out differently. Robbie, a bachelor, had a non-live-in girlfriend (this was, after all, 1962) named Vera Goss, who was older than he was and was a secretary on the *Farmer's Weekly*, a well-known journal that was part of Friend Newspapers, the publishing company in Bloemfontein that also owned two other magazines, *Personality* and *Femina*, as well as *The Friend*.

Friend Newspapers was a wholly owned subsidiary of the Argus Newspaper Company, hence my transfer from the *Argus* in Cape Town. Robbie Robertson was an untravelled but experienced, educated and balanced journalist – and a man of great charm. Sadly, he had a history of intermittent alcoholic breakdowns, one of which occurred at a high-profile banquet at the Mount Nelson Hotel in Cape Town to mark the 50th anniversary of operations in South Africa of Reuters, the international news agency. The host was Sir Roderick Jones, the chairman of Reuters, and the guest of honour was the prime minister, Dr H F Verwoerd. Apparently, Robbie looked too deeply into the bottle, as they say in Afrikaans, and lay his head wearily on the table during Verwoerd's speech, raising it occasionally to produce audible mutters of 'rubbish'. A fair comment, but it didn't please the Argus directors, who were present, and Robbie was given a warning that any recurrence would mean removal from his job.

The recurrence came about a year after I had moved to Bloemfontein. Robbie and I had adjacent offices, and he presided over a news confer-ence at 9.30 am every day. After we had broken up one morning, at about 10.00 am, he put his head around my door and said he was going out for a haircut. I did not see him until 9.30 am the next day, and then the same thing happened; he was going out for a haircut.

This went on for several days, during which time Robbie's hair became longer and greyer and he himself looked more and more haggard. At no stage did he make any reference whatsoever to his daily absence from the office, and I did not ask. Discretion being the better part of common sense, I suppose. I had my hands full trying to run the paper in the unex-pected absence of my boss, and they became even more full when the weekend arrived and I received a phone call from a distraught Vera Goss to say that Robbie had disappeared from his flat near the centre of Bloemfontein. At her request, I spent a day searching the pubs and clubs of Bloemfontein, to no avail. He reappeared at the office on the Monday, in the haircut mode again, with no explanation for his disappearance.

I suppose this kind of behaviour is familiar to people acquainted with the problems of alcoholism, but at that stage of my life I really did not know what to do about it.

Terence Trigger, the business manager of Friend Newspapers, a man 25 years my senior, knew what to do. After a phone call to the company's head office in Johannesburg, he summarily removed Robbie from office, told him he was being sent to Johannesburg for treatment, and said there was no prospect of his returning to his editorship. I was told to carry on in the meantime, with the cautionary advice that there were plenty of suitable candidates elsewhere in the Argus Company for the position.

Three months later, I was given the job. Possession is nine-tenths of the law, and in the newspaper world there is a good deal of luck in getting up the ladder. Many highly competent journalists have never become editors; and there have been editors who were distinctly fortunate to reach what is the ultimate target of almost every newspaper journalist.

I remained on good terms with Robbie, who recovered well from his difficult situation. The rehabilitative treatment proved successful, he was transferred to the *Pretoria News* and worked there for many years in a senior capacity, with only very occasional minor lapses from the strictest sobriety. He married Vera Goss and eventually retired to Cape Town, where I saw them from time to time. He died there at a good age, considering that he had been a champion smoker on top of everything else, and Vera died a few months later.

The Friend no longer exists, more's the pity. It was closed down by the Argus Company in 1985, seventeen years after I left the paper, in a move to reduce costs at a time when the company was in a novel and unwelcome period of financial stringency. *The Friend* had not made profits for years, but its losses had been balanced by profits made by magazines published from the same premises: *Farmer's Weekly*, *Personality* and *Femina*. These had been sold to another company and had moved to Durban, leaving *The Friend* exposed to heavy overhead costs and not much prospect of being able to sustain them.

All the same, *The Friend* was an outpost of resistance in what was then exceedingly hostile territory for English-speaking people of liberal or moderate persuasion. It provided the rest of the company's newspapers with news coverage from what was, and still is, an important centre; after closing the paper, the company had to open a news-service office at a cost that offset some of the savings made. The people of Bloemfontein were so concerned that the mayor made a special trip to the Argus head office in Johannesburg to plead for the paper's life. All to no avail. The deed was done, and trying to revive a dead paper is as difficult as raising Lazarus, without benefit of divine intervention.

The Friend had an interesting history. It was established in 1850 as *The Friend of the Sovereignty and Bloemfontein Gazette*, published weekly. It was bilingual, English and Dutch. Later, in the 1890s, it became an English daily called *The Friend of the Free State*, and later still the name was shortened to *The Friend*.

The paper suffered its first war casualty in 1865, when its war correspondent, Wilhelm Hoevels of Kroonstad, was killed during a Boer attack on the Basuto stronghold of Thaba Bosigo. Conflict on a much larger scale came in 1899, with the outbreak of the second Anglo-Boer War. *The Friend* was in a peculiar position, an English-language newspaper in a Boer republic that had, somewhat reluctantly, become involved with the South African Republic (the Transvaal) in a war against Britain. The youthful editor of *The Friend* at the time, Arthur Barlow, who was later to become a long-serving and vivid member of the South African parliament, decided that the paper's allegiance lay with its country, and he sided with the Boers.

This display of patriotism was not, however, allowed to last long. In March 1900, four months after the start of the war, Lord Roberts led his troops into Bloemfontein, and one of his first actions was to close down the enemy newspaper, *The Friend*. But this created a problem. Without the newspaper, there was no effective way of communicating with the large civilian population of the city during British occupation (no radio or television then). So within a few weeks, the British revived *The Friend*, staffing it with war correspondents who had accompanied them in the field.

The most prominent among these was Rudyard Kipling, who was famous then and was soon to become the most celebrated writer of his time and winner of the Nobel Prize for literature. Kipling, who had begun his working life as a newspaper journalist in India, edited *The Friend* for several weeks and was a prolific writer, giving dry advice to the British on how to cope with the greatly underestimated Boer enemy.

Copies of *The Friend* from that time became rare Africana and some-times fetch substantial prices in auction rooms in Britain and America.

Kipling, a friend of Cecil Rhodes, lived intermittently in Cape Town for several years and had a kind of romantic love of the country, memorably expressed in one of his poems:

'Under hot Constantia broad the vineyards lie –
Throned and thorned the aching berg props the speckless sky –
Slow below the Wynberg firs trails the tilted wain'.

[wain being a poetic term for wagon]

Kipling subsequently achieved great international fame and won the Nobel Prize for literature. Later, about 50 years ago, there was a reaction in the anti-imperialist mood that swept across much of the world, and he was seen as an anachronistic British jingo. Today there is, I think, a reassessment among critics in Britain in particular, and a recognition that Kipling is one of the great figures in the long history of English litera-ture. One has only to read his short stories to appreciate his stature.

Another writer who lived in Bloemfontein briefly at the time of the Anglo-Boer War was Arthur Conan Doyle, creator of the most famous of all detectives, Sherlock Holmes. Conan Doyle was a medical officer with the British troops who occupied Bloemfontein in 1900, and he and his colleagues had to cope with an outbreak of enteric fever that, in little more than a month, claimed the lives of 5 000 British soldiers who had drunk contaminated water from the old wells of Bloemfontein.

After the Anglo-Boer War, *The Friend* was staffed by a long line of distinguished editors and writers, and although it was always a small-circulation paper, it had an influence out of proportion to its sales, sometimes being described as the Manchester Guardian of South Africa. For 33 years, the editor was T W Mackenzie, a Scot who became the friend and confidant of General J B M Hertzog, prime minister of South Africa for twelve years between the two world wars. Hertzog was a Free Stater who was, in many ways, the founder of the National Party, though in 1941 they drove him out for what they regarded as his overly conciliatory attitude towards white English-speaking South Africans.

Hertzog stood for a 'twin stream' policy in the days when racial discrimination meant conflict between Boer and Brit. How times have changed. Incidentally, Hertzog's unusual combination of Christian names, James Barry Munnik, had a strange history. His mother had been a Miss Munnik, and she had been delivered at birth, in difficult circumstances, by Dr James Barry, the woman who successfully posed as a man at the Cape in the early 1800s. So General Hertzog was named in honour of a transvestite doctor.

Tom W Mackenzie, editor of *The Friend* from 1910 to 1943, created a kind of journalistic dynasty. His elder son, Wally Mackenzie, became editor of *The Friend*, then the *Daily News* in Durban and then the *Cape Argus* in Cape Town. Another son, Donald, was a well-known sports writer before his death in a motor accident. Yet another son, Pinky, worked in the printing department of *The Friend* for many years. His wife, Sheila, was widely known as president of the National Council of Women. Another of Tom's children, Mary, was an accomplished journalist who married George Aschman, later assistant editor of the *Cape Times* in Cape Town. And a grandson, Mike Mackenzie, was a photographer on the *Cape Argus* until he, too, died in a motorbike accident.

A W Wells, who succeeded Mackenzie as editor, was another immigrant from Britain, as were many English-language newspaper editors of those days. Arthur Wells came from the north of England and had made his name in Bloemfontein as founding editor of *The Outspan*, the first really successful indigenous monthly magazine in South Africa. This was his métier; he was less successful during his three-year editorship of *The Friend*, partly because he had only a limited knowledge of Afrikaans, which was the language of the Free State, although the city of Bloemfontein was, at the time, largely English-speaking.

Arthur Wells was a wonderful man whom I got to know well in the London office of the Argus company in 1953, when he was coming to the end of a long career in journalism. He was apparently a truly gifted magazine editor, a man of wide experience and knowledge, totally unpretentious and with an intuitive grasp of what interested ordinary people.

He was resourceful, too. Bill Forrest, later an assistant editor on the *Cape Argus* and *The Star* in Johannesburg, once told me, with some awe, about an experience from his youth on *The Outspan*. The magazine ran a serial fiction story imported from Britain and it was Forrest's job to prepare this for publication. In those far-off days, the material came in batches by sea, several episodes at a time. Forrest was working on the installments when he discovered, to his horror, that Chapter 7 and Chapter 9 were there, but no Chapter 8. In a panic, he rushed to his editor. Wells was perfectly calm. He read Chapters 7 and 9 and then sat down at his typewriter to write a Chapter 8 that, according to Bill Forrest, matched the style and the theme of the whole and fitted in convincingly with what went before and came after.

Wells was a man of parts. In London, he tried to teach me something about football by taking me to watch Arsenal play, and he had an acute sense of history. The Great Trek, he believed, was an overrated event. 'It wasn't a bad trek, but lots of people had treks – the Americans, the Canadians, the Australians. Now, the Boer War was different. That's the greatest event in Afrikaner history.' One day, I heard him whistling a long and fairly involved tune that I recognised as a somewhat abstruse song by Rachmaninov. Not exactly the top of the pops. He knew what it was. 'I heard someone sing it many years ago,' he explained.

Among those who followed Arthur Wells at *The Friend* were George Ferguson, another immigrant (he came from Scotland and was an obsessive lover of Shakespeare's plays); Wally Mackenzie; and René de Villiers, who later became editor of the *Daily News* in Durban and *The Star* in Johannesburg and, in retirement, a Progressive Federal Party member of parliament and president of the South African Institute of Race Relations.

René was a delightful man, a Free State aristocrat of the old order, educated at Grey College in Bloemfontein and the London School of Economics. He entered journalism young and, in a profession sometimes conspicuous for large heads and small minds, he was an exceptionally balanced and modest person, and clever too. White people who fought hard against apartheid in the 1950s, '60s, '70s and '80s do not get much credit in the new dispensation, but the way of a liberal in the Free State was hard, as I discovered in due course. For René de Villiers, who was born and bred an Afrikaner, it was even more difficult; many of the local whites regarded him as a *verraaier*, a traitor, or at best, a sad case.

His unfailing good temper no doubt helped, as must have his marriage to Moira Franklin, a member of an old and distinguished Bloemfontein family. Her father was mayor of Bloemfontein – the nature reserve on the top of Naval Hill is named after him – and her brothers were Jack, a Bloemfontein attorney, and Blen (for Blennerhassett, an old missionary family) Franklin, a Rhodes Scholar at Oxford who became a Supreme Court judge in Johannesburg and president of the South African Tennis Association. The idea of service to the community was second nature to people like these.

René was related to Dawie Marquard, one of the best people I have known. He was another old Free Stater; the town of Marquard is named after one of his forebears, a Dutch Reformed Church clergyman. Dawie spent a lifetime at Grey College, as pupil and teacher, with a break at Oxford University, where he, too, was a Rhodes Scholar. He was a true all-rounder, a lover of sport (he was president of the South African Cricket Association), the theatre, music and literature. If he had had the will and the opportunity (the Nats did not like people such as Dawie Marquard) he could have excelled in many fields. As it was, he remained a schoolmaster and became a kind of Mr Chips at Grey College until his retirement in the 1970s.

Dawie's wife, Kathleen, formerly Murray, was in charge of the editorial library at *The Friend*. They lived in a modest house in an unfashionable part of Bloemfontein, which was the focus for a stream of distinguished and interesting visitors. I never knew a middle-aged couple who had a less materialistic view of life. They had an old car and a small house and, as far as he was concerned, clothes that were functional rather than fashionable, but they ate well and drank well and their conversation was splendid.

And they begat four clever and capable children. One followed his father's example by being a Rhodes Scholar at Oxford; another became an actuary, passing, I think, second in South Africa in his final exams; one became business manager of *The Star* newspaper in Johannesburg before migrating to Australia, where he died at a relatively youthful age after an ill-advised game of hockey; and the only daughter, a joy to the eye and the ear, married Robert Molteno, son of Donald Molteno, an old-time Liberal Party member of parliament in the South African Parliament, and they ended up as academics in Zambia.

Friend Newspapers, which published the daily paper as well as *Personality, Femina* and *Farmer's Weekly* magazines, was served by some exceptional people. The women's-page editor and music critic of *The Friend* was Mary Rousseau, who was head of the South African Music Teachers' Association and who occasionally left her desk to take the piano part in chamber music recitals in Bloemfontein's Civic Theatre. Her husband was Jaap Rousseau, a real character who taught Latin at Grey College for decades. He was a most entertaining man and had been a part-time radio comedian.

The Rousseaus' daughter, Annette, was a gifted musician who became a tympanist (drum player) in the Icelandic Symphony Orchestra in Reykjavík. When she returned to South Africa, she joined an orchestra in Johannesburg and married another player, an Italian. She was Afrikaans, he was Italian, and the common language for themselves and their various relatives had to be English. Not an unusual situation, I suppose.

Friend Newspapers had an art department that was mainly occupied in producing illustrations and decorations for the magazines. Among those who laboured there were two people who became distinguished (and high-priced) artists. One was Eben van der Merwe, who left the world of journalism to become a designer of stained glass and who hit the interior décor market at the right time, when the rich of Johannesburg were becoming aware of the charms of old-fashioned windows.

The other was Alexander Podlashuc, who eventually left to become head of the Technical College art school in Port Elizabeth. Podlashuc and his wife, Marianne, were both successful artists. Pod, as he was generally known, had a fairly lofty and distant attitude to the common or garden journalists around him. After I arrived from Cape Town, he was polite but unenthusiastic when we met at the daily morning tea sessions that Terence Trigger, the manager, organised in the interests of teamwork. Pod's interest quickened, however, when he learned that I could play the piano. He himself was a clarinettist, he informed me, and if he lent me some scores perhaps we could do some duo work together. I agreed, and he produced an arrangement for clarinet and piano of a sonata by the seventeenth-century Italian composer, Arcangelo Corelli.

I worked hard at the piano part, and one Sunday morning we met at my home for our first performance. It was soon apparent that Pod was no Benny Goodman. Numerous wrong notes were punctuated by a flow of expletives that one would not have expected from the lips of a sensitive artist. Eventually, after one excruciating sound, I said with some exasperation: 'Podlashuc, you're the only clarinettist I've ever heard who can play two notes at the same time and both of them wrong.' We laughed and became better friends.

The news editor of *The Friend*, the man in charge of the reporters, was Piet Wessels, a former rugby Springbok. He had toured Britain with Basil Kenyon's famous 1951 team, and he almost shed sentimental tears every time he thought about the cold, wet playing fields of England and Scotland. He had worked on various Afrikaans and English newspapers, but at heart he was a farmer and he had a valuable property near Wepener, in the southern Free State, which he visited most weekends.

Piet was a huge man with a gentle disposition, but on the rare occasions when he became angry he was dangerous – as the chief subeditor, Ed van Olst, discovered. One afternoon, Van Olst told Wessels to 'f... off, can't you see I'm busy?' Piet's expression spoke volumes, and about half an hour later, at a news conference in my office, Van Olst deemed it wise to offer an apology. Wessels was only partly placated. 'Van Olst, I accept your apology this time, but if you ever use language like that to me again, I'll break your neck,' he said, clenching and unclenching his enormous hands. He meant it, and Ed van Olst knew it.

Piet Wessels was a treasure house of rugby reminiscences. In about 1965, an English rugby forward was sent home from a tour of New Zealand for biting an opponent, something that was less common then than it is now. The papers were full of this celebrated affair, and at our afternoon conference I facetiously asked Wessels if he had ever bitten a man during his long career as a rugby hooker. Piet had prominent front teeth, and he bared these in a smile as he said, 'Just once.' Pressed for detail, he told us about a game he had played for Transvaal against Eastern Province. Every time a scrum went down, a hand came over his eyes as the ball was put in, a vexing experience for any hooker. Piet patiently put up with this for a few scrums and found that the culprit was front-ranker Amos du Plooy, a legendary strongman in Eastern Province rugby.

After the fourth or fifth scrum, trying to hook a ball he could not see, Piet told Du Plooy (in Afrikaans): 'Amos, you stop doing that or I'll get you.' In the next scrum, the hand came over his eyes once more.

'At the next scrum,' said Piet, 'I held back until the opposing front rank had gone down. The back of Amos du Plooy's neck was below me, in thick folds. I bent down and bit as hard as I could, into the rump.' This with a vivid demonstration from those prominent teeth.

We were aghast at this appalling tale of crime and punishment. 'What happened then?' I asked.

'Ah, said Piet, 'I moved my head back as quickly as I could. Just in time. Amos's head came up like a bullet. Half a second later, no face for me.' After that, apparently, the game proceeded along orderly lines.

The Friend had a long history of interesting staff members, from Rudyard Kipling onward. One of them was Kalfie Martin, a rugby Springbok who became a general and the head of the South African Air Force. Another, for a short time, was Sir De Villiers Graaff, for many years leader of the opposition in the South African parliament. C R 'Blackie' Swart, South Africa's first state president, was an editorial contributor for years, a fact he always reminded me of on the rare occasions we met. These meetings were usually at the annual lunch the Bloemfontein City Council gave in honour of the state president, he being a Free Stater with a farm named De Aap at Winburg, 50 kilometres away.

These lunches were folksy Nationalist occasions, with a school choir singing *'Toe die sneeu val op die Maloeties'* (woorde deur C R Swart), to the tune of 'When it's springtime in the Rockies'. The state president himself would give a German impersonation that always brought the house down. He was benign, avuncular, friendly, unpompous. What strange human alchemy that people like him, so pleasant in their everyday relationships, could be so brutal and ruthless and, indeed, inhumane in devising and administering policies based solely on a person's skin colour.

Many prominent South African media people worked at one time or another on *The Friend*, among them D H 'Dum' Ollemans, who became chairman of the Argus Company; Peter McLean, later general manager of the Argus Company; Tertius Myburgh, editor of the Johannesburg *Sunday Times* for a long time; Aubrey Sussens, the doyen of the public relations industry; Ronnie Gill, editor of the *Pretoria News*; John Colman, who became deputy editor of the *Cape Argus*; David Brechin and Mike Lloyd, both editors of the *Diamond Fields Advertiser* in Kimberley.

A small paper is a first-rate training ground for young journalists, provided it is not a trivial paper. *The Friend* had an editorial staff of about 35 when I edited it, and the paper was not trivial. It was the strongest non-Nationalist voice in the Free State, a role which had some comical results.

At the time, the Free State Provincial Council consisted entirely of Nationalists. The United Party had been quite strong, in Bloemfontein particularly, until the 1950s, but the Afrikaner *trek* from the platteland into the towns, plus the usual electoral boundary gerrymandering by the Nats, changed all that. It was cosy for the Nats to have the provincial council to themselves, but even the most supine of party men occasionally hanker for an argument with someone else. This was often the reporter from *The Friend*. An indignant Nat, complaining about some real or imagined enemy, would look up at the press gallery, wave a finger in the air, and say, *'En ek sê vir jou ...'*. And I'm telling you. As the reporter had no right to reply, it always seemed to me a little unfair.

It was hard work editing *The Friend* and incurring constant and aggressive criticism from a Nationalist administration that had almost unbounded political power. I ran a campaign in the paper for a swimming bath to be built by the authorities in Bloemfontein's black township, Bochabela. This was met with withering contempt. When 'they' pay enough in municipal rates to justify the expenditure, we'll build the bath, I was told. Never mind that the wages of black people were so low and their houses so humble that there was no prospect of their ever paying substantial rates.

A campaign to establish day crèches for the children of (black) working mothers ran into another wall of hostile indifference. *The Friend* argued carefully, citing examples, that many wives and unmarried mothers in the poorer sections of the community needed to work to make ends meet. In response, I was given pious lectures about the virtues of family life. The wife of the administrator of the Free State told me that a mother's place was in the home. Never mind that the home might be made of cardboard and string, and that mother and children might be starving.

There was, of course, a fringe of concerned white people. Most of them voted for the United Party. Rightly or wrongly, they believed that, in the words of Chips Barr, a delightful man who edited the *Farmer's Weekly* for many years, the UP stood for fair play. A few people supported the Progressive Party, which, however, had no branch in Bloemfontein.

A young journalist on *The Friend*, Johan de Villiers, was one of a group who established a Progressive Party 'cell' – an appropriate word, given the risks of the time. Johan came from a distinguished and intellectual family, and was a nephew of Bram Fischer, a communist lawyer who was sentenced to life imprisonment for 'sabotage'. Bram Fischer was the son of a Judge President of the Supreme Court, and the grandson of a prime minister of the Orange River Colony. His brother, Paul Fischer, was a prominent doctor in Bloemfontein and I knew him well. Their nephew, Johan de Villiers, reporter on *The Friend*, was a clever man who left to pursue academic studies and obtained a doctorate before returning to journalism. He was the only chief subeditor (of *The Star*) I have ever heard of who was a doctor.

When I became editor of *The Friend*, I also inherited a part-time job that had, for decades, accompanied the editorship. I became correspondent of *The Times*, in London, for the Orange Free State and the Basutoland Protectorate. I was given cabling authority and was asked to supply all the news fit to print from that part of the world.

Readers of *The Times* were not much interested in Bloemfontein, Kroonstad or Dewetsdorp, but they were interested in the affairs of Basutoland, which was in the process of becoming the independent kingdom of Lesotho. My intermittent cables were quite well featured in *The Times*. The pay was unremarkable, but the big bonus was to receive, free, the airmail edition of *The Times* which, printed on thin paper, arrived in Bloemfontein within three days of publication in London.

The Times, founded in 1784, was a most gentlemanly employer. It was never a paper to rush into hasty decisions, and it was not until 1966 that it placed news on the front page instead of advertisements, something virtually every other paper in the world had done long before.

John Walter was the founder, publisher and first editor of *The Times*, and the Walter family remained the proprietors from 1784 to 1908. The last Walter, John Walter IV, relinquished his shareholding in 1966, at the age of 93.

Sir William Haley, editor from 1953 to 1967, was the first editor born in the twentieth century and the first since 1803 not to have been to a university.

Geoffrey Robinson, editor from 1912 to 1918, was the only man to occupy the editorial chair twice. He did so under different names, changing his name to Dawson to inherit from an aunt a substantial property in Yorkshire. He had been Lord Milner's private secretary in South Africa after the Anglo-Boer War of 1899–1902, and was editor of *The Star* in Johannesburg from 1905 to 1910. As Dawson, he was editor of *The Times* from 1922 to 1941 and was a close friend of Stanley Baldwin, the pre-war prime minister of Britain.

The late Roy Jenkins, former British Chancellor of the Exchequer and Chancellor of Oxford University, said in his book, *Selected Writings*: 'The *Times* has no record of impeccability. Other newspapers have quite frequently been better. But none, on average, has been so good for so long.'

Early in 1967, I had to relinquish *The Times* correspondentship. English-language newspapers in South Africa were being constantly harried by the Nationalist government, and the most frequent accusation was that they were disloyal and sent adverse and distorted news about the country to the overseas press. Given the circumstances, the Argus Company thought it best that none of its editors should be correspondents for overseas papers, no matter how august they might be. I wrote to *The Times* explaining the situation and suggested my deputy, John Colman, as my successor. The replying letter from Sir William Haley was memorable. It started off: 'Dear Mr Green, All of us at *The Times* are very sorry to hear that you have to relinquish the correspondentship ...'. I imagined them sobbing gently into their teacups at the thought that

Green was no longer working for them in Bloemfontein. As I said, *The Times* was the most gentlemanly of employers.

When I arrived in Bloemfontein from Cape Town in 1962, I found the change a depressing experience. 'The biggest cemetery in the world with lights' was one description of the central city. There were a couple of cinemas, a couple of indifferent restaurants, the Ramblers sports club, a large number of churches, and that was it. Six years later, when I left for Durban and a position as deputy editor of the *Daily News,* I was genuinely sorry to shake the Free State dust from my shoes. I had a nice house, my family were happy, we had made good friends, I played tennis at the Ramblers club, I was known in Bloemfontein and I tried, not too successfully, to make friends and acquaintances across the colour line.

I was sorry to leave all this. But, really, Durban is not to be compared with Bloemfontein. When one has left Bloemfontein, there is little reason to return. And in the past 35 years, I have spent exactly five nights there, just passing through, as they say, the city where I once lived so happily.

EIGHT

A brush with the law

Nearly 500 years of Portuguese rule in Mozambique were drawing to an end in 1974 with the Frelimo movement coming into power, and this event caused an uneasy frisson in the ranks of the government of South Africa. To the white Nationalists, it meant that protective barriers between their regime and Black Africa were going, Mozambique in the northeast and Angola in the northwest.

The Nationalists were jittery, as they had every reason to be, and they were paranoid about the rash of pro-Frelimo rallies that broke out in various parts of South Africa. The usual strong-arm tactics followed: arrests, detentions, warnings and so forth.

In Durban, the South African Students' Organisation (SASO) and the Black People's Convention (BPC) organised a pro-Frelimo celebratory meeting to be held at Currie's Fountain. This sports ground, which had traditionally been used mainly by black and brown players, is not far from the city centre, from the Greyville racecourse and from Durban's upmarket residential suburb, the Berea.

The rally was to be held on 25 September 1974 in the late afternoon, so that people could attend after work. In Cape Town the previous night, the minister of justice, Jimmy Kruger, issued a statement saying that he intended to ban all SASO and BPC meetings and that a banning order, made in terms of the Riotous Assemblies Act, would be published in the Government Gazette.

A report about all this was sent to the *Daily News* in Durban early the next morning, the day of the planned gathering, and was referred to me by the chief subeditor, Jim Baxter. I was deputy editor of the paper at the time and acting as editor on that day; the editor, John O'Malley, was attending a speech day at Hilton College near Pietermaritzburg, where his son was a pupil. Jim Baxter also sent me, for approval or otherwise, a report, written in our own office, stating that in spite of the ban the organisers of the rally intended to go ahead with it, at Currie's Fountain at 5.00 pm.

I obtained the text of the Riotous Assemblies Act from the editorial library and studied it. The Act made clear that it was an offence to 'advertise or make known' a banned meeting, but no more precise definition was given. The question facing me was whether our news report was an advertisement for the meeting.

In those days, all senior newspaper journalists had to be amateur lawyers as they attempted to evade the minefield of legislation devised by the government to suppress information and trap the unwary. It was not feasible to seek the advice of a professional lawyer every time a query arose, if only for the time factor, such as existed in this case. A legal opinion would be useless when the meeting was over.

I edited the report carefully, removing from it the time and venue of the meeting, but leaving in the essential information that the organisers intended to go ahead with it. My reasoning was that this could not be construed as an advertisement and that the public was entitled to information, including those people living or working in the neighbour-hood; the elderly in particular might wish to give Currie's Fountain a wide berth that afternoon in case of trouble with trigger-happy police-men. But my basic motivation was a desire to publish the facts, a desire shared by every journalist worth his salt.

The report was published, as edited, in the *Daily News*. O'Malley returned from Hilton College, and that evening the two of us and our wives attended a wine tasting at a Durban beachfront hotel. We had barely sipped the cabernet sauvignon when three uniformed policemen appeared, laid fairly gentle hands on O'Malley and told him they were arresting him on a charge under the Riotous Assemblies Act. He was incredulous, but he went with them to their car. I phoned the paper's attorney, Michael Hands, and arranged to meet him at the central police station in Durban.

There, we were rapidly escorted to the office of Colonel Marcus van der Merwe, who had discovered that O'Malley, who was being detained somewhere else in the police station, had been away that day and that I was responsible for the offending report. The colonel informed me that he wanted to ask me some questions but would not do so until the attorney had left the room. Hands protested about my rights and his, but the colonel was unmoved. 'Until he goes, we don't talk,' he told me. 'And I can keep you here all night and tomorrow and the next day and the next day and the next day.' So much for individual rights under the grand old Nationalist government.

Hands left and I made a statement saying, inter alia, that I did not believe I had broken the law. The colonel was not satisfied. He wanted the original report, as typed by the reporter (these were the old days) and edited by me.

It was now after 10.00 pm I explained to him that the original material would be somewhere in the proofreaders' section of the *Daily News* printing works, but I had not the faintest idea where. I pointed out that the *Daily News* was an afternoon paper and would be closed by now. He was unconvinced and insisted that we go down to the printing works. I was accompanied by three armed policemen, just in case I decided to make a break for it.

As we arrived at the newspaper building, a lone printer who had completed a late-night shift was closing the door behind him. I shouted and he waited, surprised to see me, and even more surprised at the company I was keeping. He took us into the building and quickly found the original typescript of the report, which was handed to the police. 'It wasn't so difficult after all, was it?' said the colonel sourly.

O'Malley was then released, but I was told that in my case, bail of R50 – equal to several hundred rands today – would be required; this at 11.30 pm at night. John Featherstone, assistant manager of the *Daily News,* who had been another guest at the winetasting, had followed us to the police station and was waiting there for news of our situation. He had R50 in his hip pocket and he paid the bail. He was always good with money, John Featherstone, which is why he later became the chief executive of Independent Newspapers. O'Malley and I were told to be in court at 9.00 am the next morning.

Meanwhile, in Cape Town, the minister of justice, Jimmy Kruger, the man responsible for our arrest, was attending a cocktail party at which another guest was Wally Mackenzie, editor of the *Cape Argus*. Kruger was an unusual man, superficially quite amiable in a vulgar way, and he spoke English with a Johannesburg accent rather than an Afrikaans one. He later became notorious for his crude and callous remark about Steve Biko's death in detention – 'I am not glad and I am not sorry about Mr Biko ... he leaves me cold' – and he was no lover of the English-language newspapers, not least because they had delved into his antecedents.

Many journalists had heard the interesting and amusing story – given his political background – that Jimmy Kruger's real name was Jimmy Jones, that his father was an English-speaking South African, originally Welsh, who had died, and that he had adopted his stepfather's surname when his mother remarried. The story was hardly scandalous or defamatory, but several newspapers that investigated it ran into a brick wall with Jimmy Kruger, who was anxious to be a super-Afrikaner. He would say nothing except remind newspapers that it was an offence under the Children's Act to publish unauthorised information about orphans.

So Jimmy Kruger did not love the press, but he was on quite good terms with Wally Mackenzie, the *Cape Argus* editor, and at the party in Cape Town he needled the latter, saying, 'We're arresting your fellows in Durban.' Mackenzie was horrified, and with all haste he phoned Layton Slater, chairman of the Argus Company, which owned the *Daily News*, the *Cape Argus* and *The Star*, in Johannesburg. Mackenzie told Slater that he knew Kruger quite well and that he was sure the whole matter could be settled over a drink or lunch.

Slater was having none of this. He was outraged at the treatment meted out to O'Malley and myself, and the next morning he was on the first plane to Durban. O'Malley and I made a brief formal appearance in court, the case was adjourned for further investigation, and we had a meeting with Slater at which he insisted that we should be represented by Sydney Kentridge, reputedly the best advocate in the land, and also one of the most expensive. (Kentridge is now a leading barrister in Britain, having emigrated years ago, and is Sir Sydney.)

It was a stop-start case that dragged on for months. Slater flew down from Johannesburg for every hearing, sat in the front row of the public section of the court-room, and made loud comments of 'rubbish' and 'lies' as the state witnesses gave evidence – comments the magistrate must have heard but which he chose to ignore.

Most of the state evidence concerned the promulgation in the *Government Gazette* of the notice banning the pro-Frelimo meeting, which did, in fact, take place but turned out to be peaceful and really quite unremarkable. I was the principal defence witness and spent an unpleasant but not fearful day in the witness box. The public prosecutor conceded that the offence, if any, was a technical one, and that I did not have any base criminal motives. Kentridge argued our case with his famed skill and eloquence.

In the end, the magistrate found O'Malley not guilty (he, after all, was not even present when the alleged crime was committed) and found me guilty. I was cautioned and discharged. Slater boomed out immediately afterwards that, as far as he was concerned, we were both not guilty and that the outcome of the trial was the high point in his entire 40 years in newspapers. The Argus Company, as publisher of the *Daily News*, was fined R10. An appeal was lodged before two judges in the Natal division of the Supreme Court several months later. Kentridge was highly optimistic that the appeal would succeed, but it was dismissed.

There is a postscript to the end of the case in the magistrate's court. I was about to leave the dock when a policeman's hand fell on my shoulder in a 'not so fast' way and I was told to go downstairs to have my fingerprints taken. This messy and rather demeaning experience is a common practice now, but it was not then. An elderly, fatherly looking police sergeant pressed my hands into an ink block and onto white paper before admiring his handiwork or, rather, mine. 'Beautiful prints,' he said, with the air of a connoisseur. 'You should see some of the hands that come in here. Bricklayers, workmen …' It almost made me feel better.

The last word came from an old friend and colleague, the late Arnold Benjamin, long-serving columnist on *The Star* in Johannesburg. In a letter to O'Malley and myself, he sent his good wishes and added: 'Apart from that, how did you enjoy the wine tasting?'

NINE

Sad tales

How sour sweet music is,
When time is broke and no proportion kept;
So is it in the music of men's lives.

Thus muses King Richard II in Shakespeare's play. He is right, of course. Few of us have escaped entirely those moments when harmony turns to discord and the even rhythm of life to a jarring syncopation.

For some unfortunates, the disruption of the music of their lives turns not to sourness but to total and absolute disaster. Here are three such sad tales from the 1970s and '80s, all of them involving people whom, at one time or another, I knew well.

The first is the best-known case, one of the modern mysteries of the Cape, in fact. John Wiley was a lithe and handsome young man when I first knew him. He was a member of Cape Town's elite, educated at the Diocesan College (Bishops) and Oxford University. His father was president of Western Province Cricket, which owned the famous Newlands ground, and John himself was an excellent cricketer, a batsman who scored many runs for the Western Province provincial team.

He was working at Syfrets Trust Company when I first met him, but he had distinct political ambitions. He expressed his hopes to the then-youthful leader of the United Party, Sir De Villiers Graaff, who also had Bishops, Oxford and Western Province cricket ties. Graaff told him to become fluent in Afrikaans (not exactly the language of Bishops, Oxford and Western Province cricket) and to come back when he could address a meeting in that language.

John applied himself to the task and became so proficient in Afrikaans that the United Party often used him as a public speaker in platteland towns and villages where English was seldom spoken. He was rewarded with a United Party seat in the Cape provincial council, and later with a seat in parliament, representing the then-safe UP constituency of Simonstown (the Wiley family had lived at St James, in the constituency, for many years).

That was in 1966, a few months before the assassination of the prime minister, Dr Verwoerd. Whether that event affected the 38-year-old Wiley's political attitudes is difficult to say, but it is certain that his outlook became steadily more conservative as, under John Vorster and P W Botha, the South African government trudged the dismal path of resistance at home and isolation abroad. Wiley moved steadily to the right and eventually became the National Party member of parliament for Simonstown, a conspicuous reactionary in a party that was never short of reactionaries.

He was not a popular man, especially in the Cape milieu in which he had grown up, an atmosphere of affluent and easy-going relative liberalism. But this much could be said for him, by friend or foe: when he changed parties he resigned his parliamentary seat and fought it again under his new colours.

This is a rare phenomenon in South African politics, where party-swopping by sitting members of parliament has, in recent years, been sanctioned by legislation. In the past, most party defectors sat tight and hoped for the best. One of the few who did not was Dr Bernard Friedman, an outstanding parliamentary debater who resigned on an issue of principle from the United Party in 1953 and resigned his seat, Hillbrow, to stand again as an independent.

Friedman was an intellectual and a liberal who had held the seat for ten years. Hillbrow, in the heart of Johannesburg, was generally regarded as a progressive-minded community, but an Afrikaans-speaking UP conservative from Natal had no difficulty in defeating Friedman in a by-election. It was not a great encouragement for others to follow his example. Wiley resigned Simonstown, however, and then won back the same seat. He was a difficult, often unreasonable, sometimes arrogant man in parliament, but he was an excellent constituency man. As a member of parliament, he looked after the voters' interests, regardless of their political allegiance, and they rewarded him with their support.

I shall cite one example that I heard about towards the end of his career, when he was a cabinet minister. My mother was living in a residence for elderly people in the Simonstown constituency and one of her acquaintances there was agitated because her state pension had not arrived, following a change of address. She asked my mother if I, her son, knew John Wiley. Yes, replied my mother, but why don't you phone him yourself?

The little old lady phoned Wiley and explained her problem. He took down the details and told her that if her pension had not arrived within ten days she was to phone him again. The money arrived four days later, with a letter of apology. The result: guaranteed votes for John Wiley from the little old lady and all her little old friends.

In at least one other respect, Wiley's political behaviour was commendable. He was a concerned environmentalist, particularly with reference to the conservation of marine resources. When he was a member of the parliamentary opposition, he nagged the Nationalists about the ruthless over-exploitation of fish stocks off the country's Atlantic coast. Excessive fishing quotas were granted by the government for years, a dangerous indulgence not unconnected to the fact that some Nationalist politicians and their friends were big investors in the fishing industry.

Low quotas corrected this reckless policy just in time to allow fish stocks to be restored and save the fish supplies for the future, and much of the credit must go to John Wiley, who later became the minister of environment.

But to his critics, he remained an opinionated, intolerant and potentially dangerous right-winger. In particular, he had a bee in his bonnet about the English-language newspapers, which were strongly opposed to the Nationalist government. On many occasions, members of the House of Assembly were visibly bored when Wiley produced endless cuttings and quotations to illustrate the perfidy of the newspapers.

I used to try to reason with him. One day, he let fly at the *Cape Times*, which he said was responsible for turning 'the decent, ordinary Cape Coloured people' against white people. I protested. Didn't he think, I asked, that the policies of his own government – removing them from the voters' roll in the Cape; forcibly moving them from their traditional residential areas in Cape Town to the wastes of the Cape Flats; imposing apartheid in universities, buses and trains; reserving many jobs for whites only; the list goes on – were responsible for any antipathy on the part of the Coloured people?

'No, no,' said Wiley. 'That has nothing to do with it. It's the *Cape Times* that's turned them against us.' A fruitless debate.

Wiley prospered financially, and eventually he bought a mansion at Noordhoek that had been built many years ago by Sir Drummond Chaplin, who was administrator of Southern Rhodesia from 1914 to 1923. In this baronial place, he acquired the not altogether desirable reputation of being the 'J R of the Cape', J R being the ruthless, power-hungry principal character of the long-running television serial, *Dallas*.

His private life had its vicissitudes, but it was not sensational. His first marriage lasted quite a long time but finally disintegrated because of the protracted illness of his wife, who ended up a permanent patient in a nursing home. He had a well-publicised association with the American film actress Linda Christian, and then for some years was a bachelor. His oddities aside, Wiley was a good-looking man, tall and lean, well-mannered with a gallant attitude towards the ladies, and nobody was particularly surprised when he was married again, to a quiet and retiring woman several years his junior.

He had several children, one of whom was briefly in the news when he fell under the influence of the controversial Moonies church in the United States. Wiley flew to America, extracted his son from the clutches of the cult and brought him home to general approbation.

There was nothing in Wiley's circumstances to suggest that an awful shadow hung over him. But something was there. One morning, in 1987, he was found lying dead on the floor in his home, shot through the head, with a revolver in his hand. It was, without question, suicide, and that was the finding of the official inquest a few weeks later. The inquest was notable for the paucity of information placed before it – just the essentials, nothing more. In particular, no evidence was produced to suggest why he might have taken his own life.

At the time of his death, Wiley was a cabinet minister, and the cryptic nature of the inquest looked very much like a cover-up. That, of course, did not stop the public from speculating, but every theory seemed to lead nowhere. Wiley did not have financial problems, his marriage and his family seemed to be secure, he was at the summit of his career as a government minister, and there was no suggestion of impropriety on his part, the taint of fraud or bribery that sometimes touches people in government.

There was, however, one persistent whisper about camps involving young boys; outdoor activities in which other prominent politicians were also said to have taken part. The nature of these alleged activities remain unspecified, no supporting evidence was ever produced, and the whole story seems improbable.

The question, however, remains: why did John Wiley shoot himself? There must have been some compelling reason, unless he was subject to irrational fits of depression bordering on insanity, and there was no evidence to suggest that he was a depressive.

So the mystery remains.

My second sad story concerns a couple that I grew to know, like and admire when I lived in Bloemfontein in the 1960s. They were Robert and Cicely Wahl, as dedicated a pair of English literati as you would find anywhere. He was the professor of English at the University of the Orange Free State, and she was a senior lecturer in the same department.

Their lives revolved about each other and the study and teaching of the English language. He was the son of a well-known school teacher at the Cape, she the daughter of an English professor at Rhodes University in Grahamstown. He had studied at Oxford as a Rhodes Scholar and later built a substantial reputation as an authority on the pre-Raphaelite poet and painter Dante Gabriel Rossetti, writing a book about him.

In the somewhat unpropitious academic climate of Bloemfontein, the Wahls worked hard to spread the word, so to speak, about the English language. It was a far cry from Oxford or even Grahamstown, but their enthusiasm aroused the interest of many young Afrikaans-speaking students who eventually emerged from university with an above-average knowledge of English literature.

They were the gentlest of people, quietly spoken intellectuals whose controlled reproaches could only be aroused by a gross misquotation of some well-known writer. Robert, in particular, knew the art of communicating with the young. In 1964, the 400th anniversary of Shakespeare's birth, he sat on a committee with me in a Shakespeare competition organised by *The Friend* newspaper. He was conspicuously at ease in his conversation with the schoolboys and girls who entered the competition, and you could see that they liked him.

Culture was part of the Wahls' daily diet. When I visited their home, Robert introduced me to gramophone records of Dylan Thomas's very funny thoughts about lecturing in America, and to Benjamin Britten's delightful, antique-style cantata *Noyes Fludde* (Noah's Flood). This is not to suggest that their lives were all earnest and dull. The Wahls had plenty of humour, and they enjoyed good food and drink and the company of other people. They had no children, and the bond of affection between them was touching to behold. Herein lay the seeds of tragedy.

I had left Bloemfontein and was living in Durban when the bad news filtered through to me that Cicely had cancer, with no prospect of recovery, and was in constant pain. What does a friend do in these circumstances? I said a prayer, wrote a note to them and hoped for the best. Then the unbelievably shocking denouement came in a news report from Bloemfontein. Let me relate events as they happened.

Robert Wahl became increasingly distressed at his wife's plight, until his mental and emotional anguish became as acute as her physical pain. They lived for each other. There were no children. Cicely was going to die, that was certain, and without Cicely, there was no reason for Robert to live. So early one morning, at about 5.00 am, Robert Wahl, a man who would not hurt a fly, fetched his loaded revolver, kept in a cupboard for dire emergencies, and pumped six bullets into the head and body of his stricken wife.

The deed done, he got into his Mercedes and drove at high speed to the Maselspoort dam, which supplies Bloemfontein with its water. The dam, on the Modder river, is 23 kilometres from Bloemfontein, about fifteen minutes' drive, so Robert Wahl had time to reflect on what he had done – if he were in a reflective mood, which is doubtful. At the dam, fishermen watched with amazement as his car sped along a pier, catapulted off the end and plunged into deep water. As the water entered the open windows they saw the distraught pale face of Robert Wahl looking wildly at them.

There was no hope of rescue. Filling rapidly with water, the car sank to the bottom. Robert Wahl went down with it. He made no attempt to escape.

A funeral service for Robert and Cicely Wahl was held in the Anglican cathedral in Bloemfontein, before one of the biggest congregations ever to attend such an event in the city. Murder and suicide are against the teachings of the church, but there was no word of criticism or reproach from clergyman or layman. They knew that if ever a man killed for reasons of love, that man was Robert Wahl.

All must die, but modes of departure are sometimes extraordinary, from a surfeit of small eels (King Henry I of England) to an ice pick in the head (the Russian revolutionary Leon Trotsky). I do not know of a stranger fate than that which befell a man I once worked for in London.

He was Ken Waddell, a South African and yet another Oxford graduate who won distinction at the university as a rugby scrum-half. He joined the Argus Newspaper Company in Johannesburg and, in due time, became the company's London editor, heading a team of about a dozen journalists based in an office in the Reuters building in Fleet Street. That was in the 1950s, when a South African pound was worth the same as an English pound and when South African newspapers could afford to maintain big offices overseas (they have shrunk greatly since then).

As a young journalist, I was seconded to the Argus's London office in 1953, to spend a year there widening my horizons and improving my skills. Ken Waddell was my boss. He was a dapper, small man of about 50, amiable, efficient as far as I could judge from my junior vantage point, and understandably rather conciliatory to some of the old hands who had been there a long time.

Eighty percent of the daily editorial output was produced at night, extracted from British newspapers to whom the Argus company paid fees for publishing rights, so that the material was waiting on South African editorial desks first thing in the morning for use in the afternoon papers. Unfortunately, eighty percent of the London staff had some good reason or another for not being available for night duty. I was one of the twenty percent who worked at night. There were three of us, sometimes two, and for ten of my twelve months in London I worked five or six nights a week from 10.00 pm to 5.30 am, the worst hours imaginable and not conducive to widening one's horizons in the metropolis.

I was not really resentful about this – in those days the young did as they were told – and I saw that Ken Waddell was in a difficult position and that it was easier to draft me, a newcomer, into night duty than to argue with the veterans.

We parted on good terms at the end of the year, and I exchanged Christmas cards with him for a couple of years after that. Then he retired, with the customary plaudits conferred on an employee with long service. I think it fair to say that he was an honest, dependable, hard-working journalist rather than an inspiring one. He did not seem to me to be a commanding or confident personality, and I doubt whether he would have had the temperament to edit a newspaper in South Africa.

Fast forward about ten years, and another person enters the scene in a strange drama. Ernie Christie was a skilled Johannesburg news cameraman known for his somewhat eccentric behaviour. He came from a humble background, being raised in an orphanage, and established a reputation as a fearless and enterprising press and television photographer in the turbulent and dangerous Congo of the 1960s. He was a volatile and unpredictable man. His domestic life was one of upheaval; he was married and divorced three times.

On the night of 5 March 1979, he was having a bad time. He phoned a woman friend, Isobel Yvonne Rorich, several times and asked her to marry him. When she tried to stave him off, pointing out that this was an important decision not to be taken lightly, he threatened to take his own life. It was at this point that Ernie Christie took off, in more senses than one.

He was a licensed private pilot, and at about 5.00 am on 6 March 1979 he drove to the Lenasia airport, climbed into one of the light aircraft parked on the airfield (security wasn't what it is today), took off and began circling aimlessly over the quiet and well-wooded residential areas of northern Johannesburg. A man out of control, a man seeking death.

Meanwhile, Ken Waddell and his wife, Doreen, were asleep in their ample apartment on the sixth floor of a Sandton block when the unthinkable happened. The deranged Christie flew his plane straight at the building. It roared across a balcony and into the Waddells' bedroom, instantly killing them both, as well as Ernie Christie. They must have had a moment's warning, a terrifying noise, a glimpse of the plane, a flash of fire, then oblivion.

It is hard to visualise a more tragic end for an elderly couple living in peaceful retirement. The ironies were, of course, profound. Ernie Christie did not know Ken Waddell, but he might have heard of him, and vice versa. And it was never suggested that he might have aimed his aircraft deliberately at the Waddells' flat. No, the Waddells were like characters in a Greek tragedy, victims of an event that was unjust, unforeseeable, unavoidable, yet in some way almost predetermined by forces over which they had no control.

There is no moral to be read into these three sad tales, except, perhaps, that man may be noble in reason and infinite in faculty but (if I may mix my literary sources) he is born unto trouble, as the sparks fly upward.

TEN

Sweet music

Music has been the strongest single interest in my life, a recreation, a discipline, an absorption, an ever-present companion, friend and solace.

I started learning to play the piano when I was eight years old, and more than 60 years later I still play every day. As a child, I was no Mozart or Chopin, and after all these years I am no more than a tolerably competent amateur pianist. Perhaps the only unusual thing about my amateur piano playing has been its persistence. So many people I know studied the piano at school or university and then neglected it, finding it too difficult to pick up the notes years later.

The piano is a hard taskmaster. Sergei Rachmaninov, one of the greatest players of the twentieth century, said that if he missed one day's practice he noticed the difference; if he missed two days, his wife noticed; and if he missed three days, the audience noticed, and that was bad news. Accomplishment at the piano is five percent inspiration and 95 percent perspiration. I remember once, in the Cape Town city hall, hearing the blind Greek pianist Themeli practise. As a young reporter, I was waiting for a statement to emerge from a long city council committee meeting when I heard the sound of a piano in the main hall.

Taking a seat in a bay, I watched and listened for a time. Themeli, a gifted pianist who, I think, had been born blind, was by himself on the platform, practising the opening bars of Schumann's piano concerto, which he was due to play with the orchestra that night. This opening consists of twenty massive chords descending down the keyboard, not too easy to play but no problem for a virtuoso. Themeli must have played these three opening bars twenty, thirty times in succession, making sure that the notes were absolutely secure in his hands. I left after about ten minutes and he was still at it, playing one line of music. There really is no substitute for hard work.

People like myself, who have other jobs and play the piano for pleasure, are never likely to reach great heights of performance. But they add an important dimension to their lives, and with a bit of luck they may even provide some entertainment and instruction for others.

Chamber music, performed by anything from two to twenty players, is the ultimate pleasure for most instrumentalists. Well, almost. As I used to say when introducing little two-piano recitals at my home, playing the piano is my second favourite occupation. Music for small groups of players with modest skills was a common form of home entertainment in the eighteenth and nineteenth centuries, up to the first World War, in fact. After that, radio and then television provided music at the press of a button and amateur music at home became an almost forgotten art.

Not quite. In Durban about 30 years ago, four amateur string players approached me, said they had heard of my pianistic prowess (!) and asked if I would care to join them in sessions of chamber music. Of course I would, I said. Ah, said the spokesperson, a medical man who probably made more money than the entire brass section of the KwaZulu-Natal Philharmonic Orchestra, they were thinking of playing Brahms's piano quintet in F minor (for piano, two violins, viola and cello) and perhaps I would do the piano part. And with a little flourish he produced a score for me to peruse.

While the five of us chatted over a drink, I glanced through the score with a sinking feeling. I did not know the music at that stage, but the most cursory look was sufficient to tell me that it was a very difficult and very long work, the equivalent of a full-blown piano concerto, with pages of thundering octaves and tricky thirds and sixths. 'We thought we would get together next Sunday to run through it,' said the medical viola player. I blanched and explained that it would take me several weeks to work up some kind of account of the music. They reacted badly to this, clearly believing that they had been landed with a dud, and I went away somewhat chastened.

I worked at that quintet every day for six weeks, an hour to two hours a day. I bought a record and followed the music intently with the score. Concert standard, or anything like it, was beyond my abilities, but finally I had the music in rough working order and told my new-found friends that I was about as ready as I would ever be.

We met at somebody's home and launched forth. Within the first three bars there was a pained cry from my companions: 'You're going too fast!' (I was trying to maintain approximately the tempo of the gramophone record.) So we tried again at half-speed, or less, and the dreadful truth dawned on me: they were very limited performers, no better than I was, maybe worse. But we soldiered on, over many sessions, and in the end we could play, in a fashion, through the entire quintet, with maybe a breakdown here and an argument there. And each of us knew this great music like the back of his or her hand.

The Brahms quintet provided an amusing episode at my house one evening. As we banged and sawed away, my Boxer dog, Lucy, stirred from her sleep and began to utter piteous cries, the sound of an animal in pain. It was embarrassing, so I took her into the dining room next door, where my then wife, Molly, was studying French, and shut her in, with a desperate plea to Molly to keep the beast quiet. After our music-making, when the players had gone home, I found Molly convulsed with laughter. Lucy had sat on the floor next to her, head on her lap, whimpering sadly while Molly patted her. Then she put her paws up, then her chest, and eventually, by a slow process of wriggling upward, she ended up sitting on Molly's lap, moaning gently into her ear. The direct form of music criticism.

Skilful or not, our group of five drew great pleasure from playing Brahms and Beethoven until a new job temporarily prevented me from carrying on. Years later, I was fortunate enough to play occasional sessions with four members of the Durban orchestra, Jitske Brien (violin),

Jenny di Paoli (violin), Barbara Aitchison (viola) and Nancy Greig (cello). We would meet at my home, with some other guests, for an hour or so of music followed by lunch or dinner.

They were all top-class professionals, and I would practise diligently beforehand for my modest part, usually in one of the early Beethoven trios for piano, violin and cello. Young Ludwig van Beethoven knew what he was doing when he wrote these delightful works and used them as a kind of musical visiting card after departing from Bonn, his birthplace, in 1792 to seek fame and fortune in Vienna. They are tuneful, elegant and relatively comfortable to play (Beethoven, a pianist of immense powers, would have handled them without sweating hard), and they are quite showy in performance. Just the thing for the ambitious amateur.

Later still, I formed a vastly rewarding association with a gifted young Durban pianist, Lara Jones, who by the time she was seventeen was a fully fledged concert performer, with half a dozen concerto performances with orchestras and several solo recitals behind her. In recent years, she has been a piano student in Germany, working and competing with the best. Lara's parents and grandparents are old friends of mine, all of them well-known Durbanites. Her father, Craig Jones, is an attorney. One grandfather, Frank Jones, was a prominent man in the sugar industry and chairman of the Clairwood Turf Club. The other grandfather, Vernon Drake, is a well-liked retired businessman.

When it was suggested that I should try some two-piano music with Lara, then aged fifteen, I jumped at the opportunity. This rather quaint partnership has continued intermittently for more than a decade. We have given Sunday lunch recitals at my home or hers, attended by disparate audiences ranging from the menacingly knowledgeable (such as David Tidboald, the conductor, who was Lara's piano teacher for some time) to the cheerfully ignorant. As David Tidboald observed, referring to my playing rather than Lara's, the right audience is one that is enthusiastic but not too critical.

I suppose we make an odd pair. As I observe in my preliminary announcements on these occasions, Lara has, in sporting parlance, the age advantage – she is nearly 50 years younger than I am! She is a professional; people pay to hear her. I am a rank amateur; I have to bribe people with food and wine before they will agree to listen to my playing. Nevertheless, these little recitals, each about an hour long, have, I think, given pleasure to quite a large number of people, partly because of Lara's playing and partly because the two-piano repertory contains a feast of lovely music. We have played Bach, Schubert (the wonderful F minor *Fantasy*, which was written for four hands at one piano), Saint-Saens (a brilliant set of variations on a theme from one of Beethoven's piano sonatas), Faure (the *Dolly* suite), Brahms (the famous waltzes), Granados, Arthur Benjamin's Jamaican Rumba, and much more. Twenty fingers can make imposing sounds at the keyboard, and for those of us with playing limitations, there is some scope for errors and omissions. Perhaps that is why the repertory is so rich; much of it was composed for amateur players in the days before television.

Not long ago, we made a public appearance, as distinct from our home performances. This was to raise funds for the Frere Road Presbyterian Church in Glenwood, Durban, of which Lara is a member. It was old hat to her but a big deal for me, with people actually paying money to hear us play. Nearly five hundred people attended. Our efforts were enthusiastically received, especially the Brahms waltzes, which brought forth cheers and whistles of approval; applause is the sweetest music of all to a performer. And we raised more than R10 000 for the church.

The great amateur musical activity is, of course, singing. Nearly everybody can sing in tune. I am amused when people describe someone as 'musical'. My definition is simple: anyone who can sing *God Save the King*, *Die Stem* or *Nkosi sikelel'iAfrika* in tune is musical. A very small proportion of people cannot do it because they are tone deaf.

One such is a dear old friend of mine. When we were young, we used to go to Saturday night dances at Kelvin Grove, the sports and social club at Newlands, near Cape Town. In those distant imperialist days, the band would end at midnight by playing *God Save the King*, at which point my friend would push his unwilling partner into a brisk fox-trot, pausing only when he noticed that everybody else was standing to attention. He was unmusical. For the rest of us, musicality is inherent. Whether you end up listening to Bach fugues or a pop group or a ceremonial drum depends on environment and taste. One is not likely to develop a sophisticated musical ear by listening to the radio or the television, but if you are brought up in a home and school where classical music is heard and played you will probably come to recognise that this is something far greater and more complex than the ephemeral excitement of pop music.

Choir singing is a most enjoyable way of expanding one's musical horizons. It is a great tradition in the north of England and in Wales, where thousands of people without any real musical training give public performances of Handel and Bach, Beethoven and Mendelssohn. You do not have to be able to read music to sing in a large choir; your ear teaches you the melodies as they become familiar with repeated practice. It's like singing hymns in church, an enjoyable occupation marred for me by the fact that Anglican Church hymns are always pitched awkwardly for natural baritones, so that one is forced into a high falsetto or into a strained and uncertain basso profondo. But, of course, singing in a choir is much easier if one can read musical notation.

Apart from the church choirs of my youth, my choral experience has been limited to one work, but a massive work. In the mid-1970s, a former newspaper colleague of mine, John Torres, then a lecturer in African government at Natal University, persuaded me to join a choir that was preparing to perform Verdi's *Requiem* in Durban. As the choir's director, Heather Brandon, was an old friend, I went along with the idea. For weeks we practised at night, in a kind of large dungeon in the Durban city hall, about 120 of us from many occupations. *The Daily News* had two representatives, myself and the man who was in charge of the car pool.

We bellowed and whispered the Latin text of Verdi's great work and thought ourselves fine fellows until, one evening, the man who was to conduct us with the Durban orchestra appeared to apply the finishing touches at rehearsals. He was Mendi Rodan, a distinguished Israeli conductor, and he swiftly put our efforts into perspective. '*Requiem aeternam dona eis, Domine,*' we sang softly in the work's opening phrase. Eternal rest give unto them, O Lord. Rodan stopped us. 'Too fast, too loud.' And so it went until, by the time we came to sing with the orchestra, he had reshaped our entire performance. Next time you see a conductor waving his arms while the orchestra plays, you might reflect that he has earned his fee before the concert, not during it. The hard work is done at rehearsals when the conductor painstakingly, bit by bit, leads the orchestra into his interpretation of a composition.

In classical music, one is always learning. I was about 45 when I sang in Verdi's *Requiem* and I had been well acquainted with the composer's operatic music for 30 years. I thought him a tuneful, dramatic, popular composer. *The Requiem* opened my eyes. Written in 1873–74 to mark the death of Alessandro Manzoni, a novelist, poet and campaigner for a united Italy, it is, in many ways a stupendous work, rather like a painting by Michelangelo. In my judgment, it places Verdi in the ranks of the really great composers.

The Requiem runs for about an hour and three-quarters and we gave two performances in the Durban city hall, with four distinguished soloists, including Joyce Barker and Sjoerd Beute. For me, there were two unrelated sequels of varying importance. The music critic of *The Mercury* (formerly the *Natal Mercury*), Tim Aitchison, wrote a review that included a somewhat disparaging reference to the choir's 'half-hearted hosannas', a phrase that caused my newspaper colleagues endless mirth. And one of my fellow choristers was a blonde named Heather whom I did not know and did not notice and whom I married a dozen years later.

I grew up in Cape Town and was for many years a part-time piano student at the university's College of Music at Rosebank. My teacher was Minnie Seabridge, who had guided many gifted students, among them Rachel Rabinowitz, Yvonne Endler, Yvonne Roux and Estelle Strijdom, daughter of the prime minister, J G Strijdom (she later married the distinguished pianist Lamar Crowson). Minnie Seabridge was a good pianist who broadcast occasionally on the radio. In younger days, she must have been something of an actress; she was in the cast of the first play ever produced at the Cape Town Little Theatre, Chekhov's *The Seagull*, in 1931.

At the age of 22, I went to work in London and the music lessons ceased. Five or six years later, I was married and living in a very pleasant thatched cottage in Dean Street, Newlands, having bought the property from Sonny Heseltine, who was the first of the 'Chelsea' restorers of old houses at Newlands and Wynberg. I discovered that Minnie Seabridge, who had retired from the university, was living and teaching in another restored cottage at the upper end of Dean Street. So off I went for more lessons, twice a week from 7.30 to 8.30 pm, which was more often 9.00 pm.

It was a wonderfully instructive experience. As I was a grown man, I was excused from five-finger exercises and was taken slowly and carefully through some of the great works in the piano repertory, including Beethoven's Op. 109 sonata, Brahms's F minor sonata, the Brahms D minor piano concerto and the Beethoven G major concerto. I never mastered these works completely, but I could play through them in a rough and ready way, and when accompanied in the concertos by Minnie Seabridge, playing the orchestra part on her second piano, I felt like Vladimir Horowitz.

My musical inclinations led to my writing concert reviews for the *Cape Argus* not very long after I had joined the newspaper as its most junior journalist in 1947, and I have been an intermittent music critic ever since. In recent years, my musical activities have expanded to include giving occasional pre-symphony concert lectures in Durban. I am on a panel of lecturers, and I discuss the works to be played, with taped excerpts from the music. This is quite hard work – it involves borrowing scores from the university's music library and studying them carefully, plus research into the composers' lives and work – but it is vastly rewarding to help spread a wider appreciation of music and expand one's own knowledge in the process.

In the 1950s and early '60s, there was intense musical activity in Cape Town, focused on the symphony orchestra and the university's opera school. For two years, Enrique Jorda, a young Spaniard, was conductor of the orchestra and he revitalised the Thursday night concerts, not without upheaval. He decided almost at his first rehearsal that the players needed reshuffling to bring the best performers to the fore and relegate the weaker elements to less prominent positions. There was consternation from the latter. Promotion in the ranks of the orchestra depended, it seemed, on years of service, not playing ability. The aggrieved players complained to their employer, the Cape Town City Council. The matter was eventually settled Jorda's way, but he was never very happy in Cape Town and left to take charge of the San Francisco Symphony Orchestra, where, apparently, he was better appreciated.

As a perk of the job, Jorda and his wife lived in a beautiful old Oranjezicht homestead, then owned by the City Council and long since demolished to make way for urban improvements. On one memorable evening, in 1951, I think, they gave what used to be called a musical soiree. About fifty people, myself among them, were invited to Oranjezicht to hear a young pianist, followed by supper. Dressed in evening clothes, we sat on chairs and the arms of chairs in the drawing room, looking rather like one of those society paintings from the mid-nineteenth century. The pianist was an Australian named Noel Mewton-Wood who was passing through Cape Town on his way by sea to England, where he would seek to establish a concert career. He looked like a rugby player and played like an angel. I was particularly impressed by the fact that, during the brief interval, he refreshed himself with long draughts of beer from a glass tankard. (My own experience has always been that alcohol and piano playing do not mix; I can tell the difference in finger dexterity after half a tot of whisky.)

We had a lovely evening and wished Noel Mewton-Wood well. He had friendly manners and in London he quickly established himself as a front-rank concert pianist. But within two years he was dead. At the age of 31, he put his head in a gas oven after a bitter argument with his close friend, another young man.

After Jorda's departure, the orchestra had several conductors in rapid succession, including the charismatic Edward Dunn from Durban (whose son, Napier Dunn, became a well-known cartoonist on the staff of *The Mercury*). Edward Dunn was not the greatest musician of his time, but he had a rare flair for publicising and promoting the activities of the orchestra. He was a pioneer in taking music to the people, just as many orchestras are doing now with concerts in parks and at sports grounds. His occasional city hall concerts for the old folks were hilarious affairs, with the conductor leading the audience in song.

Not many people remember now that the Cape Town Orchestra was conducted, once only, by one of the greatest of modern composers: Igor Stravinsky. In 1962, Stravinsky, then aged 80, visited Cape Town with Robert Craft, his assistant – acolyte would be a better word, really – of many years' standing. The orchestra gave a concert devoted entirely to works by Stravinsky and the great man himself conducted one of them; Robert Craft conducted the others. Stravinsky, who died in 1971, had to be helped to the podium, and his conducting consisted of short rhythmical movements of his hands as he peered at the orchestra through thick glasses. The rest of his body was immobile.

A short while later, Reg Clay, one of the orchestra's woodwind players, told me that there was a theory among orchestra members that Stravinsky had actually died ten years before, had been pumped full of formalin and given an electric shock before being wheeled on-stage to conduct. Cruel, but quite funny, if you like macabre humour. All the same, it is something to see in action a man whose ballet music, *The Rite of Spring*, was shouted down when it was performed in Paris in 1913 (popular vindication came 35 years later from, of all people, Walt Disney in his musical film, *Fantasia*).

Musicians generally are not short of a sense of humour. One group of orchestral musicians whom I knew used to sing 'I am a teenaged werewolf' to a tune from one of Beethoven's piano concertos. And Barbara Aitchison, long-serving viola player in the Durban Symphony Orchestra, used to quote a neat (though rude) jest about a well-known conductor from Johannesburg: what's the difference between a chiropodist and Anton Hartman? A chiropodist bucks up the feet.

Benno Moiseiwitsch, one of the great piano players of the twentieth century, had an acerbic wit. Born in Russia, resident for most of his life in Britain, he was Jewish, and on one occasion was asked by a naïve and irritating interviewer whether he encountered much anti-Semitism. 'Only from the Jews,' snapped Benno.

Moiseiwitsch visited South Africa in the 1950s. He was at the peak of his powers and gave memorable performances, but on one occasion, in the Cape Town city hall, he completely lost his way in Beethoven's *Andante Favori*, a piece he had probably played hundreds of times. Like a true trouper, he improvised impassively and expertly until he found his way back to Beethoven's score. I imagine that most of the audience were blissfully unaware of the problem.

For many years, the director of the University Opera School in Cape Town was Gregorio Fiasconaro, a man who has done much for music in South Africa. He came to this country in the least propitious circumstances – as an Italian prisoner of war. He stayed, married, produced a family that included a son, Marcello, who became a world champion athlete, and made opera part of the cultural life of Cape Town.

The Little Theatre, just off Government Avenue, is, as its name suggests, not a big place, but Fiasconaro filled it with big ideas and sounds. He was a baritone of high quality and a director imbued with the best operatic traditions of Europe. His production of, and singing in, Mozart's *Don Giovanni*, the greatest of all operas, is still fresh in my memory after more than 40 years. During his directorship, a stream of exquisite operatic productions flowed in the Little Theatre: more Mozart, Menotti's *The Consul*, Pergolesi's *La Serva Padrona*, Puccini's *Suor Angelica*, Bartok's *Bluebeard's Castle*. No *Carmen*, you will notice, no Traviata, no Flying Dutchman. It would not have been possible to stage operas like these with the available human and physical resources. Making a virtue of necessity, Fiasconaro gave Cape Town the purer air of masterpieces that relied on music rather than mass effects (not that there was anything wrong with his effects in the final scene of *Don Giovanni*, when the erring don is swallowed up by hellfire).

In the post-World War II years, South Africa had many excellent resident musicians. Foremost among them was the Australian-born pianist, Elsie Hall, who died in 1976 at the age of 99. She was a legendary person. As an unusually gifted young girl, she was taken to Germany to further her studies and there she was introduced to Johannes Brahms, one of the towering figures in the history of music, who died in 1897.

She married a psychiatrist, Dr F O Stohr, and produced a son, Philip Stohr, who was a friend and colleague of mine on the *Cape Argus*. She survived her husband by nearly 30 years. She always played the piano under the name Elsie Hall and she made an ample and striking figure. Her nimble and eloquent fingers introduced me to many of the great works of the piano repertory – for example, Schumann's *Fantasy* and

Beethoven's sonata Op 31, No. 3 – and she retained her skills to a great age. She gave her last recital, in Rustenburg, about 150 kilometres west of Pretoria, at the age of 97!

Elsie Hall owned a taxi service operating from Rondebosch station and she was an astute business woman; folklore has it that, as she strode on to the concert platform she could, with one imperious glance around the auditorium, assess the takings to the nearest shilling. On one occasion, the story goes, she was giving a recital with a gentle and slightly nervy violinist named Ivy Angove when, in the middle of a soulful, slow movement, she startled her partner by muttering over her shoulder, 'Not much money in the house tonight.'

The stories may be apocryphal. Elsie Hall was a much-loved personality and she made a huge contribution to the advancement of music in South Africa.

Harold Rubens, a small, dark Welshman who taught at the College of Music in the 1950s, was a brilliant pianist who gave a public performance in Cape Town of the entire *Iberia* suite by Isaac Albeniz, twelve piano pieces that are among the most difficult ever written for the keyboard. Like many concert artists, he was highly strung and at one stage worked himself into such a state of worry about his fingers that he gave up playing in public for a while. It was only a temporary anxiety and he was soon back in the concert hall.

The remarkable Lili Kraus from Germany was also with us for a while, skipping jauntily to the piano and tripping archly through the music, a mannered player if ever there was one.

Lionel Bowman from Cape Town, Adolf Hallis from Johannesburg, Glyn Townley from Durban, these were some of the gifted pianists who built big reputations over the years. Glyn Townley, now in his nineties, told me not long ago that in his heyday he had 30 piano concertos in his repertory, all of them played from memory. That's a lot of notes. Among singers, Albina Bini of Cape Town was an opera prima donna for about 30 years, from the thirties to the sixties. As her name suggests, she was of Italian extraction and she married an Italian; her son, Ugo Bergomasco, was at school with me. She was a pupil of the renowned Cape Town-based Giuseppe Paganelli, formerly a member of the Sistine

Chapel choir in Rome. Albina Bini was a beautiful soprano. She was also a first-rate pianist, good enough to have played concertos with the Cape Town orchestra.

One of her contemporaries was Cecilia Wessels, a big-voiced and big-bosomed Wagnerian soprano who was the daughter of Sir Cornelius Wessels, Administrator of the Orange Free State. During World War II, she was a witness in a divorce case in which the Supreme Court judge ordered that her identity be concealed and that she be referred to in the press as 'Madame X'. In those wartime days, there were notices everywhere saying, 'Don't talk about ships or shipping', in case idle chatter about what had arrived in port might be of use to enemy agents. Everybody in Cape Town seemed to know who Madame X was, and the comment on street corners was, 'Don't talk about ships or Wessels'.

Another major singer of half a century ago was Rose Alper, later known by her married name Rose Magid. She had sung with the Carl Rosa opera company in London. A petite person with a beautiful, controlled lyric soprano voice, she later became a good friend of mine in Durban, where she was an indefatigable supporter of the arts. She married a Durban attorney and her son, Alan Magid, became a High Court judge.

A surprisingly large number of international celebrities came to South Africa in the first twenty years or so after the second World War, before the cultural boycott of apartheid began to bite. The great violinist Yehudi Menuhin came, before conscience and pressure made him keep away for decades, and he played Beethoven and Brahms beautifully in Cape Town. Then he gave a recital at Stellenbosch, dutifully attended by the faithful from Cape Town, your scribe included.

Somebody must have told him that Stellenbosch was a cultural centre, for he inflicted on his unfortunate audience a very long sonata for unaccompanied violin by the modern Hungarian composer, Bela Bartok. Menuhin himself had commissioned the composer to write the sonata, and it was advanced stuff. The first movement lasted perhaps ten minutes, then the violinist paused to mob his brow and launched into the equally impenetrable second movement. After several more long minutes, another pause, this time punctuated by what one can only describe as hopeful applause from the audience.

But the violinist was not through yet, not by a long shot. Another mournful movement was followed by more determined applause and another determined resumption of hostilities by the violinist. The comment of the evening came between the third and fourth movements from a Stellenbosch dowager sitting behind me. In a loud stage whisper, she said to her companion: *'Man, hy speel vrot vanaand.'* ('Man, he's playing rubbish tonight.')

Yehudi Menuhin was only one of many distinguished artists who refused to come to South Africa as the apartheid policy trudged to its eventual and inevitable demise. You could hardly blame them. It seems impossible that apartheid could have thrown its ugly shadow over the noble art of music, but it did. For example, an acquaintance of mine, a person of colour, was denied admission to the main part of the Durban City Hall when he wanted to attend a performance of Handel's *Messiah*.

In 1970, the South African Broadcasting Corporation organised a national competition for performers to mark the bicentenary of the birth of Beethoven. Entries were restricted to whites only. I wrote an article about it at the time speculating on what Beethoven, a fierce individualist, would have said about this, and pointing out that the first performance of one of his most famous works, the *Kreutzer Sonata*, was given by a violinist who was a man of colour, Joseph Bridgetower, who was born in the West Indies.

These apartheid restrictions were, of course, imposed by the politicians and the bureaucrats, not by the music-loving public, who by and large had a much more civilised approached to life and art. Now we are living in a normal society and the international celebrities are returning to our shores, including some remarkably gifted performers from the East, from Korea and Japan and China. Their role, incidentally, gives the lie to the political myths about 'Eurocentricity'. I have read that Beethoven's fifth symphony is played, on average, once a week somewhere or other in Japan. The Japanese don't have hang-ups about Eurocentricity. The reality is that great art is universal in its appeal.

Some of the greatest pianists of the era came to South Africa before the cultural boycott: Solomon, the Englishman who never used his first name (it was actually Cutner); the moustachioed Arturo Benedetti

Michelangeli from Italy, looking like an army colonel and shaking the rapidly ascending chords in Beethoven's third sonata from his sleeve, like a conjuror with cards; Claudio Arrau from Chile, big technique and lush romantic tone; Gina Bachauer from Greece, playing Beethoven's *Waldstein* sonata with the muscularity of an athlete; Julius Katchen; and, later Alicia de Larrocha, a pocket Hercules who played with apparent ease some formidably difficult music by her Spanish compatriots, Albeniz and Granados.

Claudio Arrau was a pianist in the grand manner, with the kind of magnetism that audiences find irresistible. I met him in London in 1953, at a post-concert party given by Miss Rose Standfield, one of two sisters who owned the famous Augener music publishing firm. I asked the virtuoso how he managed to cope with a performance schedule running to a concert every three days, year in and year out, in many parts of the world. 'By standing on my head,' he replied. He practised yoga, and no doubt this helped him to survive.

Simple responses are often the most telling. I went with my old friend, Dirk de Villiers, a South African journalist who has lived in London for about 50 years, to an Arrau recital in the Royal Festival Hall, on the south bank of the Thames. One of the items on the programme was Schumann's *Carnaval*, which starts with a series of massive, rich chords. Arrau played these with almost startling sonority, and an awestruck De Villiers whispered to me, *'Dis darem lekker'*, which I suppose translates as 'That's really nice'. Quite so.

Another of my acquaintances in those London days was the composer, Arthur Benjamin, an Australian who settled in England after the first World War, in which he flew with the Royal Flying Corps and was shot down and captured by the Germans. He and a friend, Jack Henderson, a Canadian who worked for a music publishing firm, lived in a mews apartment at Regent's Park in London, a pleasant lifestyle varied by occasional journeys to Sicily in their Armstrong-Siddeley car. Benjamin was a gentle and humorous soul and, in spite of an age gap of 40 years, we got on well together – in, I hasten to add, the most proper and innocent way. Arthur was not the marrying type, but if he took a fancy to me he never showed it in any overt way. As for me, at the tender age of 23 in the pre-permissive and pre-information age, I was hardly aware of such matters.

Benjamin was a substantial composer before he died in 1960, and is remembered today by his 1938 *Jamaican Rumba* and some other catchy pieces with origins in the West Indies, which he visited often as a music examiner. He took me and several other guests to the premiere of his imposing opera, *A Tale of Two Cities*, which was based on the Charles Dickens novel of the same name and produced by the BBC in 1953. He wrote a harmonica (mouth organ) concerto for Larry Adler, the American harmonica virtuoso, an attractive personality whom I met in London at the time, and he achieved a different kind of fame, and income, by writing the music for the film *The Conquest of Everest*, the story of the first ascent by Edmund Hillary and Tenzing Norgay in 1953. Benjamin was also a teacher of the aforesaid Lamar Crowson, the man who many years later married Estelle Strijdom, who had the same piano tutor as I did in Cape Town. It's a small world.

Another visitor to South Africa was Julius Katchen, the American pianist who lived in Paris and was one of the great virtuosi. He was a collector of netsuke, little Japanese ivory carvings originally made in the eighteenth century as clasps for robes and belts. I had learned something about these intriguing statuettes from my old friend Harry Wight, a rich man who spent the European summer at his home in Yorkshire and the southern summer at his other home, a beautiful house on the hillside at Gordon's Bay, near Cape Town. I was in London and Harry Wight, down in town for a sale of netsuke at Sotheby's, invited me to lunch at his club. By arrangement, I arrived early so that he could tell me about his other guests. There was so-and-so, whom I knew; and so-and-so, who was a book dealer; and so-and-so, who was a retired brigadier. And, said Harry Wight in his broad Yorkshire, 'there's a feller called Julius Katchen. Got a lovely collection of netsuke. Bought some today'. Pause, then rather vaguely, 'I believe he plays the pianner for a living.'

I sat next to Julius Katchen at lunch and tried my best to get him to talk about his music, but all he wanted to talk about was his netsuke, and especially the commercial advantages of buying in Rome and selling in New York. No problem with customs, just put them in your pocket and say they are toys for children.

Julius Katchen died in 1969 at the age of 42, a grievous loss to the world of concert music.

Sir Thomas Beecham, one of the most vivid personalities among all twentieth-century conductors, came to South Africa and conducted here, giving press interviews that contained his usual withering and bombastic wit on all manner of subjects. Stories about Beecham are legion. Asked by a bright young thing at a party whether he had conducted any music by Karlheinz Stockhausen, the tuneless modern German composer, he replied: 'No, but I stood in some once.' And he managed to demolish two of his rival conductors in one phrase when he described Herbert von Karajan as 'a kind of musical Malcolm Sargent'.

Another celebrated visitor to South Africa was involved in a hilarious dispute with a Johannesburg music critic. Many critics are anything but bashful, and I have often been surprised by the dogmatic attitude of some of them. One of the most famous examples arose from the first performance, in Boston in 1874, of what was to become perhaps the most celebrated of all big compositions, Tchaikovsky's piano concerto No. 1 in B flat minor. One of the American critics didn't like it at all and said that, fortunately, there was not much chance of its ever being played again, anywhere.

In about 1960, an American harpsichordist named Ralph Kirkpatrick visited South Africa and stunned audiences with his playing of the music of Domenico Scarlatti, one of the underrated geniuses of musical history. Scarlatti (1685–1757) wrote about 550 short pieces that he called exercises but which are now called sonatas. They encompass a vast range of techniques and emotions and moods, from the melancholy to the exultant. More than half of them were written by Scarlatti between the ages of 67 to 72, an extraordinary late burst of creative activity.

The harpsichord is a limited instrument, not really to be compared with the piano. The strings are plucked with quills, producing a metallic, buzzy sound that dies away almost instantly. One unappreciative Englishman said it sounded like a performance on a birdcage with a toasting fork. But in Ralph Kirkpatrick's hands, the harpsichord opened the door to a new world of brilliant and poetic effects.

Kirkpatrick was one of the significant virtuosi of the twentieth century. He was also the final authority on the music of Domenico Scarlatti. About 1900, an Italian named Alessandro Longo classified all those sonatas by Scarlatti, to avoid confusion, and for half a century they were numbered L (for Longo), for example L465, in what Longo presumed was chronological order. Kirkpatrick's research showed that this chronology was often wrong and he revised the entire system. Nowadays, the Scarlatti sonatas are numbered K for Kirkpatrick, not L for Longo.

A formidable character, this Kirkpatrick, but that did not daunt the critic of the *Rand Daily Mail* in Johannesburg. This was Dora Sowden, well known in her own right and also because she was married to Lewis Sowden, novelist, poet, playwright and an assistant editor of the *Rand Daily Mail*. After Kirkpatrick had given the first of two recitals in Johannesburg, the *Rand Daily Mail*'s critic noted that the style of his playing was really better suited to Bach or Handel and that he did not really reflect the spirit of Scarlatti, or words to that effect.

This caused a stir among the concertgoers of Johannesburg, but it was nothing compared with what followed. At his second recital a few days later, Kirkpatrick strode on to the stage, immaculately clad, as usual, in white tie and tails, but he didn't sit down to play. Instead, he gazed searchingly around the audience and said, 'Is Mrs Dora Sowden here tonight?' Mrs Sowden, sitting a few rows from the front, looked embarrassed but she put up her hand. 'Ah,' said the harpsichordist in tones of deep sarcasm. 'Before I play, perhaps you would like to come up here and give us a brief lecture on the differences in interpreting Scarlatti, Handel and Bach.' There was an audible gasp from the audience. Dora Sowden, now red-faced, sat tight, and Ralph Kirkpatrick sat down to play the harpsichord with controlled fury.

As you may imagine, this interlude was the sole topic of conversation at the interval. After the audience had filed back into the hall for the second half, there was a long and inexplicable delay. It became all too explicable when, on the stage, from the wings, there appeared two angry, slightly built, well-dressed middle-aged men, making feeble and unsuccessful attempts to exchange punches. Lewis Sowden, it seemed, had gone backstage to avenge his wife's honour but got short shrift from the enraged harpsichordist. As the latter tried to go on stage to resume his recital, he was hindered by the avenging husband; blows were attempted, and the two stumbled out from the wings into the full view of the fascinated audience.

Ushers at the hall promptly escorted Mr Sowden back to his seat; Mr Kirkpatrick dusted himself off and sat down to finish his recital.

I was not present but those who were say the whole business was an unforgettable experience. The best show in town, in fact.

In sombre mood John O'Malley (right), then editor of the Daily News, *and the author, then his deputy, walk to the Durban Regional Court in 1974 to face charges under the Riotious Assemblies Act.*

Robert Wahl (right), professor of English at the University of the Orange Free State, and Michael Green when he was editor of The Friend *in Bloemfontein. Robert Wahl and his wife Cicely came to a tragic end.*

Duo pianist Michael Green and a young Lara Jones, who has since studied in Germany for several years and become a distinguished concert pianist.

Two old friends: Ian Wyllie, former editor of the Sunday Tribune *(left) and Ramon Leon, former Supreme Court judge and father of Tony Leon, Leader of the Opposition in Parliament.*

My 1952 Fiat Cub at the top of the Maloja Pass in Switzerland. The little car took Douglas Hoffe of Johannesburg and me on a four-week, 10 000 km trip through seven European countries in 1953.

This London taxi, a 1934 Austin, was brought to South Africa by Philip Stohr and bought by me in 1960. The idea was to use the capacious interior, complete with two back-facing opera seats, as a mobile changing booth at the beach. The car gave no problems but it was heavy on petrol and after about two years I sold it to another colleague, the late Max Leigh. He smartened it up and hired it out to bridal couples, with himself as chauffeur.

A fond handshake for the author from Robert Mugabe. The photograph was taken in Harare in 1982, when the Zimbabwe leader was generally regarded as a bright hope for the future. On the right is Harvey Tyson, editor of the Johannesburg Star.

Auckland, New Zealand, is with justification called the city of sails. In relation to its population it has a higher proportion of yachts than any other city in the world.

117

Vineyards in a broad valley with Hawke's Bay in the background. This New Zealand scene resembles the winelands of the Western Cape.

(Above left) Molly Green, well-known Cape Town journalist and the author's first wife. (Above right) John Patten, former editor of the Natal Mercury.

(Above left) Pippa Green, the author's daughter, a journalist who has become head of Radio News at the SABC. (Above right) Aubrey Sussens.

(Above left) The author's son Geoffrey Green, a physician in New Zealand. (Above right) Jock Leyden, doyen of South African cartoonists.

Michael Green and his wife Heather (2004)

(Above left) Heather Green, the author's wife. (Above right) Michael Green, a portrait by Veronica Mackeson.

Gerry Ferry, Mayor of Cape Town, looks at a foundation stone laid by Cecil John Rhodes, whom he greatly admired.

Cartoon by Jock Leyden depicting people who worked on the *Daily News,* Durban, between 1927 and 1980. The comments were written by Jock Leyden when he drew the cartoon in 1980. The central figure in the front with black-rimmed glasses, not identified in the key, is Jock Leyden himself.

1. **Harold 'Buttons' Emerson** as he was when he first joined the News and did his 'Royal Tour of Duty'. He's a big boy now'.
2. **Bob Cooper**
3. **June Vigor**
4. **Travers Barret**
5. **Graham Linscott**
6. **'PCB' – P.C. Bishop** the first news editor I knew on the old 'Tiser' in 1927.
7. **EFG 'Brud' Bishop,** his nephew, who was in the magazine section office, under FFG Bettle. As a matter of interest, I recommended him to apply for a motor editor's job on *The Daily Dispatch.* He was

out of work, during the Depression, so I cajoled him into applying. He got the job and then went on to inaugurate the SA Gran Prix car racing series. But for me ..!
8. **W. Urquhart,** manager of *The Star.* I did a lot of work for *The Star* in the early '30s and nearly joined *The Star* staff in 1932. But you won't find that very interesting story in *Today's News Today* book. Pity, it's a good one.
9. **Creighton Mandell,** who got me to join the SASJ in 1939 – God knows why. They didn't recognise cartoonists then. I'm probably one of the oldest on their books of members. They recently made me an honarary life member.
10. **Baron Boyel,** part-time motor editor during the '30s, who showed me much of South Africa in company with
11. **Julius Wharton,** motor editor about the same time.

123

12. **Laurie Bloomfield**
13. **Scott Haigh**
14. **Florence Bayman** – 'Bay' – librarian for many years with her inevitable jar of biscuits to keep body and soul of JL together.
15. **Barbara Strachan,** librarian now.
16. **Cliff Scott**
17. **Rhys Meir** of *The Rhodesia Herald.*
18. **Harvey Tyson**
19. **Gordon Makepeace** complete with beret – a sign of Battle on Saturday evenings. He was editor of the *Sunday Tribune*. Note cigar – and coffee to keep the staff from flagging.
20. **Richard Cluver**
21. **'Mossie' van Schoor**
22. **David James**
23. **Jack Moore**
24. **Terry Green**
25. **Harry Burgess,** works manager for many years.
26. **John Vigor**
27. **Charles Still**
28. **George Muller**
29. **Les Hutchison**
30. **George Hutchison,** Les's father.
31. **Ramsay Milne** – 'Here's a ski in your eye' – New York Bureau.
32. **Ronnie Gill.**
33. **Colin Cowan,** editor of *The Rhodesia Herald.* I did several stints for the company in Rhodesia.
34. **Ken Nicholson,** deputy overseer.
35. **Dave Brechin**
36. Dear old **Charles Collins,** trying to tempt.
37. Mike – now The Rev. – **Michael Lloyd,** with a lemon. Charles did the rounds every Monday with a bag of lemons dispensing them and the latest Van der Merwe jokes for many years.
38. **Roy Rudden**
39. **Sjoerd Meijer**

40. **Reg Sweet**
41. **Hubert Huxham,** with whom I co-operated for a long run of humerous articles for the *Sunday Tribune* under the title Leyden and Huckbert.
42. **John Gittens**
43. **John Hennessy**
44. **Louis** 'Cut-Yourself-a-Piece-of-Cake' **Duffus.** He always received me with that welcome when I paid him my daily visit in the sports office. He still does (in retirement).
45. **Dom Ollemans**
46. **Liff Hewit**
47. **Dave Ramsay,** manager of the old *Natal Advertiser* when I first came on the scene in 1927.
48. **'Mac' McCarthy,** accountant at the same time.
49. The one and only 'Brokie' – **Les Brokensha.** He broke his knee playing in a Press v. musicians charity match – war fund-raising effort that packed old Kingsmead.
50. **Peter McLean**
51. **Jolyon Nuttall**
52. **Charles Barry**
53. **'Buck' Buchanan** – financial editor, who loved golf and speaking, savouring his words as would a Napoleon brandy.
54. **Fred Marshall Long,** who ran the process department later taken over by the Argus Company.
55. **Judith Hewetson,** first woman's page editor I knew.
56. Dear old **PW 'Tinkle' Bell,** a true-blue old Tory, and all, a magnificent writer of English. I found this out only when I read it in the paper for I could never decipher a word of it when he brought his copy into my office for me to read. A completely and utterly impossible task for me. The CID must have helped the lino men with it.

57. **Layton Slater**
58. **'Black Mac' Macintosh**
59. **René de Villiers.** I always remember him with a smile on his face. Those must have been 'the good old days in SA' that people are always talking about.
60. **Michael Green**
61. **John O'Malley**
62. **Justice 'What Ho!' Alexander,** whom I've known since before he first entered a newspaper office.
63. **Don Stayt**
64. **Ray McCall**
65. **Morris Broughton** with his typical Napoleonic 'lord of all he surveys' look.
66. Des, the inimitable, unflappable chief sub, **Des Prior**
67. **Gerald Pauli,** the last real friend I ever made among journalists – and the only one likely to know all the people depicted here.
68. **Austin 'Perpetual Motion' Ferraz**
69. Little **'Mac' Simpson**
70. **Horace Flather** waiting to see if I've finished the cartoon and retouched the first radio pictures (usually of such poor quality they often finished up as 'paintings' which I felt like signing!) before giving me some maps to draw. He loved maps. I often did two a day. North Africa front, Russia front, I must have been the only person who didn't keep shouting for a second front in Europe!
71. **Wally Mackenzie,** who always found time to discuss the latest sporting event, after I'd handed in my cartoon. Those were the days.
72. **Ronnie Tungay,** a news editor in the Ferraz tradition.
73. **Len Pickles**
74. **'Challis',** the puckish little lift operator who had a smile and a cheery word for everyone, usually asking after 'the missus and the piccanins'. In later years he loved to stand with a Bible in his hand gazing intently at the words. One day I asked him what the Bible said. Solemnly he looked at the page 'Je-sus says – E says ...'. 'Why don't you turn the book the other way round Challis? It's easier to read that way', I said. Dear old Challis. He's still around.

75. **Cyril Simons,** photographer in the days when he did the lot – photographing, developing, printing. An all-round sportsman, Currie Cup swimmer, scratch golfer. He rode in the first 1913 Jo'burg to Durban motorcycle race. I got Peter Knowles to do a piece about him and as I wanted to illustrate it, I told Cyril I'd like to do a sketch of him. 'When?', he said. 'Tomorrow'. 'Tomorrow may be too late', came a sad-sounding reply – so unlike the very active little man I had known for 30 years. I did the sketch. He was dead within weeks.

76. Last, but by no means least. **Peter Murugen,** chief messenger for years, who hopped around the office with chest puffed up like a little blackbird and knew all about everybody – maybe too much. For he knew the office on the days when more of the staff were to be found in the Bodega Bar than anywhere.

ELEVEN

Grape juice

'**G**o easy on the grape juice,' my physician, an old friend, used to say after my annual medical check-up. Consciously or otherwise, he was reducing the mystique of wine to what it really is: grape juice, fermented.

More pretentious claptrap has been written and spoken about wine than about almost any other subject, with the possible exception of contemporary art. I have been a wine writer for the past 25 years, for a daily newspaper, a weekly and a website, and no doubt I have contributed occasionally to the bull that baffles brain when wine is under discussion. The other side of the coin is that the subject is a big and complex one, and there are, of course, dozens of excellent and knowledgeable commentators who have spread an appreciation and love of wine among an ever-widening circle of consumers.

To me, the expert commentator is one who draws attention to a quality in a wine that you had perceived, albeit dimly, but could not identify. The annual *John Platter's Wine Guide*, which is a local bestseller, contains many examples. You may taste a red wine and get a certain distinctive flavour that is difficult to pinpoint. Turn up the Platter guide and there you see the taste and aroma described accurately: raspberry or plum, chocolate or tobacco.

That little bull appears with the high-flown phrases so loved by some writers and winemakers. They talk about 'trenchant tones' of wine, 'honestly crafted', 'rich and serious', 'deep draughts of chalk' 'tongue-thumping plums' and a thousand other flights of fancy. My favourite extravagance comes from the pen of Auberon Waugh, a brilliant British journalist and wine writer who died some years ago. Describing a Spanish rioja wine, he wrote, tongue in cheek no doubt: 'Riojas are growing more sophisticated and European in style, but this is a splendidly hairy, short-legged example with swaggering, low-slung bottom and eyebrows that cross over each other.'

The bull looms larger on the very rare occasions when the experts submit to a blind tasting, when you cannot see the labels, as I shall demonstrate a little later.

Wine is a fascinating subject. It is the most ancient of all beverages. It goes back to the Romans, the Greeks, the Pharaohs and earlier. Even censorious old Paul advised Timothy, two thousand years ago, to take a little wine for his stomach's sake. It is the product of nature and man, and winemakers have intense debates about the relative importance of the soil, the vines, the climate and the cellar, where the juice of the grape is fermented and turned into wine and matured.

My own experience of wine goes back more than half a century to my days as a young reporter on the *Cape Argus*. Some colleagues and I formed a syndicate to buy wine occasionally from Simonsvlei cellar near Paarl, the place that today has an outsize bottle, visible from the N1, as its landmark.

It seems incredible now, but in those days you needed a permit from the Department of Excise to transport, as a private citizen, twelve or more bottles of wine at a time. We would obtain the necessary permits, drive out to Simonsvlei and load up with the only two wines they sold then, a quite robust Cape riesling and a pale, delicate clairette blanche. The price was twelve shillings a case, one shilling a bottle, equal to ten cents of decimalised money. A little later, the wines won prizes on the Paarl wine show and the price was increased to fifteen shillings a case, amid much moaning from customers.

Not many people in those days, the late 1940s and early '50s, regarded wine as an everyday accompaniment to food. The bottles I bought were reserved for Sunday lunch with my parents, roast chicken and riesling.

For the rest of the week, it was beer or whisky in the evenings before dinner, maybe a sherry, and that was it.

My habits have changed since then, for better or worse. Travelling in a train in Britain during the second World War, Winston Churchill, while absorbing his daily intake of champagne, jocularly asked his scientific adviser, Lord Cherwell, to calculate how much champagne he had drunk in his life. After some fiddling with a slide rule Cherwell announced, much to Churchill's amusement, that it was enough to fill two railway carriages.

I don't know how I compare, in wine-drinking, that is. I suppose that over the past 50 years I have averaged two-thirds of a bottle a day (with not much other liquor, I hasten to add). That's more than 12 000 bottles up against that well-known wall, or over a thousand cases; at today's prices for a middle of the road wine, about R300 000. That's a fair sum, but it was spread over a long period and it provided a lot of fun, not to mention relaxation and tranquillisation. A teetotaller would have saved enough to buy a Mercedes, but we're all different, and if you're lucky enough you get the Mercedes and the merlot.

I don't think my consumption is particularly imposing. A few years ago, I was the guest speaker at a big function to celebrate the 25th anniversary of the Stellenbosch wine route, and I mentioned that my wife and I consumed a bottle of wine every evening, two-thirds for me, one-third for her. To put this into perspective, it is four glasses and two glasses. Afterwards, a farmer who is well known for the quality of the grapes he supplies to the wine industry, someone who is much younger than myself, came up and spoke to me. 'I was interested in your drinking statistics,' he said. 'You look quite well on it.' I acknowledged this back-handed compliment and said that I supposed he was in the same category. 'Oh no,' he replied. 'My wife and I drink a bottle each every evening.'

I should perhaps add that since then my consumption has decreased somewhat. The caution induced by the passing years, I suppose.

Wine tastes today are much more sophisticated than they were even twenty years ago. The Cape riesling that we enjoyed for so long is very much a back number today. The favoured white wines are Rhine riesling, which is the authentic type (Cape ricsling is really a remote cousin correctly called crouchen blanc); chardonnay, the basis of the great whites of Europe and California; sauvignon blanc, which has reached a peak of quality in the cold climate of New Zealand; and, latterly, chenin blanc, an underrated wine grape that is widely planted in the Cape and has attracted favourable attention among connoisseurs from abroad.

Red wines, too, have multiplied and prospered in the Cape. Fifty years ago, there were Nederburg cabernet, Zonnebloem cabernet, Chateau Libertas and a handful of 'dry reds' of varying quality. Tassenberg, then as now, set a standard for a kind of acceptable vin ordinaire, an inexpensive, palatable everyday wine. I can remember the days when Tassenberg sold in the bottle stores for 1s 8d (about eighteen cents) a bottle and its more upmarket relative from the same producer, Chateau Libertas, for 2s. 4d. (about 24 cents).

Today there is a profusion of good reds: cabernet sauvignon, pinotage, shiraz, merlot, and blends encompassing seemingly endless permutations.

John Platter's first wine guide listed, in 1980, 1 250 different Cape wines. The 2004 Platter guide lists about 5 000. John Platter, an old friend of mine (his wife, Erica, worked with me on the *Daily News* in Durban), sold the guide some years ago, but it retains his name and his services on a panel of highly qualified and experienced tasters.

Many of the Cape wines are today of very high quality – in our judgment. Foreign visitors are often less impressed, but then wine is like food, or houses, or street signs, or newspapers; you tend to prefer those with which you are familiar. It is difficult to make absolute judgments. I used to think that the only European wine that could not be successfully emulated at the Cape was champagne. The original, which comes from the Champagne area of France, was different from and superior to South African sparkling wine (in terms of an international agreement the Cape product may not be called champagne). Now, with the foremost Cape producers using the identical raw materials (chardonnay and pinot noir grapes) and the identical winemaking process (second fermentation in the bottle itself), it is not so easy to tell the difference.

Which brings me back to that little bull. Some time ago, the South African magazine called *Wine* published an analysis by a panel of brandy experts of the merits and demerits of about 25 different brandies from South Africa and elsewhere. The tasting was blind, which means that the tasters were given glasses of neat brandy and were not told which was which. They could add water if they wanted to; a little water, not iced, often brings out the flavours in brandy or whisky.

The expert panel scored the brandies in the method used for wine tastings: three points for colour, seven for bouquet and ten for taste, a total of twenty When the scores had been totted up and the identities of the brandies revealed, it emerged that the one they liked best was a South African Bols Reserve priced at the time at about R35 a bottle. A Courvousier cognac from France, priced at more than R200 a bottle, was placed twelfth in the estimation of these experts. Why waste your money on cognac, you might well ask.

This report in *Wine* prompted me to write a letter to the magazine unfolding some of the wilder moments of a Durban wine-tasting group to which I have belonged for many years. There are ten of us and we meet at each other's houses every month for a blind tasting of eight to twelve wines, followed by dinner. Each taster is given a list of the wines and brief descriptions of their qualities, usually taken from the John Platter wine guide. Generally, but not always, the presenter sticks to one type, a cabernet sauvignon, for example, or a chardonnay. The tasters score the wines out of the standard twenty points, and after they have done so the identity of the wines is disclosed.

Five of us are involved with the liquor industry and we think we know something about wine. It is not unusual for most of our tasters to correctly identify five or six wines out of eight, and our higher marks nearly always go to wines that are widely regarded as having high quality (and high prices; in wine, as in most things, you usually get what you pay for).

But things went comically awry at my house one night. Our tasters like to have three or four tasting glasses each, so that they can compare differences as they work their way through the wines poured by the host from concealed bottles or plain decanters. It was a red-wine night, and wine number four was being compared with wine number five, which was generally reckoned to have a better colour, stronger bouquet and more flavour. Backstage in the kitchen, I realised that I had made a mistake; I had poured the same wine twice from the same bottle. Red faces to go with the red wine, and much laughter; we don't take ourselves too seriously.

I told this little tale in my letter to *Wine* magazine. But, I added, don't jump to the conclusion that we were ignorant idiots. I went on to relate how our group had, on one occasion, invited a guest to our tasting, he being one of the Cape's most distinguished winemakers. He sportingly agreed to take part in the blind tasting, which was of eight Cape sparkling wines and three authentic French champagnes. Our guest could not identify the three expensive imports from France (at today's prices, more than R200 a bottle). Moreover, he could not identify one of his own wines that had been included in the tasting. And when the tasters' scores and the identity of the wines were revealed, the situation became quite embarrassing; he had given a relatively low score to his own highly esteemed product and had awarded high marks to some much more plebeian wines.

He shrugged and said cheerfully that his competitors' wine must have improved in quality. A good sport, as I said, and it would be unfair of me to say who he was, but the facts are correct, as our tasting group well remember. Over the years, we have had other winemakers as guests at our tastings, but they have all resolutely refused to try to identify the wines or to score them. There is a time when silence is best.

My letter to the magazine set a cat among the pigeons. In the next issue, a letter from Dr Isidor Mofson, a Durban radiologist, related the experiences of his tasting group, which includes some expert palates. On one occasion they decided to try a literally blind tasting. The tasters were blindfolded and glasses of wine were set down before them. The test was very simple: tell which are the red wines and which are the white. Nobody succeeded in getting them all right.

A few weeks after this, I attended a big function at the beautiful La Motte estate at Franschhoek. There was some amused talk about totally blind tastings and one of the Cape's well-known winemakers, not the one involved with us earlier, said ruefully that he and three of his colleagues, all winemakers, had taken part in a blindfold test. Each was given eight glasses of wine, four red and four white, with plenty of time to work out the colours. Eventually all four tasters came triumphantly to the same conclusion: these were the four reds, those the four whites.

They were all one hundred percent wrong; the fellow who had presented the wines had chilled all the reds and had served the whites at room temperature. In the final analysis, these experts were judging on temperature.

You get my drift when I talk about a little bull? Having said that, let me add that my criticism applies only to the pretentious wine snobs, of whom there are quite a few, and to those in the wine industry whose habitual mood is one of self-congratulation.

Moreover, blunders of this kind are by no means confined to wine. It is sometimes difficult to tell the difference between brandy and whisky, and even beer can pose problems. The late Laurie van der Watt, a senior executive at South African Breweries, was reputed to have an excellent palate for beer. One evening, some friends asked him to perform a one-man blindfold tasting of different beers. He identified the different types with impressive accuracy, but the ninth or tenth glass had him guessing. Those unkind friends had put in a glass of water at this juncture. Laurie van der Watt tasted it long and hard, and eventually screwed up his face and said: 'I don't know what it is, but I'll tell you this: it won't sell.'

One more true story, and a quite recent one. At a big wine function in the Cape, one of the guests was an internationally known expert who has written books on one aspect of French wines. Somebody poured him a glass of pinotage red wine, the one wine that is indigenous to South Africa, which he sipped with displeasure. 'I don't know how you can hope to sell this rubbish overseas,' he remarked sourly. A fellow guest, an Australian, said obligingly, 'I'll get you something else', took the pinotage bottle away and, out of sight, decanted the contents into an empty cabernet sauvignon bottle, from which he poured a fresh glass for the critic. 'Ah, that's much better,' said the great man.

There are, of course, hundreds of wine experts, professional and amateur, who have wonderfully educated palates and whose guidance and comments are of great value to anybody who is interested in this complex subject. To give just one example, I remember Gunter Brozel, the legendary cellarmaster at Nederburg, Paarl, taking a group of us through a tasting of as yet unlabelled whites. They all tasted much the same to me, but when the third or fourth wine was poured, Brozel sniffed, tasted and complained immediately: 'Wrong wine.' A flurry among the pourers revealed that they had, indeed, made a mistake.

Gunter completed the tasting in the elegant, wood-panelled tasting room, then went outside and took a long, long drag at a Gauloise cigarette. Most wine drinkers shrink in horror at the sight and smell of tobacco, but rules are made to be broken.

One of the truisms of the garden-variety drinker is that the best wine is the one you like best. Yes, and don't be unduly abashed if you think you're drinking chardonnay and it turns out to be chenin blanc. As Duimpie Bayly, a former wine-industry executive and one of the best palates in the business, sagely observes: 'A glance at the label is worth 25 years' tasting experience.'

In spite of the huge increase in wine drinking in South Africa over the past 25 years, it is still very much a minority drink. Sales of brandy and beer far exceed those of wine. But wine is a fascinating subject and a healthy drink available at relatively low cost to all who are not intimidated by the mystique of the bull-shooters.

For those who may be tentative about trying wines, or unfamiliar wines, here is a rough guide to smells and flavours that you may find in different types.

--------- **Red wines** ---------

Cabernet sauvignon: Dark colour, berry, fruity, nutty, tobacco, woody, blackcurrant, sometimes peppery.

Shiraz: Peppery again, smoky, chocolaty. Used to be likened to sweaty saddles until some jokers pointed out that this was too close to the bone.

Merlot: Fruity, softer than cabernet sauvignon, but can be sharp and astringent when young.

Pinot noir: Fruity, cherry, damp leaves, decaying vegetation. It tastes much better than it sounds.

Cinsaut, formerly called hermitage: Dry but with a sweet undertone. Plummy.

Ruby cabernet: A less expensive alternative to cabernet sauvignon. Developed in California but now grown in the Cape in increasing quantities. A good-quality red with a slightly sweetish flavour. I like it.

Pinotage: A South African hybrid, developed half a century ago from pinot noir and hermitage. It used to be rather astringent, with a distinctive and not particularly pleasant smell of acetone or nail polish. Much refined in recent years. Now usually fruity and full-bodied.

─────── **White wines** ───────

Chardonnay: The great white grape. Buttery, toasty, citrus. Chardonnay wines often have a strong lemon flavour and smell.

Sauvignon blanc: Grassy, flinty, fig, gooseberry, asparagus. A wide range of flavours and, in general, a somewhat controversial and ambivalent wine. In New Zealand, a country famed for its sauvignon blanc, I bought a bottle that was labelled, accurately, 'cat's pee on a gooseberry bush'. It was delicious (I thought).

Rhine riesling: Aromatic, spicy and often quite sweet. Sometimes has a distinctly terpene, oily character, not much liked here in South Africa but valued in Europe.

Cape Riesling: Formerly called plain 'riesling' and in fact not a German riesling at all but related to the French grape, crouchen blanc. Very dry, can be refreshing, can be sharp on the palate.

Blanc fumé: A fancy name for sauvignon blanc.

Chenin blanc: The most widely grown grape in the Cape. It produces a huge range of wines, from sweet dessert wines to ultra-dry whites. At its best offers very good value. Often has peach or guava flavours.

Gewurztraminer: Usually off-dry. Strong litchi and rose petal scents and flavours.

There are many more. It may be important to consider vintages when dealing with red wines. A good cabernet sauvignon may need five or six years of bottle maturation, or more, before it will do justice to its maker in the cellar and its Maker in the vineyard. Before that, it may be bitter and sharp. On the other hand, most South African red wines are now made for early maturation. The winemakers have taken cognisance of the fact that more than 90 percent of all the wine sold in South Africa is consumed within 24 hours of purchase. Most people just don't have the time, the money, the patience or the space to store bottles of wine for long periods in the optimum conditions. Optimum means air conditioning, but I have had good results from wines kept in a darkish study on the shaded part of the house, with windows on both sides for cross-ventilation, and this in Durban's humid and hot climate. Many experts believe, and it has been my experience, that a steady temperature without hot and cold extremes is the most important factor.

Red wines other than cabernet sauvignon require lesser periods of maturation, but there are very few that do not improve with a year or two of gentle rest on a cool shelf, in a well-ventilated room with a more or less even temperature. Look at the vintage year on the label before buying. Some reds are only released by the producers two or three years after bottling.

If the wine is really old, it may have developed a sediment in the bottom of the bottle by the time you open it. There is nothing wrong here. The best plan, I have found, is to decant the wine into a plain bottle or flask using a little funnel and coffee filter paper. The true-blue connoisseurs (I know one who carries his own wine glasses around with him, in a little leather case) open red wines an hour or two before serving, so that they can 'breathe'. It can improve the wine quite a bit, but I wouldn't regard it as essential. I think it is much more important not to serve red wine too warm. Room temperature is what the textbooks say, but room temperature in Europe is likely to be ten to fifteen degrees Celsius, not the 25 to 35 common in many parts of South Africa. In hot weather, red wine is greatly improved if it sits in the refrigerator for half an hour or so before pouring.

Don't be afraid to express an opinion on wine. And don't be persuaded, as I was when I was young, that the drier the wine the better. Tastes change, and the trend these days seems to be towards fuller wines with ample flavours. Maybe it's my age. Patrick Grubb of Oxfordshire, who has conducted the Nederburg wine auction at Paarl for the past thirty years, says his palate has broadened as the years have gone by. I feel the same way.

And drink wine because you like the taste, not because you're thirsty or because you're trying to escape from something else. Over-consumption leads to what is delicately called palate fatigue.

--- TWELVE ---

Odd fellows

All journalists meet unusual people from time to time, from the man who has a genuine seventeenth-century Stradivarius violin (made in 1955) to the woman who has discovered the secret of perpetual motion.

I've had my share. One of the first was a man I shared a railway compartment with in 1950, on my way from Cape Town to Kimberley to do a three-month-stint on the *Diamond Fields Advertiser*. On the occupants' ticket outside the compartment window, his name was given as Dr J van Rensburg. He turned out to be a neatly dressed man in his fifties, chatty, amiable and hospitable (he bought us a bottle of wine at dinner).

We had spoken for some time when it dawned on me – or doomed on me, as Judge Rudolf Erasmus used to say – that he might be a very well-known person indeed. 'You're not *the* Dr van Rensburg of the *Ossewa-Brandwag?*' I asked. He gave a courtly little bow and said, 'I believe I have achieved a certain notoriety.'

An understatement. To English-speaking white South Africans involved in the 1939–1945 war against Hitler, and to many Afrikaners too, he was a monster, an enemy, a fifth columnist. He was the founder and leader of the *Ossewa-Brandwag* (Sentinels of the Ox-wagon) which was formed in 1938 and which became, in the words of the historian Arthur Keppel-Jones, 'an avowedly Nationalist-Socialist organisation, working for a totalitarian republic and the abolition of the party system'.

Nationalist-Socialist was, of course, the polite abbreviation for Nazi, and the OB, as it was known, made no bones about its enthusiasm for the Nazi cause. Its members and supporters sabotaged the South African war effort wherever they could. Some, like the wrestling champion Johannes van der Walt, were killed in battles with the police. Some were jailed. Others, like B J Vorster, the future prime minister and state president, were interned in camps. And here I, an 'English' youth from Cape Town, was ensconced in a railway compartment with the head man.

I learned a good deal on that train journey; the type of lesson that has been learned and applied half a century later in the new South Africa but not by everybody. Lessons about wisdom and folly and, above all, about trying to look into the minds of those one could regard simply as 'the enemy'.

J F J van Rensburg, Hans, was born at Winburg in the Free State in 1898. He was educated at Stellenbosch University, where he eventually became a doctor of law, and then joined the public service, where he made rapid progress. At the age of 35, he was appointed Secretary for Justice – this was an era in which it usually took a lifetime of hard work to reach such a position – and three years later he became Administrator of the Free State.

At this time, 1936, he made a trip to Europe that was to change his life and the lives of many other South Africans: he went to Germany and met the heads of the Nazi government, including Adolf Hitler.

Van Rensburg, like many Afrikaners of his time, was no great lover of the British or the democratic system. He admired militarism and author-itarianism and notions of a master race, and he found his soul mates in Germany. In 1940, the year after the outbreak of World War II, he left the public service to become leader of the *Ossewa-Brandwag*.

Today, more than 50 years later, it is difficult to envisage the extreme bitterness generated between those who supported and those who opposed South Africa's participation in the second World War. The decision to enter the war on the side of Britain and her allies had been taken by a vote in parliament in which the majority was only thirteen votes, 80 to 67. It was only by chance that parliament happened to be sitting in Cape Town at the time, 5 September 1939; a special session had been called for reasons totally unconnected with the war in Europe. The prime minister, General J B M Hertzog, argued that it was not in South Africa's interest to take part and that, in any case, the question should be put to the (white) electorate by way of a general election. The leader of the opposition, General J C Smuts, believed it was imperative for South Africa to join the allies and said parliament should take the decision there and then.

At the start of the debate, opinion in the House of Assembly was evenly balanced, but Hertzog's speech degenerated into angry criticisms of British behaviour in the past, and feeling against him hardened. After the vote had gone against him, Hertzog resigned and Smuts became the new prime minister. Nevertheless, a large segment of the country's white population, most of them Afrikaners, shared Hertzog's view (the black people were not consulted), and the uncompromising *Ossewa-Brandwag* grew in influence.

The *OB* was opposed to parliamentary government. In spite of its anti-war propaganda and activities, Smuts did not ban it, probably because he saw it as a fairly harmless channel of criticism. Some if its leaders were interned, including B J Vorster (an irony, in light of his later Draconian house arrest and detention without trial of members of liberation movements). Hans van Rensburg was never interned. Some of the younger members of the *OB* formed the *Storm-jaers*, the storm troopers, and they committed acts of sabotage. Johannes van der Walt, the wrestler once known as the Masked Marvel, died after being shot by the police during such adventures.

The white English-speakers, most of whom had family members serving in the army 'Up North' (North Africa and later Italy), hated Van Rensburg and his *OB*. The feeling was reciprocated. Young soldiers who had volunteered for service outside South Africa wore red shoulder tabs on their uniforms. They were called *rooi luise*, red lice, by the *OB* people, and it was dangerous for them to sally forth in uniform in certain parts of Johannesburg and Pretoria and in some country towns.

Ironically enough, the *OB* faded away after the Nationalists came to power in 1948. The Nat leader and new prime minister, Dr D F Malan, had long viewed the *OB* with deep suspicion because of its extra-parliamentary role; after all, the Nats were committed to winning power in parliament by what were then called 'democratic means', even though more than half the population were excluded.

Hans van Rensburg was still the leader of the *OB* when I shared that train compartment with him in 1950. What was he like, this monster? He was a charming conversationalist, very interesting on some abstruse aspects of South African history. We didn't talk much about recent politics, but eventually I asked him: 'You met Hitler?' 'Yes.' 'What did you think of him?' A short pause and then, 'I thought I was face to face with a god.'

I was taken aback, to put it mildly. To my generation, Hitler was an ugly and evil man, aptly described by Winston Churchill as a blood-thirsty guttersnipe. Van Rensburg's hero worship seemed absurd. So I inquired further: 'And have you changed your mind since then?' The war was over, Hitler was dead.

'Well, yes, to some extent. But he was a very remarkable man.' On which cautious note we dropped that aspect of our conversation.

Hans van Rensburg went back into the civil service, in a relatively minor role, after the disbandment of the *OB* in the 1950s and eventually settled on his farm on an island in the Vaal River near Parys. He died in 1966, a man of high ability perverted by poor judgment and misguided beliefs.

Sidney Robey Leibbrandt, another extreme right-winger, was a different kettle of fish, a man of infinite courage but limited intelligence. He was born in Potchefstroom in 1913, but spent much of his youth in Bloemfontein, which was where I encountered him many years later. He matriculated from Grey College, Bloemfontein, about the same time as Bram Fischer, the communist lawyer who was sentenced to life imprison-ment after evading the police for a long time. I think it says something for Grey College that it could produce, at opposite ends of the political spectrum, a Robey Leibbrandt and a Bram Fischer.

From his schooldays, Leibbrandt showed great prowess as a boxer, and in 1936 he represented South Africa at the Olympic Games in Berlin, the Games that Hitler intended to be a showpiece for the Nazi state (the master race theory was badly jolted when Jesse Owens, a black

American, won four of the main events). Leibbrandt did well in the heavyweight division, but lost his fourth fight to a German after what seemed to be a home-town decision by the judges. More importantly, he fell under the spell of Hitler and the Nazis. Like many Afrikaners of his time, he had a strong dislike of the British and an equally fervent admiration of German discipline. His father had served in the Anglo-Boer War of 1899–1902 with General Smuts, who later became a great friend of Britain and was the so-called handyman of the Empire. It was a link that would eventually save Robey Leibbrandt's life.

After the Olympics, Leibbrandt stayed in Germany to take a course in physical education in Berlin. Returning home, he became a professional boxer and in 1937 won the South African heavyweight title. Then he was off to Europe again, to Britain, Denmark, Sweden, Finland and Germany for more studies in physical education. He was in Germany when the second World War broke out in September 1939, and by now he was a Nazi fanatic. He offered his services to Germany as a spy in South Africa, a saboteur and an assassin who would kill General Smuts.

On April Fool's Day in 1941, he sailed for South Africa as a passenger in a German military yacht called the *Kyloe*. His orders were to take the yacht's wireless operator ashore with him in South Africa and make contact with a German agent in Lambert's Bay, on the Cape west coast.

Leibbrandt ignored these instructions and disembarked alone on the Namaqualand coast (the yacht's captain thought he was entirely mad). He tried to make contact with Hans van Rensburg's *Ossewa-Brandwag*, but the *OB* were distinctly mistrustful of this interloper. Leibbrandt then embarked on a mainly unsuccessful mission of sabotage, with troop trains as a main target.

After six months, he was ambushed and arrested by the police near Pretoria. In March 1942, he was convicted of high treason and sentenced to death. He lost an appeal, which he conducted himself, but some months later the sentence was commuted to life imprisonment; Smuts said privately that he could not hang the son of the bravest comrade he had had in the Anglo-Boer War.

When the National Party came to power in 1948, one of their first acts was to release Leibbrandt from prison. The decision caused a huge uproar in South Africa. Leibbrandt, apparently unperturbed and certainly unrepentant, bought a flower farm at Honeydew, near Johannesburg, later opened a butchery and then went to Bloemfontein to run a motor business and a shop, all the time pouring out vituperative pamphlets about the danger of communism.

I first met Robey Leibbrandt in Bloemfontein in 1963. I had published an editorial in *The Friend* criticising John Vorster, then minister of justice, who claimed to have the 'communist menace' under control but at the same time wanted even more restrictive laws than those that already existed. He couldn't have it both ways, I had written, and in any case, he was already armed with more than enough laws and regulations that infringed basic liberties and rights.

Two days later, Piet Wessels, news editor of *The Friend*, told me that Leibbrandt wanted to discuss the editorial with me. He said he knew Leibbrandt quite well. 'He's a very nice fellow,' said Piet, using one of his favourite phrases, 'but he's a bit unpredictable – sometimes just gives you a clout for no reason.'

I agreed to see Leibbrandt on condition that Piet, a large former Springbok rugby forward, was present throughout the interview. It went off amiably enough. Leibbrandt, a short, powerfully built man, wore thick glasses, spoke English well, and had an obviously aggressive temperament. At the time, he was running his shop in Bloemfontein, but he considered himself a political pundit. I was bemused when he congratulated me on the editorial and said I was quite right to point out that Vorster was too soft on the communists! This was not at all what the editorial had said, quite the contrary in fact, but it seemed unwise to debate the point too vigorously with a man of obviously limited reasoning power but equally obvious physical strength. We parted noncommittally and after that he would visit me occasionally to ramble on about the sins of the Nationalist government, which he regarded as left-wing. These were trying discussions, but I felt almost sorry for this man who had once alarmed the Smuts government and was now an incoherent nonentity.

Perhaps I shouldn't have wasted my sympathy. Robey Leibbrandt was convicted of assaulting a black person and was occasionally in the news with anti-Semitic utterances before he died in 1966 at the age of 52.

From the ridiculous to the, well, sublime, in some respects anyway. The Fancourt hotel and country estate near George is well known now to many affluent South Africans and visitors from abroad. The old manor house is now about 150 years old, but for 40 of those years it stood neglected and decaying after a sudden and unexpected family tragedy.

The man who restored Fancourt and saved it from total collapse was one of the most extraordinary people I have ever encountered. His name was Rowland Anthony Harold Krynauw (pronounced 'crayno'), and I met him in 1960 when I was covering a week-long conference at the Wilderness Hotel, on the southern Cape coast. I got to know him and wrote, on the site of a Fancourt very different from the sophisticated scene of today, a story for the *Cape Argus* of the old house and its saviour.

Rowland Krynauw, the descendant of a French Huguenot family who settled at the Cape in 1689, was a neurosurgeon, a pioneer of brain surgery in South Africa and an international authority on this subject. He was born in Johannesburg in 1907, the only son of a prominent mining man, and from King Edward VII School in Johannesburg he went to Balliol College, Oxford, and then to Edinburgh University, where he took medical degrees. He then spent several years at Oxford in research and the practice of neurosurgery, a field of medicine that was then in its infancy. In 1940, he returned to South Africa and was, at the age of 33, appointed head of the Department of Neurosurgery in the Johannesburg General Hospital.

Displaying an endless capacity for meticulous patience and precision in examination, surgery and after-care, he became a world-renowned figure in his profession. He evolved an operation, hemispherectomy, in which half the brain is removed to cure certain spastic and epileptic cases, and he played an important part in the development of the 'brain wave' machine, the electro encephelograph. He reduced the brain-surgery mortality rate from close to 90 percent to below ten percent, and thousands of patients returned to useful lives instead of dying on the operating table. His work was acclaimed internationally, and in 1950 Krynauw lectured on it at the National Hospital for Nervous Diseases in London. For a dozen years, he worked in Johannesburg, treating patients from many parts of the world, performing operations that could last from eight to eighteen hours.

Then he retired in 1952 at the unusually early age of 45. Many people thought he was a serious loss to the medical profession, but Krynauw himself told me: 'Nobody's indispensable. I had built up a good unit in Johannesburg and I had done all my best work by the time I retired.' He was also, no doubt, influenced by the enormous mental and physical strain of that work, and by the fact that he had inherited a large fortune from his father.

Rowland Krynauw was not a man to sit back and relax. He had bought a farm between Wilderness and Knysna, and here the surgeon became a farmer. He ran a prize dairy herd, spent three months in New Zealand studying pasturages and applied his findings to make his farm, Woodfield, a showpiece.

Then he sold it at a large profit. He bought a hotel at Wilderness, then another hotel, then a company that owned much of the land at this quiet resort, then houseboats and caravans, and finally, in 1958, the derelict Victorian mansion called Fancourt. This double-storey house, about eight kilometres from George, started life in the 1840s as a modest single-storey home. It was built by Henry Fancourt White, an Australian roads engineer who in 1844 was hired by the Cape colonial secretary, John Montagu, to build a road across the Outeniqua mountains. The road was opened in 1847 and was officially named the Montagu Pass. White's workmen had their camp near here and, when the job was done, it was suggested that the little settlement be named White's Village.

Then, as now, it was an ambiguous and perhaps indiscreet name, so the village became Blanco (for White) instead. Henry White built his house close by and gave it one of his family names, Fancourt. After White's death in 1866, the place had several successive owners until 1903, when White's son, Montagu, bought it for three thousand five hundred pounds, the equivalent then of R7 000 today, and brought the estate to full flower.

Montagu White was, like the pass, named after John Montagu, as was the town of Montagu. White had done well on the Witwatersrand in the 1890s and before the Anglo-Boer War was the consul-general in London of the Transvaal republic. He retired to George and built additions to Fancourt, which included a coach house and stables.

There he lived with his family in baronial splendour, with the immaculately dressed Montagu White usually sporting a Panama hat and buttonhole. Wildfowl swam in the serpentine pond in front of the house; there were tea parties under the oaks or on the wide lawns. For the sportsmen, there was a private polo ground, the ladies could rest from the heat in a garden pavilion, and a butler saw to the smooth running of the dinner parties in the stinkwood-lined dining room.

It was a dinner party that ended Fancourt's days of glory with one swift blow. Montagu White grew mushrooms as a hobby. One day in 1916, he put mushrooms on the menu – but poisonous field fungi had been inadvertently mixed with the cultivated mushrooms. The next day, three people were dead, killed by the wild mushrooms: Montagu White himself, aged 58; his sister, Mrs Ham; and a member of the Vintcent family who then lived at Oudtshoorn and are still well-known in the Mossel Bay area.

Understandably, Fancourt decayed after that. It had a succession of owners who could not or would not face the high costs of its upkeep. For many years, locals refused to go near the place because it was said to be haunted. The house began to crumble away. The lawns disappeared under weeds and bushes; gum trees overwhelmed the oaks. For a time, the estate was used as a riding school, but eventually the polo ground lay neglected and forgotten. By the 1950s, the house was an empty derelict.

Rowland Krynauw heard about the deserted house. He told me in 1960: 'My interests at Wilderness were running smoothly and I was becoming bored. I was thinking about buying a yacht and cruising in the Pacific. Then I heard about this house, took one look and decided to buy it.'

It was some months after his purchase that he took me around the property. Workmen were painting the house. A tractor hauled a plough near a new lawn. A bulldozer was making short work of a clump of bluegums. Irises and azaleas had been planted in front of the house.

The house as it then stood had an entrance hall, two drawing-rooms, library, the ill-fated dining room, six bedrooms, three bathrooms, butler's pantry, kitchen and servants' hall. Dr Krynauw told me: 'I think I bought her just in time. The old girl was on her last legs. We had to prop up a section of the roof and rebuild one wall. Elsewhere, we used steel girders as a reinforcement.'

Krynauw had the advice of an architect, but he was his own planner and foreman. Every day for more than a year, he drove the 24 kilometres from Wilderness, where he lived, to Fancourt to supervise the work.

At the time I knew him, he was a short, balding man who spoke in clipped English tones and favoured tweedish country squire clothes. He seemed conventional enough, but his private life was far from conventional, at least by the standards of the mid-twentieth century. He lived in a double-storey house on the beach at Wilderness and had most of his evening meals at the Wilderness Hotel, which he owned. He was divorced and had no children, but he had company in the form of two pretty young Afrikaans girls, aged about twenty, daughters of a foreman on one of his farms. They lived in his house, causing much intense and indignant speculation in the neighbourhood, and they dined with him every evening at the hotel. From my table nearby, I could hear him explaining that *zuppa* was Italian for soup and that *coq au vin* was chicken cooked in wine. A latter-day Professor Henry Higgins, it would seem.

Krynauw had exceptional intellect and energy, and was obviously a man ahead of his time, in more ways than one.

In later years, Fancourt, the derelict that he saved, was owned by a property company that collapsed and was then occupied for many years by the film producer, Andre Pieterse. Eventually it became the present luxury hotel and golf resort, a fitting destiny, really, for the grand old lady.

—— THIRTEEN ——

The Book of Judges

Newspaper reporters often have contact with the law and lawyers. The pitfalls of publishing information that is often controversial and open to challenge or criticism mean that a newspaper journalist should have a broader and better grasp of the law than, say, an architect or an engineer. This is particularly true of a person who reports on the proceedings in a court of law. Most of my generation of journalists started their careers by being assigned to cover the magistrates' courts, where speed and accuracy, particularly the latter, were prerequisites. Many of us covered the Supreme Court (now the High Court) as well government boards, commissions and committees that conducted inquiries in the manner of the courts. One had to be a good reporter to unravel the complicated mysteries of litigation involving companies, insolvencies, major fraud cases, and so forth. And to this day I have a prejudice in favour of reporters who were brought up the hard way, producing high-speed copy from court cases, rather than the dilettantes with English Honours degrees who want to glide effortlessly into political analysis or drama reviews.

It is not unusual, then, for newspaper journalists to be friendly with lawyers. I had a close association with many lawyers and judges in Cape Town, Bloemfontein and Durban, and the closest of all came with my marriage (not the first) in 1987 to Heather, who was law librarian at the

University of Natal, had passed her law degrees and had been admitted to the bar as an advocate. She never practised there; she is not the inquisitorial type. My first wife, Molly Green, was for many years a well-known journalist on the staff of the *Cape Times* in Cape Town. There was somebody in between, but it was a matter of no consequence.

The legal profession has always had humorists and wits. One doesn't often hear uproarious stories from or about accountants or land surveyors or harbour pilots, but the tales of lawyers are legion. Perhaps it's because their calling often brings them into contact with some of the less pleasant aspects of life: crime, accidents, disputes. A veneer of cheerful cynicism may be a good protection in this kind of environment.

One of the famous court retorts was uttered by Judge Leopold Greenberg, who was a judge for 31 years, from 1924 to 1955. A murder trial jury had brought in a verdict of guilty but insane. 'What?' said the judge. 'All nine of you?' An even drier Greenberg comment was his reply to an intemperate attack on the Appeal Court in Bloemfontein by the then minister of justice, C R Swart, in 1952. Angered by the court's rejection of the government's High Court of Parliament Act, intended to remove Coloured voters from the electoral roll in the Cape, Swart said: 'The old men in Bloemfontein cannot hold up matters in South Africa.' Greenberg, a member of the court, responded: 'I can only say that this has not caused me or any of my brother judges any loss of sleep at night or in the afternoon.'

I once reported on a case in the Supreme Court in Cape Town in which three traders were charged with receiving stolen property. They were defended by H H Bloch, Queen's Counsel, later a judge. 'Bobby' Bloch was a persuasive advocate, and by the time he'd finished with the jury trying the case they would have convicted themselves rather than the not-so-innocents in the dock. At the end, the presiding judge said disagreeably: 'I think you're lucky. The jury have found you not guilty. You can go.'

Outside the courtroom, grinning advocates congratulated Bloch on his success. He accepted the tributes gravely. 'This case,' he said, 'has restored my faith in the jury system.'

Perhaps it's as well that the jury system was abolished in South Africa in 1969.

The most quoted South African judge over the past 30 years has probably been Mr Justice Rudolf Erasmus of Bloemfontein, not because of the sagacity of his words but because of his inimitably eccentric use of the English language. Erasmus, whom I knew slightly when I lived in Bloemfontein, was educated at Oxford and was always rather proud of his mastery of English. But he had a rare gift for finding an idiom that was close to correct but not quite close enough, with comic effects. Some examples of Erasmusiana:

Judge to counsel, in court: 'Your argument is like a duck's water off my back.'

Judge to distressed woman plaintiff in divorce case: 'Don't worry, my dear, your case is as safe as a house on fire.'

Expressing surprise: 'Suddenly it doomed on me that ...'

On one occasion, an expert witness was giving evidence in a case concerning mining rights. He was asked by counsel about his qualifications and experience. 'I studied geology at McGill University in Canada,' said the witness, 'and then I worked as a geologist in Canada, South Africa, Ghana, Australia, France, Bolivia ...'

'Really?' said the judge with acute interest. 'Seems to me you've been right round the bulb.'

The most celebrated Erasmus story bears repeating here. A property agent known for blowing his own trumpet (I heard him in action often) was discoursing at length in the bar of the Bloemfontein Club about his recent business triumphs: bought this, sold that, assembled these sites, syndicated that property, made a profit here, sold out there. Most of his listeners were stone bored, but not Rudolf Erasmus, who, after the garrulous one had left, observed to the company: 'Remarkable fellow, remarkable. Seems to me he has a finger in every tart in town.'

The Administrator of the Free State, Sand du Plessis, gave a party in his imposing new official residence. Mrs du Plessis proudly conducted groups of visitors around the house and I happened to be in the one that included Rudolf Erasmus. At the bottom of the stairs, he paused before a large painting of flowers in a vase and, after careful study, said knowledgeably: 'Now that's a really good example of a quiet life.' Quiet, still, what's in a word?

One of the formidable brains on the Appeal Court bench during my time in Bloemfontein was Frans Rumpff, who became Chief Justice. He came from a highly conservative Afrikaans background and was seen as such, but as the years passed he became conspicuously more liberal in his attitudes and judgments. An example was a dissenting judgment he gave in 1962 in a case involving Wilbur Smith's book, *When the Lion Feeds*. The Publications Board, in effect the censorship board, had ruled that the book was obscene and undesirable and should not be sold in South Africa, a ruling that seems hardly believable by today's standards. The publishers appealed and eventually the Appeal Court upheld the ban. Judge Rumpff disagreed, however, and gave his reasons in a judgment that became something of a watershed in the centuries-old battle in South Africa for free or freer speech. He argued that public taste did not remain static, and that books should not necessarily be judged from the responses of country clergymen or old ladies. In his judgment he quoted extensively from Smith's book, and Joel Mervis, editor of the Johannesburg *Sunday Times* – never one to miss a point – seized the opportunity to publish these excerpts from a book that was banned. Rumpff's judgment was, of course, a court document and as such publishable.

Frans Rumpff was an attractive character. He was tall, lean, fair and blue-eyed and he had an alert and sprightly manner. He also had a mischievous sense of humour. After I had left Bloemfontein for Durban, one of my friends, Leonora van den Heever, was appointed to the bench, becoming South Africa's first woman judge. Leo van den Heever is the daughter of F P 'Toon' van den Heever, in his day a distinguished Appeal Court judge and a respected Afrikaans writer and poet. Leo married Chris Neethling, a cheerful, practical man who was a salesman for a tyre company and spent much time doing business with farmers in the Free State.

By convention, the judges in Bloemfontein met for lunch every day at a big round table in the dining room of the Bloemfontein Club. On one such occasion there was a newcomer at the table, Michael Corbett from Cape Town, an acting judge of appeal who subsequently became Chief Justice. Rumpff was sitting next to him, and presiding over the conversation was the then Chief Justice, Ogilvie Thompson.

Enter, at the other end of the room, Chris Neethling and two farmers, in jolly mood, to celebrate the successful conclusion of a business deal. Rumpff nudged his companion and nodded towards this trio sitting some distance away. 'Do you see that round-faced man with the glasses in the middle of those three, the one laughing?' Corbett turned briefly to look. 'What about him?'

'Do you know that that man regularly sleeps with one of our judges?' After which Rumpff deftly turned his attention to the Chief Justice, droning away on the other side of the table.

Judge Corbett had an unhappy lunch, glancing furtively every now and then at the party in question. By the time the coffee arrived, he could contain himself no longer. He whispered to Rumpff: 'I've been watching that fellow. He doesn't even look odd.'

'Oh, nothing odd about him,' said Rumpff blandly. 'He's married to our lady judge.'

A sexist story, I suppose, especially these days, when openly homosexual judges of both sexes sit on the bench. It was not always like that. A Johannesburg lawyer told me this story, possibly apocryphal, about G J Maritz, judge-president of the then Transvaal from 1947 to 1959. A senior advocate was doing his first spell on the bench as an acting judge and had to adjudicate in an unpleasant case involving a male homosexual. In those days, the police and the law were totally intolerant; homosexuals were often spied on and brought to court, even when they conducted their activities in private and with consenting adults.

The acting judge convicted the accused man and deferred until the next day the difficult matter of sentence. That night, he phoned Maritz and asked if he could have some informal advice.

'Certainly, my boy,' said the judge-president.

'Tell me,' said the younger man diffidently, 'have you ever tried sodomy?'

A short pause. 'Well, yes.'

'Oh, then you can help me.' The words came rushing out nervously. 'Tell me, what did you give your man?'

Another short pause. 'Five bob and a box of chocolates.'

Sexist again, I suppose. Let me ward off any accusation that I am anti this or that. Like King Edward VII, I don't care what people do as long as they don't do it in the streets and frighten the horses.

Two reporters who were on the *Cape Argus* during my time there subsequently became prominent judges – Pat Tebbutt of Cape Town and John Didcott of Durban. Many a young advocate has supplemented his earnings by writing court reports for the newspapers, among them Petrus Wessels, who became an appeal court judge, and Gerald Friedman, who became judge-president of the Cape.

Another who had a stint in journalism was Henry Fagan, Chief Justice, politician, novelist, inventor of a shorthand system, and chairman of the Fagan Commission, which in the 1940s produced a report saying that total segregation in South Africa was impracticable and recommending interracial consultation instead. The report was discarded by the Nationalist government in 1948, with much woe to humankind.

I knew Judge Fagan slightly and wrote a long article about him for the *Cape Argus*. He was a delightful man, natural and unassuming and singularly free of pomposity. Every person has a weakness, however, and I was amused to discover that Fagan's was a minor, insignificant vanity. He wore a hearing aid, rather more visible in those days than it would be now, and he would not allow a posed photograph to be taken showing that side of his face.

Years later, I heard an entertaining story about this distinguished man (who, incidentally, had two distinguished sons, Hannes Fagan, another judge, and Gideon Fagan, an architect well known for his restoration of old Cape buildings). Henry Fagan was presiding in a criminal case in the Cape Supreme Court in a courtroom that had been equipped, for the first time, with microphones for witnesses and counsel and small earphones for the judge. On the judicial bench was a set of dials to adjust the volume and source of the sound, and in his typically alert and inquiring way Judge Fagan fiddled with these continuously to obtain the best results.

At the end of the trial, the accused was convicted of robbery and was asked by state counsel if he wished to say anything in mitigation before sentence was passed. The miscreant gazed at the bench and replied mournfully: 'What's the good of saying anything to him when he just sits there listening to his radio?'

By common consent, Albert Centlivres, Chief Justice from 1951 to 1957, was in the front rank of South African judges and so, for that matter, were all his colleagues in the Appeal Court who resisted the Nationalist government's attempt to remove Coloured voters from the Cape roll: Oliver Schreiner, O D Hoexter, Leopold Greenberg and F P van den Heever.

Centlivres was a big, heavy man, rather rustic in appearance, quiet in manner, his appearance belying his intellectual powers. I well remember being told to phone his home in Cape Town one Saturday morning to obtain a brief comment on an important matter. His wife answered and said he was at the shops but would phone me back when he returned. I said I would ring again – I could hardly expect the Chief Justice to phone a junior reporter on the *Cape Argus* – but she was insistent and I reluctantly left my name and number. Half an hour later, my phone rang. 'Centlivres here. I believe you wanted to speak to me.' How many really big shots would behave like that today?

Oliver Schreiner would have become Chief Justice if his reputation as a liberal had not been indigestible to the government of the time. Many senior appointments went to people not because they were good judges, but because they were good Nats. Even then, the aura and traditions of judicial office often proved greater than the individuals, and the political appointees did not always behave as expected. As Oswald Pirow, pre-war minister of justice, observed cynically: 'Put a man on the bench and in six months he thinks he's been appointed on merit.'

As we have seen in the new South Africa, certain preferences are inevitable. My old friend Hendrik van Heerden ended a distinguished judicial career as deputy Chief Justice. Earlier it had seemed logical that he would succeed to the top job. When the time came, however, the appointment went to Ismail Mohamed, and one can well understand the government's desire to appoint a person of colour. In any event, Judge Mohamed occupied the post with distinction until his premature death.

Hendrik van Heerden was born in the Free State village of Edenburg and was awarded a doctorate in law by Yale University in the United

States. He was a member of the legal team that appeared before the World Court at the Hague in 1966 to argue in favour of South Africa's continued occupancy of the then South West Africa, and scored an unexpected victory. During the case, the lawyers often spent weekends in London, where they were entertained by friendly Britons. At one such party, Van Heerden was asked by a plummy Englishman where he came from: 'Edenburg,' said Hendrik, pronouncing it in the correct Afrikaans way. 'Ah, I thought you had a Scottish accent.'

Several of the judges I have known consider Solly Miller the beau ideal of their profession. He was indeed a man of rare quality, keen in intellect but modest and gentle to a degree. He was a Free Stater and went to school in Bloemfontein at Grey College, which has produced so many prominent men. He became a senior counsel at the Free State bar and suffered the silent mortification of seeing various people who were his juniors appointed to the bench ahead of him. The fact that he was Jewish no doubt had something to do with this.

In 1961, he was finally given a judgeship, in Durban. B J Vorster, then minister of justice, phoned Miller from Cape Town, told him he would be offered the appointment and said it was long overdue, an action that reflects some credit on a politician not generally remembered for his grace and generosity. Miller later became an Appeal Court judge and displayed what every good judge should have: an abiding concern with the rights of the individual. He was a cultured man, with a great love of Shakespeare and Mozart; he left a performance of the film *Amadeus* because he couldn't bear to see the great composer being depicted as a foolish and capricious juvenile.

On occasional visits to London, one of Miller's greatest pleasures was to read a bedtime story to his grandson, then aged four or five. One night (he told me) he decided, by way of variation, to invent a story. 'This is a story made up by grandpa,' he began, and proceeded to create characters, a plot and development – all very credibly, he thought. Eventually, he found a way to round it off satisfactorily, the child listening intently all the while. 'And that,' said Judge Miller, 'is the end of the story.' Whereupon his grandson said, 'I've never heard such a load of crap in all my life.'

Solly Miller died of a heart illness at the age of 67. At that time, I lost several friends who died far too young, among them Frank Martin, one of Natal's leading politicians, and Charles Still, deputy editor of the *Daily News* for many years. I mentioned this in sorrowful tones to Solange Raffray, who comes from France and became a wine consultant in Durban. She replied with a phrase in French. 'What does it mean?' I asked. 'The beautiful flowers die young, the weeds go on for ever.'

Another old friend of mine, Ramon Leon, was a judge in Natal for more than twenty years before becoming Chancellor of Natal University. His son, Tony, is leader of the opposition in parliament and another son, Peter, is a prominent lawyer in Johannesburg. In retirement, Ray Leon became a member of the courts of appeal in Lesotho and Swaziland, the other members being retired South African judges. Eventually, they ran into a problem in Swaziland, a country with a king who is virtually an absolute monarch and a government that is less than emphatic about individual rights. The government decided to ignore two rulings by the court, and when they refused to alter their position, Ramon Leon, the president of the court, and his six judges resigned en bloc. For the citizens of Swaziland that is a pity, but it is hard to see what else the appeal judges could do.

John Milne, one of the country's most distinguished judges, was another who died too soon, of an unexpected heart attack while on holiday in Britain. He was the quintessential white Natalian. His father was the Judge-President of Natal, he was educated at Hilton College and Oxford, he practised at the Natal bar, he was equally at home in Durban or Pietermaritzburg, and he himself became Judge-President. But when he was appointed to the Appeal Court in Bloemfontein in 1988, he immediately made an impact in the wider sphere, with his acute mind, balanced outlook and ardent defence of human rights. At a time when the English-language newspapers were subjected to a barrage of criticism, he was strong on freedom of the press. On the Natal bench, he ruled in favour of Rex Gibson, then editor of the *Rand Daily Mail*, when Rex was sued for defamation by an aggrieved lawyer, and Milne's written judgment was a carefully phrased analysis of the right to criticise and be criticised, and included an apt quotation from John Donne:

'… on a huge hill, Cragged and steep, Truth stands and he that will Reach her, about must, and about must go.'

In a long and close friendship I only once had an altercation with John Milne and the fault was mine, though inadvertently. As Judge-President of Natal, he had given formal permission for press photographs to be taken on court premises and in the courtrooms themselves, in accordance with the belief that justice should be open and should, literally, be seen to be done. There was one proviso: under no circumstances should a photograph be taken while the court was actually sitting, that is when the presiding officer, the judge or magistrate, had taken his seat. This was a great advance on the situation that had existed previously (and that still existed then in other parts of South Africa), in which press photographers were quite likely to be arrested and charged with contempt of court if they were seen within the sacred precincts.

Alas, the concession was short-lived. John Milne himself was sitting in a Supreme Court case when my newspaper, the *Daily News,* incurred his extreme wrath by breaking the rule. I was away in Cape Town for a few days when the incident occurred, and I learned about it on my return. The case was a sensational one about a Bonnie-and-Clyde-type couple, man and woman, who wantonly murdered four people on separate occasions, tying them to trees and shooting them, apparently for the sheer thrill of doing it. They showed no remorse, there were no extenuating circumstances, and John Milne passed death sentences on both the accused, as he was obliged to do in terms of the law – and the *Daily News* published a photograph of him doing so, taken through an open window of the courtroom.

I was aghast when I heard of this, but was told that the matter had been settled to the judge's satisfaction. The next day, the judge phoned me. I said that I regretted the offending publication but that I gathered he was satisfied. He informed me icily that he was far from satisfied. Chastened, I explained that, while I was not trying to shake off responsibility, I should point out that I was away in Cape Town at the time. Still icy, he said that he was aware of that and that he had instructed the police to trace me in Cape Town (they were unsuccessful), and he suggested that the error would not have occurred if I had been in my office.

It is the hard lot of newspaper editors to accept responsibility for their publications whether they are there or not, and I made no excuses. John Milne went on to say, in somewhat calmer tones, that he was withdrawing permanently the permission for any newspaper to take photographs on court premises and that he was issuing a statement to this effect to the South African Press Association (the national news agency that serves all papers with news).

I wrote a formal letter to him expressing my regret, and I made sure that his statement was published with prominence in the *Daily News*. The statement referred to 'a newspaper' that had breached the rule but did not mention the *Daily News*. I added an editor's footnote stating that the erring newspaper was, in fact, the *Daily News*, that I regretted the error, and that I had tendered a private apology to the judge that I now repeated publicly.

As you may imagine, my fellow newspaper editors were not overjoyed, for the ban had been reimposed on all of us, and for good. I had to answer a number of embarrassing phone inquiries from reporters on other papers, and all I could do was repeat my acknowledgment of error and apology.

All this happened on a Tuesday. By a long-standing arrangement, I was due to attend a party at the Milne home in Pietermaritzburg the following Saturday and to spend the weekend there as a house guest (I was unmarried at the time). It was with considerable trepidation that I set off for the party. I need not have worried. John Milne was friendliness, warmth and hospitality itself. He made no reference whatsoever to the newspaper contretemps and his anger, nor did he ever do so again. As Chief Justice Michael Corbett said after his death years later, he was a true gentleman.

Did the South African judiciary serve South Africa well during more than 40 years of repressive and authoritarian government by the National Party? Yes and no. Many judges did what they could to blunt the cruel, sharp edge of apartheid and to maintain civilised principles. They spoke out from time to time, reasonably secure in the knowledge that a South African judge may be removed from office only by Act of Parliament, something that has never happened. Other judges showed more or less consistent support for the policies of the government, often relying on the dictum that the security of the state was paramount and had to be placed before the rights of individuals (never mind that 'the state' represented only a small minority of the people).

Some judges have shown a tendency to be self-congratulatory. This is understandable enough in the changed circumstances of the new South Africa, when it is obviously better to have opposed the old government than to have supported it. In addition, the judiciary of the apartheid years was all white. The first black judge, Hassan Mall of Durban, was an acting appointment made by John Milne when he was Judge-President of Natal.

Have the judges performed as noble a task as some of them would have us believe? Not everybody thinks so. They upheld the law, as their oath of office demanded, even if they did try to ameliorate the effects of cruel and unjust laws. They sometimes had harsh words and deeds for newspapers that were struggling to publish legitimate news and views in the face of government suppression.

It is a bias that survives. Some years ago, the Appeal Court ruled against publication of certain material and had sharp words to say about newspapers that were allegedly more concerned with their own interests than with the public interest. An odd criticism, as Ken Owen pointed out in the *Sunday Times*, coming from an institution that upheld the laws of apartheid for 40 years and directed against an institution that opposed apartheid for 40 years.

In the heyday of apartheid, government spokespeople would sometimes hail South Africa's judges as the finest in the world (along with our finest soldiers, rugby players, helicopters, power stations, dams, etcetera, etcetera). As one grizzled veteran of the bench remarked to me, why should our judges be any better than those of, say, Australia or Switzerland or France or Canada?

The balanced view is, I think, that our judges were certainly people well versed in the law, fair-minded, generally compassionate, conscientious and not consciously oppressive even when they were sentencing political offenders to long terms of imprisonment in the interests of apartheid. But they were not martyrs or sufferers or champions in the battle against apartheid. They were, and remain, a protected species. No judge ever lost his job, or was visited by the police, or was threatened with prosecution or detention in jail because he had spoken out about the government and its laws, a fate that was commonly experienced by a great many other people. They helped, in difficult circumstances, to maintain reasonably just standards in the courts, but unlike the English-language press, universities and churches, they were not a significant influence in bringing about change in South Africa.

Perhaps this was inevitable, given the non-political role that judges are expected to play. The challenges that await them now will, I suspect, be as daunting as those of the apartheid years. They may have to be the prime protectors of human rights. They will be assisted by a Constitution that guarantees those rights but that may be subject to change in the future; who knows? And their actions will always be under close scrutiny. One of the many improvements in the new South Africa is the free, bold and critical comment about the courts that is now accepted as the norm, compared with the timid, obsequious, exaggerated respect of the old South Africa. Should the need arise for the judges to be the watchdogs of individual rights, one hopes they will generally be more effective in the future than they were able to be in the past.

FOURTEEN

East is east

When Arthur Sydney Anthony East died in Cape Town in 1996, his passing went almost unnoticed in the media, except for the ordinary death notice advertisements in the newspapers. Yet there was a time when hardly a day passed without his name appearing somewhere in the papers.

Sydney East was born in Cape Town, the son of an immigrant who had done well out of a fisheries business. He practised as an attorney, was married with children, had some vague cultural and literary pretensions, and eventually, in the 1950s, became a Cape Town city councillor, an ordinary enough curriculum vitae. What he also had, however, was a lust for personal publicity almost unparalleled in my long experience of such matters.

As a councillor, Sydney cultivated every journalist he met. Day after day he would be in the newspaper offices, giving his (unasked for) opinions on various topical matters, beginning and ending with 'You can say: "Mr A S A East said …".' A pain? Yes, but he was a pleasant and courteous man and, oddly enough, much of his proliferation of comments made good sense.

Whether he made much money out of his legal practice I do not know, but he always seemed to have time to stroll into the news room of the *Cape Argus*, usually at about three in the afternoon, so that he could depart with, tucked under his arm, a copy of the *Argus* stamped 'Staff copy – not for sale'. He occasionally appeared as an attorney in minor cases in the magistrate's court, sometimes with hilarious effect. I remember reporting a low-grade case in which the owner of a hot-dog stall on the Grand Parade was charged with damaging his neighbours' property by throwing rubbish over their fence. It had been a long-standing feud, and was totally unedifying, but Sydney rose grandly to the occasion. Addressing the court on his client's behalf, he told the bemused magistrate: 'Here, Your Worship, we have before us enacted once more the immortal story of the Montagues and the Capulets.'

Sydney had an ample house in Bishopscourt, and it was typical of him that he should name it Hughenden, after the Buckinghamshire mansion that once belonged to Benjamin Disraeli, the celebrated prime minister of Britain in Victoria's time. It was typical, too, that he should take up horseriding and, on a visit to England, parade mounted down Rotten Row in London's Hyde Park, in full scarlet hunting regalia. Asked by a curious newspaperman where he came from, Sydney replied that he was the Count of Oranjezicht from South Africa, all of which was duly reported.

He was not a bad city councillor, quite a good one in some ways, but his ceaseless quest for publicity earned him the abiding enmity of many of his council colleagues in the 1950s and '60s. The Eastern Boulevard, the 3,5-kilometre highway that runs across the lower slopes of Table Mountain from De Waal Drive to the Cape Town foreshore, was originally, in the long planning stage, called Boulevard East. Many councillors became obsessed with the idea that people would think it was named after Sydney East, and so the name was changed to Eastern Boulevard.

This road caused, through forced removals of families and shopkeepers, great hardship and grievance, but I was told that its conception was as casual as could be. A French town planner who was a consultant on the development of the foreshore in the 1940s and '50s was looking at a map with some city councillors and officials when somebody said, 'But when all this is finished how will we get the traffic down to the foreshore without clogging up the city's streets?' 'Oh, that's easy,' said the planner, 'you build a road along here.' Taking a pencil, he drew a line from a point just above Groote Schuur Hospital to the middle of the Foreshore. And that was the birth of the Eastern Boulevard.

I don't know whether the Cape Town City Council, which had a relatively liberal reputation, fully understood the social and political implications of building that road, which was completed in 1968. I'm pretty sure that the Nationalist government and its officials saw it as a golden opportunity to implement apartheid by moving the inhabitants of this area to the Cape Flats, a process that culminated in the destruction of District Six, one of Cape Town's most colourful and historic neighbourhoods. The damage in human terms was incalculable, creating a generation of bitterness.

The Cape Town City Council of the 1950s and '60s was an odd mixture of impersonal idealism and personal advancement. The council of 45 members included six people of colour, and they were elected not as 'Coloured representatives' but on a common municipal voters' roll, a fact not often remembered when the history of apartheid is discussed. The government eventually put an end to it, of course, but for many years after the Nationalist election victory in 1948 the six, led by the redoubtable Mrs Zainunissa Gool, made full use of their right of free speech in the council chamber and often belaboured their white colleagues mercilessly. Others in this group included Edgar Deane, a trade unionist with a good sense of humour; H J M Holmes, a business man at Athlone and a tenacious debater; and R E Viljoen, a rather avuncular former schoolteacher.

Mayors came and went every two years, but the real chief of the council, the power behind the throne, was Major Aaron Zalman Berman. Russian-born, he was a businessman who had served with distinction in World War II and became the chairman of the council's finance committee, in effect the holder of the city's purse strings. He was also a United Party member of the Cape Provincial Council and, later, a senator. He was an aggressive man, highly literate (he was reputed to have one of the biggest private libraries in Cape Town) and highly articulate, albeit with a marked Middle European accent. His modus operandi generally was to bully the council into his way of thinking, but if he saw the tide

was running against him he would switch into a mode of sweet reasonableness: 'I'm asking councillors, don't they understand the King's
English?' – this in an accent far removed from the playing fields of Eton.

A Z Berman owned two bottle stores. In those days, holding a liquor
licence was widely regarded as the key to untold riches; it is apparently
rather different today, with hot competition from the supermarkets.
Anyway, Berman was rich and powerful. His son, Harold, a gentler soul,
became in the fullness of time a judge of the Cape Supreme Court (now
the High Court).

Many of Berman's close friends and colleagues are commemorated in
the names of streets in and around Cape Town: Louis Gradner, Martin
Hammerschlag, Isaac Albow, and others. It's not a good idea, really, to
name streets after local or national politicians. Durban has a street
named after a mayor who went to jail for dishonesty. How many
Capetonians know anything about Oswald Pirow, he of the Oswald
Pirow Boulevard? He was a pre-war Nationalist minister of justice who
became something perilously close to a Nazi when he later founded the
New Order party.

Fritz Sonnenberg, a humorous and sophisticated attorney, stood outside the power clique but he became a successful mayor of Cape Town.
I was at school with his three sons, one of whom, Dr John Sonnenberg
of Sea Point, became a prominent councillor.

Another school acquaintance, David Bloomberg, followed in his
father's footsteps by becoming mayor in the 1960s. Father and son were
both attorneys. Abe Bloomberg was mayor in 1947 when the British
royal family visited South Africa, and he marked the occasion by having
the Mayor's Parlour at the City Hall fitted with splendid and expensive
wood panelling. He was a suave and amiable man with impeccable manners, softly spoken, and a generous host at his palatial home at Fresnaye,
above Sea Point, but his critics called him Honest Abe. This was a reference not to Abraham Lincoln but to the tough interior that lay behind
Abe Bloomberg's smiling face. He was, for a time, United Party member of parliament for the Castle constituency in Cape Town. Most of the
voters in the constituency at that time were members of the Coloured
community, and the story was that it was distinctly risky to vote against

Abe Bloomberg; you might run into trouble at the hands of some of his more zealous supporters.

His son, David, was a gifted and cultured man who, among other things, established the Barn Theatre at Constantia, a venue where the distinguished actress Yvonne Bryceland first appeared on stage, in knockabout farces. On one occasion, when my wife and I were visiting Cape Town from Bloemfontein, David Bloomberg entertained us in perfect mayoral fashion. We were invited, with about twenty others, to drinks in the Mayor's Parlour, followed by a symphony concert given by the Cape Town Orchestra, with seats in the mayoral bay. Another round of drinks at the interval, and at the end of the concert a finger supper at which the orchestra's conductor and several players joined us. I thought this was an excellent way of entertaining officially and displaying the City Council's prize asset, the orchestra.

David Bloomberg left South Africa many years ago, and he has not returned. His wife, Toby Fine, was a brilliant ballet dancer.

The most vivid of all the councillors, the one who became the most successful mayor of all, the one who was the least sophisticated of them all, was Gerald Edgar Ferry. The village blacksmith, his critics called him, and indeed there was something of the old-fashioned smithy about Gerry Ferry. He owned a small iron-and-steel business, the Atlantic Foundry, on the mountain slopes of Woodstock. He was a huge man who always looked vaguely as if he had just been hammering some metal in his foundry. He was Mr Woodstock. He had lived in this suburb, I suppose you could call it a working-class suburb, all his life. Everybody knew him, and he seemed to know everybody.

Today Woodstock has become faintly fashionable, 'Woodies' in property agents' language. In those days, 40 years ago, it was a fairly tight-knit community of hard-working people – no grand houses, but no bad debts either. Gerry Ferry was involved with ratepayers' associations, youth organisations, school committees, boxing clubs, just about everything. As a councillor, he protected his ward like a watchful Alsatian, and he never tired of espousing the cause of what he called the decent working man. He was not a racist; Woodstock was too mixed a community for that, and Gerry's heart was too big for that. He was not an intellectual, but he was no fool, not by a long chalk. He was an effective public speaker but not a polished orator.

He understood the meaning of transparency long before it became a buzzword in public affairs. Cape Town councillors and officials who for various reasons wanted to keep some matters secret would have these placed on the agenda on green paper and headed 'Strictly Confidential – Not for Publication'. Very often, the reasons for secrecy were far from convincing, and sometimes they were positively sinister. Gerry Ferry ensured that I, as the municipal reporter of the *Cape Argus*, received all the green paper that was worth having. It would come anonymously in the post, in a plain envelope, but the large black fingerprints on the envelope and on the documents themselves instantly revealed the source. Gerry Ferry had very big hands, and when you are working in a foundry it is difficult to have hands like lilies. But he was not scruffy. At mayoral functions he would appear resplendent, like a British trade unionist of the old school, in black jacket, striped trousers and grey silk tie.

If Gerry Ferry was a symbol of Woodstock, he was also a symbol of Cape Town. His father, Driver Ferry, had been one of the drivers of the trains on the Cape Town-Simonstown line in the days of steam, and he had been one of the two drivers of the ceremonial train that took Cecil John Rhodes's coffin from Cape Town to be buried in the Matopo hills in Rhodesia, now Zimbabwe, in 1902. Gerry Ferry was immensely proud of this, and he also cherished his long-standing association with the naval dockyard in Simonstown. When many Afrikaans people grew beards to commemorate a Voortrekker celebration, Gerry Ferry grew his own beard, which he called a Francis Drake.

I had left Cape Town by the time he became mayor, rather against the odds, but I kept in touch with him. He was obviously the most popular mayor the city had had, showing a natural dignity and friendliness and common sense to all, regardless of rank or colour. An old friend of mine, the wife of a member of Chris Barnard's original heart transplant team, told me about meeting Mayor Ferry at the funeral of the first transplant patient, Louis Washkansky, in 1967. She said the mayor's dignity, sincerity and sympathy had made a great impression on her and on everyone else at the funeral.

After becoming mayor, Gerry Ferry visited Durban, where I was living, and I entertained him at my home. He struck up a friendship, with my son, then aged about ten, and in due course Geoffrey received in the post a parcel containing a magnificent coffee-table book on Cape Town inscribed on the fly leaf, with a few fingerprints, in Gerry's sprawling hand, 'To Geoffrey Green, from his friend Gerry Ferry, Mayor of Cape Town.'

Not that they saw eye to eye all the time. I took Gerry and Geoffrey for a drive around Durban and made a stop at the end of the Bluff, where one has a splendid view of the harbour and the city. 'Nice, isn't it?' said Geoffrey, as he and Gerry ate ice creams bought by the latter. 'Yes,' said Gerry Ferry. 'Nice, but no Table Mountain.'

FIFTEEN

Wheels

I would not describe myself as a car enthusiast – I hardly know the difference between a spark plug and a big end – but, like most people, I like driving a nice car. South Africa must be one of the few countries in the world where many people are prepared to spend almost half as much on a car as they do on a house. It wasn't always so. Forty years ago, newly married couples often managed without cars, giving preference to a deposit on a house or a flat. They relied on friends for lifts at night or took buses, trains or taxis (quite expensive in the days before the ubiquitous minibus taxi, but not as expensive as running a car).

Even the big shots were not averse to using public transport. Mervyn Williams and Rex Walker, respectively Cape Town's town clerk and treasurer in the 1950s, both had large official cars as a perquisite of their stations, which, along with the positions of city engineer and medical officer of health, were the top jobs in the municipal service. Messrs Williams and Walker both lived at St James, and every morning they would drive their big black cars to the St James station, on the False Bay coast, board a suburban train, disembark at the old Cape Town station and walk across the Grand Parade to their offices at the city hall.

Times change, and it would probably not be easy or wise for them to do so today. But what has changed the most, I suspect, is the attitude of South African middle-income earners to the question of private and public transport. Many people seem to regard it as demeaning or humiliating to catch a bus or train, even though they do so without blinking when on holiday in London or New York. Not everybody shares this view, of course. I know white Durbanites who regularly use Zola Budds, the cheerful name given to the black-owned minibus taxis that career about our streets. They have had no problems.

So we are car snobs, and our snobbery is fed ceaselessly by the world's motor manufacturers, who produce 60 million new cars each year, and by dealers, advertisers and motoring writers – an army of salesmen trying to entice us into buying newer, better and faster cars. The truth is that any reasonably well-made car should last at least ten years, maybe a lot longer. And they are nearly all well made today. The history of motoring is littered with car makes and models that fell by the wayside because they did not last. Many British cars had a poor reputation after World War II. You don't see the names of the duds any more, not in South Africa, anyway. By contrast, the motor manufacturers of the Far East have long put behind them the reputation of being cheap and nasty imitators of European and American products.

The two most interesting cars I have ever owned were the two least expensive. In 1952, having saved assiduously from my modest salary at the *Cape Argus*, I bought my first car, a new Fiat Cub. It cost me £380, equal to R760. Fiat, based in Turin, is of course Italy's biggest motor manufacturer. The Fiat Cub was a very small car designed for two occupants. Luggage went on to a shelf behind the two front seats, and at a pinch you could put two small children there, provided you had no luggage and they had short legs. There was a rather handsome lockable boot at the back, but this was entirely occupied by the spare wheel. The engine, in front, had a capacity of 500 cubic centimetres. Most modern small cars have engines at least twice that size. Flat out, the car could do about 60 miles an hour, about 100 kilometres per hour. Its pulling power uphill was negligible, and you had to work at the four-speed gearbox to keep the speed at a respectable level. It had a canvas roof that folded down easily, so it was a convertible of sorts. With the roof down and the breeze blowing over the fixed side windows you could, with a considerable stretch of the imagination, feel that you were in an MG or an Alfa.

Nearly a year after I bought the Fiat I was seconded to the newspaper's London office for twelve months. I flew there, in a Constellation aircraft that took 24 hours to make the journey from Johannesburg via Salisbury (Harare), Nairobi, Khartoum and Rome, and my employers benevolently agreed to ship my car to Britain, at a cost, I think, of £20, or R40.

In London, my car often created a minor sensation. Foreign cars were rarities in England in those days, and my little Fiat was something strange and wonderful. For a year I parked in the street outside my lodgings in Bayswater and didn't lose so much as a hubcap. Occasionally I drove to Fleet Street, where I worked, and on one occasion I risked leaving the car for a few minutes in a No Parking area. When I returned, a London bobby was standing there. 'Where did you get this thing?' he asked in lofty tones. My feelings were bruised, but I called him officer and told him that I was from South Africa and the car from Italy. Mollified, he let me off with a warning not to park like that again.

The Fiat really proved its worth on a long holiday trip in continental Europe, which I made with Douglas Hoffe of Johannesburg. He was the son of Brigadier C M Hoffe, who had been general manager of the South African Railways. Doug Hoffe was working as a lawyer in London and later returned to South Africa and became a prominent businessman. He was an ideal travelling companion: entertaining, good humoured and equable in temperament. I never heard him lose his temper or say angry words.

Together we covered about 10 000 kilometres through Belgium, Holland, France, Germany, Switzerland and Italy, the sort of eye-opening trip that many young people make at some time or another. The Fiat didn't falter in the traffic jams of Paris, along the magnificent banks of the Rhine, over the Alps or down to southern Italy. We lowered the canvas roof every day and after four weeks had developed expensive-looking suntans. Our luggage, minimal, nestled on the shelf behind the seats and we were never in fear of losing anything, except in Naples, which had a bad reputation. There Doug Hoffe sat twisted around with his hand on the bags to make sure nobody stole them at traffic lights. A sign of things to come in many parts of the world.

Our four-week trip cost us less than £100 (R200) each, and our only real alarm was registered in a narrow Paris side street. I parked in the road outside our small hotel and the next morning, having checked that the car was all right, we set out on foot to explore. When we returned that afternoon, the car had moved a little distance down the street to the opposite side. It was still locked, and we were baffled. The locals explained, mainly by sign language. In this particular street, parking was permitted on only one side, and the side alternated from day to day. By leaving my car where it was, I had broken the rule and caused a traffic blockage. Eventually two gendarmes arrived to sort out the problem. Unable to find the errant owner, they had enlisted the aid of two able-bodied bystanders, picked up the car, and dumped it on the other side of the street.

It was a lovely car. I sold it after five years, and did so through a colleague on the *Cape Argus*, Hughe Mackinnon, who had once been a successful motor dealer. I wanted £180 for it and agreed to pay him commission for finding a buyer and handling the whole deal. He advertised the car in the smalls columns of the *Cape Argus*, and at the same time I saw another advertisement for another Fiat Cub, with a higher mileage, asking price £220. 'I should get my price,' I said to Hughe, 'somebody's asking more for an older Fiat.' 'Ah,' said Hughe, 'Alma put in that advertisement.' Alma was his wife.

My second really interesting car was a 1934 London taxi, an Austin, which I bought from my colleague Philip Stohr in 1961 for £25 (R50). Philip had been a newspaper journalist in London and had bought the old car there from a cab driver who was upgrading to something newer. Whereas the Fiat Cub was strictly a two-seater, the London cab was easily a six-seater. Philip Stohr drove it about London for a year, then returned to Cape Town and brought the taxi with him.

I bought it because I saw it as a kind of mobile changing room for use at Muizenberg beach. It had done about 800 000 kilometres, having worked the streets of London for nearly 30 years. It was a solemn, uncompromising, rather faded black, with cracked red leather upholstery. In the back were a wide bench seat and two rear-facing folding opera seats. The driver sat in dignified seclusion with a sliding window behind him for when he wished to talk to the passengers, or they to him. The engine was a massive four-cylinder unit and the gearbox was designed specifically for slow London traffic; the car could pull away comfortably in top gear at ten miles an hour. The controls were minimal and functional. Dipping the headlights was literally that: you pushed a lever on the driver's door and the headlights dropped forward with a heavy thud. Outside the driver's window was an old-fashioned horn. You squeezed the red rubber bulb and it gave a loud parp.

Next to the driver was the luggage platform, where suitcases were strapped (a roof rack provided additional luggage space). The only part of the car that was not original was a pole at the edge of this platform, from floor to roof. This was for Philip's wife, Flora, to hold on to. When Philip drove the car in London, Flora would sit on a kitchen chair on the luggage platform – it was more sociable than having her in the cab at the back – and every time he turned a corner she would grab the pole he had installed to avoid sliding off the platform and on to the road.

When I bought the taxi it had a problem starting, and I soon became familiar with the crank handle. There was a knack to this. The car started easily with one swing of the crank, but you had to slip the handle loose quickly to avoid sustaining a broken wrist. I paid a mechanic at Woodstock £15 (R30) to overhaul the engine and fix the starter, and after that we travelled in relatively modern style.

I took the taxi to Muizenberg many times. The cab was so big that it was easy to change in it while parked at Sunrise Beach. And, of course, it attracted attention everywhere, especially among the children of Newlands, where I lived.

I had at the time another car that was in many ways the exact opposite: a new Volkswagen Beetle, small, sensible, compact. Eventually, I sold the London taxi to another *Cape Argus* colleague, Maxwell Leigh, charging him exactly what I had put into the car: £40 (R80). He smartened it up a bit, drove it for a year or two, used it sometimes as a carriage for bridal couples, managed on one occasion to transport two paraplegic athletes and their wheelchairs, and then sold it to an old car enthusiast in Bellville. I'd like to think that it is still rumbling away somewhere in the Cape, but, 40 years on, I have my doubts.

SIXTEEN

Harvard

Harvard is the oldest university in the United States and probably the most famous; it is among the nine universities that predate American independence in 1776 and that are called the Ivy League, because they are ancient enough to have ivy growing on their walls.

In recent years, a large number of South Africans have attended short courses at Harvard's business school, a celebrated institution that is a good demonstration of how education must keep up with the times; tradition is not enough, teaching must embrace modern ideas as well as old wisdom.

A rather more rarefied group are the Nieman Fellows of Harvard University, beneficiaries of the most cherished award that a journalist can win. Lucius W Nieman was the publisher (equals owner) of the *Milwaukee Journal*, one of America's major newspapers. From humble beginnings he became a very rich man, and he built for his newspaper an enviable reputation for accuracy, fairness and responsibility. He died in 1935, and when his widow, Agnes Wahl Nieman, died the following year, she bequeathed US$1-million, then a huge sum, to Harvard University to commemorate their name and 'to promote and elevate the standards of journalism in the United States and educate persons deemed specially qualified for journalism'.

The university authorities decided that running a journalism school was not quite their style, and they allocated the money to bursaries for senior, qualified and experienced journalists to study anything they liked (except journalism!) at Harvard for a year. The university was less than totally enthusiastic; the Harvard president, James Bryant Conant, described the whole enterprise as 'a dubious experiment'. Time has resolved all doubts.

This grant to Harvard was in accordance with a long and admirable American tradition of giving to good causes. The United States has long been the richest country in the world, and most of its leading citizens have been aware of their duty to plough back their profits, so to speak, into the broader fabric of American society. Names like Carnegie and Rockefeller are remembered today not so much because they were fabulously rich men but because they represent public generosity on the grandest scale in projects ranging from relief for the poor to the acquisition of Renaissance art.

Harvard has been the recipient of great generosity and indeed the university owes its name to the first such good deed. The first group of the Pilgrim Fathers – that brave, highly principled and unusually intelligent band of pioneers – arrived in what they called New England in 1620. There were 102 of them, in a little sailing ship called the *Mayflower*. I have seen its replica at Plymouth, Massachusetts, which was built in 1957 and was sailed across the Atlantic Ocean in a commemorative voyage. It is hardly believable that more than a hundred people crowded into this little boat, only 25 metres long. I think they must have slept in shifts. Privacy must have been impossible. And two children were born during the voyage, boys named Oceanus and Peregrine (from the Latin for traveller).

Several waves of pilgrims (who had left Europe, mainly England, to seek religious freedom, though they themselves were an intolerant lot) arrived over the next few years. Among them was a clergyman named John Harvard, a graduate of Cambridge University in England. He died in 1638, aged 31, and in his will left £780 and his collection of 260 books to a college that had been established two years earlier in a little town that the settlers called Cambridge because about 70 of their leading citizens had been educated at the famous English university. His hope, his vision and his bequest brought him immortality. The settlers forthwith named their new college after their late preacher.

Harvard prospered, as did Cambridge, which is now virtually a suburb of Boston, one of America's most historic and attractive large cities. The spirit of giving continued. For example, the Harvard library, which has thirteen million volumes and is the largest university library in the world, is largely focused on the imposing Widener Library, a huge classical building donated in memory of a graduate, Harry Elkins Widener, who died when the *Titanic* sank after hitting an iceberg in 1912. Mrs Nieman's gift followed a well-established tradition.

Initially, her money was used to bring a handful of American journalists to Harvard every year, the idea being to broaden their perspectives and knowledge. After the second World War, the programme was extended to include a few foreign journalists. In 1960, South Africa was invited to send a representative, the costs being met by an organisation called the United States-South African Leader Exchange Programme. Since then, South Africa, alone among foreign countries, has had a Nieman Fellow every year, and there are now more than 40 of them.

Aubrey Sussens was the first South African Nieman, and his successors included many well-known names in South African journalism. About 25 of them became editors of South African newspapers at one time or another. Among the early ones were Tertius Myburgh, later editor of the Johannesburg *Sunday Times*; Allister Sparks, *Rand Daily Mail*; Ton Vosloo, the Johannesburg *Beeld* and later chairman of the Sanlam insurance company; Percy Qoboza, editor of the mass circulation Johannesburg paper, *The World;* Hennie van Deventer, the Bloemfontein paper, *Volksblad*; Obed Kunene, the Zulu paper, *Ilanga*; and Aggrey Klaaste, of the *Sowetan*. More recent Niemans included another batch of editors: Richard Steyn (*The Star*), Brian Pottinger and Mathatha Tsedu (both *Sunday Times*), Tony Heard (*Cape Times*), Joe Latakgomo (*Sowetan*), Dennis Pather (*Daily News*, Durban), Barney Mthombothi (*Sunday Tribune*) and Tim du Plessis (*Beeld*).

Perhaps inevitably, in so disparate a group, there have been curiosities, and one tragedy. In 1964, a gifted black journalist named Nat Nakasa was awarded the Nieman Fellowship but the narrow, constricted South African government of those days refused to allow him to leave the country. Finally, they granted him a one-way exit permit; he could go, but he could not come back. Nat Nakasa went to Harvard, spent a bitter-sweet year there, understandably suffered depression and in 1965 fell to his death from a building in New York. His memory is honoured today by a journalistic award named after him.

The unusual stories include that of Sebastian Kleu, an Afrikaans financial journalist who went to Harvard in 1961 and stayed there for three years after completing his Nieman year, eventually emerging as a doctor of economics. Another Nieman left South Africa after his Harvard year and has not been heard of since, not by the Niemans, anyway. Another is Moeletsi Mbeki, brother of President Thabo Mbeki. Yet another is Zwelakhe Sisulu, son of the late Walter Sisulu; as with Nat Nakasa, his movements were hampered by a vindictive government bureaucracy, but he came back from Harvard and became a senior executive with the South African Broadcasting Corporation. During the apartheid years, several Niemans had to endure, at the hands of the Nationalist government, detention in prison without trial. They were regarded as troublemakers, a kind of inverted compliment for courageous journalists.

I was the eighth Nieman Fellow from South Africa, in 1967–1968, and my daughter Philippa (Pippa) Green, was the 39th, in 1998–1999. We are the only parent-child combination to have been awarded the fellowship in South Africa, and I do not know of any other such cases elsewhere, though there may be some among the several hundred fellowships awarded worldwide since 1938.

Typically, a Nieman Fellow would be in his thirties, with a spouse and a couple of young children. What does such a person do when moved from the hurly-burly of a newspaper office to what Milton called the olive grove of academe? Most of them find it a rare opportunity to take a deep breath and look at the world with new eyes. Scholarship is everywhere at Harvard, of course, but so is debate – strenuous, earnest, cool, hot, wise and foolish debate. The motto of the university is one word, *Veritas*, truth, and the search for truth is paramount. It is stimulating for the Americans; and for the foreigners, most of them visiting the United States for the first time, it is something of a revelation.

Perhaps I should explain that Nieman Fellows have a special status at Harvard University. The university has two main divisions: Harvard College, the undergraduate section; and the university proper, which has specialist post-graduate schools ranging from architecture and music to medicine and law and a myriad other learned subjects. The Nieman Fellows have access to anything they want in this vast educational array. There is nothing to stop a Nieman Fellow from spending his time in the faculties of divinity or physics, biology or zoology. The only discipline placed upon him or her is the obligation to complete the work of one course in one semester, or term. As a typical undergraduate might complete four or five courses in a semester, this is hardly an onerous duty.

I decided to get it over with in the first semester (there are two terms in the university year). I wrote for my politics professor a gripping account of the rise of Afrikaner nationalism in South Africa, this off the top of my head; I filled in the learned references later. The professor was delighted, congratulated me, and no doubt filed my paper away for future quotes in a book of his own.

The Nieman Fellows are a fairly serious-minded bunch who tend to concentrate their academic efforts on political science, history and economics. Some of the older students like me (I was 37) combine cultural entertainment with instruction. I attended a fascinating course of lectures on the music of Igor Stravinsky, who had special ties with Harvard and was periodically a visiting lecturer there. The dismal science of economics was greatly enlivened by the dry humour of John Kenneth Galbraith, one of many Harvard professors who have become world famous, in his case mainly because of a book called *The Affluent Society* which put a new phrase into the English language. A highly popular series of lectures was a course on Samuel Johnson by Walter Jackson Bate, who later produced a big fat biography of the formidable Doctor Johnson. Johnson is, of course, one of the greatest and most cantankerous figures in English literature, and these lectures kept huge student audiences in fits of appreciative laughter.

Aside from lectures, the Niemans have a busy time at Harvard, partly because they are treated with considerable respect. Staff members seek out the opportunity of fraternising with the Niemans. Who knows, I suppose, when it might pay off in the future? When I was there, busy people like Bobby Kennedy and Henry Kissinger were very willing to accept invitations to address Niemans and attend their dinners and seminars.

Nieman Fellows spend a full academic year at Harvard University, which in practical terms means about nine months. The original bequest intended to pay their academic fees and a subsistence allowance is now supported from other funds. In the case of South Africa, the money comes from various sources and until recently was channelled through USSALEP, that Leader Exchange Programme that I mentioned earlier and which for many decades has, as its name suggests, sent South Africans on visits to the United States and vice versa. The wives (or husbands) of Niemans are entitled to attend, without charge, any lectures at the university, and most of them seize the opportunity.

These days, the annual intake consists of about a dozen Americans and a dozen foreigners. When I was there, six non-Americans were Niemans. They came from Japan, Korea, Britain, Canada, the Philippines and South Africa.

For non-Americans, the experience is widened immeasurably by contact with the United States in general and New England in particular. In travel terms, the world has shrunk in the past 30 or 40 years, and America is not as remote as it once was. Nevertheless, I suspect that many South Africans who have visited countries in Africa and Europe are still strangers to the New World. It is a fascinating society, and one not to be judged by the films emanating from Hollywood.

I think the unbiased observer would be most impressed by the authentic feeling for democracy that exists everywhere. Americans seem to me to be very well aware of the fact that their forebears set the highest public and personal standards in the knowledge that their actions were being keenly scrutinised elsewhere. John Winthrop, who led a group of a thousand Pilgrim Fathers who crossed the Atlantic in 1630, said it in a famous phrase: 'We must consider that we shall be as a City on a Hill – the eyes of all people are upon us.' John Winthrop was the founder of the town of Boston, was governor of Massachusetts for fifteen years, and laid the foundations of American politics. One of the 'houses' at

Harvard, similar to colleges at Oxford and Cambridge, is named John Winthrop House, and I was appointed a member of it during my year at the university, so I learned something about the old gentleman.

The City on a Hill syndrome still prevails and is at the core of the vigorous debate and controversy that permeate American political life. I am sometimes wryly amused when people in other parts of the world lecture the United States about democracy, as has happened frequently since the military action in Afghanistan and Iraq. The truth is that many of the critics are anything but democratic, whereas the US is still a pillar of freedom and egalitarianism. The fact is that 95 percent of the world's population would give their eye teeth to live in the United States, perceiving correctly that there they would have a better chance than anywhere else of prospering and living in a true democracy.

To give two simple examples, one public, one personal. The US has a huge number of public posts that are filled by election, not by the appointment of political friends as rewards for services given. There are far more such posts than exist in any other country, posts in local government, the administration of justice, and other fields. At the personal level, I can do no better than cite the example of my landlord in Cambridge, Massachusetts, when I was at Harvard. His name was Patsy Umanzio and he was about 50, the son of immigrants from Italy, married with a son who was a student. He owned the small semidetached house I rented, he and his wife occupying the other half. His elderly mother helped in a shop around the corner.

Patsy Umanzio himself had a wonderfully pragmatic working life. In winter, he donned a warm blue uniform and a blue cap and drove a small truck from which he sold oil for the heaters in houses in the neighbourhood, a do-it-yourself job (no assistant), from making the hose connections to keeping the books. In the summer, he changed this for a white uniform and drove another truck from which he sold ice-cream. Almost a microcosm of American enterprise. His brother was the medical superintendent of a big hospital elsewhere in New England and was a medical graduate of Harvard. Patsy thought this unremarkable and in conversation made it quite clear that he thought his job was just as good as his brother's. Which, of course, it was – just different.

This kind of classless scene is duplicated all over the US. There are great differences of wealth and education, and due respect is paid to the prestige of an institution like Harvard. But if equality of opportunity exists anywhere in the world, it does so in the United States. Those huddled masses of the inscription on the Statue of Liberty at New York have really found themselves in the City on the Hill, and the Americans never forget it.

In New England, so named because nearly all the early settlers came from old England, the semi-permanent visitor soon realises that life is not altogether easy there. Winters can be extremely severe. The Gulf Stream, the great current of warm water from the Gulf of Mexico that flows across the Atlantic and moderates the climate of western Europe, misses that little top right-hand corner of the United States. Boston is roughly the same latitude as Madrid and Rome, but its climate is very different. South Africans who complain about the rigours of a London winter probably have very little idea of the harshness of winter in Massachusetts. The 102 Pilgrim Fathers who landed in 1620 lost half their number to illness and exposure in their first winter on the new continent. They buried the bodies in the snow at night, and in the spring planted grain over the graves, so that the local American Indians, about whom they felt uncertain, did not see how their numbers had been reduced.

Today, people have warm clothes and central heating, but life is still often unpleasant. Cars have to be fitted with thick-grooved snow tyres, and you carry a gadget to chip ice off the windscreen, plus a spade in the boot. At home, I learned to park off the road but as close as possible to it. That way, there wasn't so much snow to be shovelled off before driving away in the morning. Car batteries lose their efficiency when the temperature drops below freezing, which means just about every winter's day there, so one takes a long electrical lead with a caged inspection lamp at the end and rests the lamp on the battery all night in an attempt to keep it warm. One evening, I emerged from a lecture to find that a sudden heavy snowstorm had created havoc with the traffic and that my parked car was totally blocked in by snow and an apparently insoluble traffic jam. I walked home – it took about half an hour – and retrieved the car the next day. The papers reported that some people took seven or eight hours to get home that night.

I bought a Ford Falcon station wagon for my stay in America and with my family made many fairly long trips in it in New England, to Canada, and down the East Coast to New York, Philadelphia and Washington. It had done a low mileage when I bought it but it was very cheap, because it was about five years old. Americans change their cars frequently and, at that time anyway, there was not much demand for second-hand vehicles. You have to be careful when driving in winter. For example, I was intrigued by signs that said, ambiguously, 'snow heaves'. It turned out that this did not mean that the snow was heaving but that it had formed into 'heaves', lovely, soft-looking mounds of snow at the side of the road that seemed totally innocent but had in fact hardened to rock-like consistency. Driving into one of these would mean serious damage to the car.

As I have indicated earlier, the vast majority of South African Nieman Fellows have returned to this country and achieved senior posts in the media and some in communications jobs in government. Out of more than 40, I can think of only three who decided to live abroad. About 30 years ago, we formed a loose association that met once a year to discuss relevant matters, usually complaints about the way the Nationalist government was treating the press, and to hold an annual black-tie, formal dinner. The first of our Niemans, Aubrey Sussens, continued the tradition of giving to a good cause. He paid the considerable bills for accommodation, food and drink when we met at places like the Wild Coast, Swaziland, Sea Point, the Chobe game lodge in Botswana, or a resort on the Vaal River, and he did so for many years.

Predictably enough, these gatherings have generated their own folklore over the years. Journalists are generally gregarious, and they certainly like the cup that cheers. They also like arguing and declaiming, and they are seldom shy and withdrawn. We had one gathering, during the apartheid era, at which one of our number walked out after another had delivered a speech that developed into a heated attack on white people and their sins. The rest of us sat tight and either cheered or had another drink. A political journalist of impeccable Nationalist credentials had to make a speech of thanks to the critic, which he did with long teeth, as they say in Afrikaans.

There was the evening when one of our number, a well-known political writer, became tired and emotional, stood up to make a speech, uttered a dozen disjointed words and then collapsed in a swoon, head on the table. Ton Vosloo, later the chairman of the Afrikaans press group, Nasionale Pers, described it as a speech that had no noun, no verb, no clauses and no closure.

Then there was the night when, during an argument about a Nieman Fellow who was being detained in prison without trial, Percy Qoboza, one debater threw a glass of wine at another. It missed him and hit me.

One year at the Wild Coast Casino, one of our group, an Afrikaans editor, departed for bed, opened the curtains, and was startled to see a couple on the lawn outside engaged in what the British satirical magazine *Private Eye* used to call Ugandan discussions. (Private Eye's euphemism stemmed from a report about a Ugandan diplomat in London who, taken by surprise while busy with his secretary, explained, 'We were just having discussions.') The unnerving experience of our Nieman colleague caused much discussion (non-Ugandan) the next day, and he was called upon several times to re-tell his strange and wonderful story.

Of course, amid the jests, the jokes, the drinking and the fighting, much that is serious and beneficial has emerged from these Nieman gatherings over the years, especially in the constant defence of press freedom and the stout resistance against intrusions and threats of intrusions on that freedom. Aubrey Sussens almost single-handedly kept the early Niemans together, and his contribution was recognised after he died in 2001. Nearly all the Niemans attended his memorial service or sent messages, one correctly describing him as 'a giant personality'. Today the Nieman organisation thrives, and we are the biggest single congregation of Nieman Fellows in the world outside the United States – a curiosity indeed, considering that there is hardly a major country anywhere that has, over the years, not sent Nieman Fellows to Harvard.

SEVENTEEN

Aubrey Sussens

Awell-known American magazine used to publish a series of articles entitled 'The Most Unforgettable Character I Have Ever Known'. The Character involved was almost invariably a member of the family of the writer of the article, his or her father or mother or sibling, and the perspective was fond and sentimental.

Most of us feel like that about close family members, and I am therefore excluding that entire category when I write about a friend who left his unforgettable stamp on a great many people. When he died, one of those people said to me, with some awe, 'I thought he was indestructible.'

The indestructible one who finally went the way of all flesh was Aubrey Sussens, who was my friend for more than half a century. He made his career and his reputation as a pioneer of the public relations industry in South Africa, but I think his heart was always in newspapers, which was where he started. And I think he would have been an outsize character no matter what he had done in life.

Aubrey Sussens was born in 1923 at Skeerpoort, a village about 40 kilometres west of Pretoria, so named because in the old days the Boers used to stop and have a shave – *skeer* means shave – and a wash before riding into Pretoria to do some shopping or chat to the old president. Notwithstanding his rather grand full name of Clarence Aubrey Sussens, his parents were humble folk. His father was a small man, gentle and softly spoken, a builder and odd-job man by trade. His mother was a rural housewife typical of the time, homely and loyal. They were religious people, observing members of the Seventh Day Adventist Church, and the young Aubrey was sent to a school run by that church, Helderberg College at Somerset West, near Cape Town. They had quiet and unassuming daughters, and as far as I know there was nothing in the background to suggest that their son would become a larger-than-life character; indeed, in later years, the old couple often seemed bemused at their son's success and affluence.

At Helderberg College, a strict vegetarian diet was imposed on the pupils, in accordance with the rules of the church. The effect of this, as far as Aubrey Sussens was concerned, was to turn him into a convinced carnivore from the day he left school. That day came early. At the age of sixteen, just after the start of the second World War, he joined the South African Air Force and served as a flight engineer on combat missions in the skies above North Africa and Italy. It may have been this early knowledge of aircraft machinery that engendered his lifelong enthusiasm for the internal combustion engine. He owned, at various times, a remarkable assortment of cars, from the very grand, a Rolls Royce, to the very small, a 1952 Fiat Cub that the Italians called *Topolino,* which means little mouse. He understood car engines very well, but he was always a wayward driver, with the disturbing habit of turning round to conduct long conversations with back-seat passengers while driving in heavy traffic.

On one occasion when we were all young, Aubrey unnerved a woman passenger with a display of enterprising and innovative driving in his baby Fiat. A group of us had been to the Saturday night dinner-dance at the Blue Peter restaurant at Blaauwberg – it is still there, still flourishing – and everybody had had a fair quantity of wine. In those days, you didn't worry too much about roadblocks and Breathalysers; provided you didn't have an accident you were okay.

We left after midnight and arranged to regroup at Aubrey's house in Hof Street, Gardens. He and his companion didn't pitch up for a long time, and when they did she was incoherent with annoyance and anxiety. At that time, the road alongside the Blaauwberg beach was a narrow strip of concrete that took a sharp turn at the Cape Town end. Aubrey had missed the turn and had plunged on regardless, through sand and bushes and brambles, until he eventually hit the tar again a couple of kilometres further on. Rough on the car, and rough on the nerves, except for Aubrey, who thought the entire experience highly amusing.

After the war, Aubrey decided to become a journalist and worked on *The Star* newspaper in Johannesburg while studying at night to complete the matric that he had abandoned at school (he passed). He was posted to a remote branch office at Benoni and, in the fullness of time, the news editor of *The Star* informed him that he was the most useless apprentice journalist he had ever encountered. Aubrey was offered a posting on the *Pretoria News* as a last resort, where he thrived and established the foundation of a highly successful career in journalism. He was always a political animal, and I think the intensely political atmosphere of Pretoria stimulated his interest and latent abilities. He soon became a political reporter, and when I first met him, in 1951, he was the political correspondent of the *Cape Times* in Cape Town.

He was then 27 years old and was as large in personality as he was in body. He was well over six feet tall, to use the kind of measurement that everybody still understands, even in the metric era, and he must have weighed about 230 pounds, over a hundred kilograms. He had a ruddy complexion, curly black hair, and twinkling eyes that creased into almost oriental slits when he was amused, which was often. He looked as if he should have been a rugby player, but in fact he was not a deft sports player, judging by the faintly comical games of cricket and tennis we occasionally played together. But he was immensely strong, unaggressive but well able to look after himself when trouble loomed in the form of an argument that threatened to turn violent.

Aubrey had a small, five-metre yacht at Hout Bay and sometimes three or four of us would go sailing with him in the beautiful bay, under the imposing cliffs of Chapman's Peak. On one occasion, I was giving him an inexpert hand during a maintenance session in which he had removed the boat's small motor and placed it on the quayside. 'Just bring the engine over here,' he called out while attending to some other bit of equipment. I tried to pick it up and was staggered, literally, by its weight.

After carrying it a metre, I put it down to regather my strength. I was reasonably fit, a rugby player, six foot, but this was something else. Aubrey turned absent-mindedly from what he was doing, saw the engine on the ground, said, 'Ah yes, that's what I was looking for', picked it up without any apparent strain and strolled around with the motor clutched to his chest. I was impressed. Obviously a good man to have on your side.

His large frame was, no doubt, the reason for his large appetite. For more than 50 years, he ate and drank more than was good for any normal person, but he didn't seem to bat an eye, not until his last couple of years, when he suffered chronic illness for the first time in his life. He never smoked, but just about everything else was consumed with gusto, regardless of time or circumstance. In 1987, when he was 64, the two of us and Nigel Bruce, then editor of the *Financial Mail* and later a member of parliament, visited Portugal in our official capacities. Our flight back from Lisbon to Johannesburg originated in Frankfurt and was delayed for several hours. We were flying first-class and were well looked after in the lounge at Lisbon airport, and supplied with drinks and an ample dinner. We eventually took off from Lisbon about 1.00 am. In accordance with the inflexible routine of airways all over the world, dinner was served at that awful hour, a full and elaborate meal. I picked at some caviar and sipped a glass of wine unenthusiastically. Aubrey, replete from the airport meal, set to with a will, ate everything that came along and drank copiously of beer, French champagne and wine, and all this without any apparent after-effects.

On the same visit to Lisbon, the three of us visited the wonderfully ornate fifteenth-century Jeronimo church, which contains many relics of Portugal's greatest days as a world power. Nigel Bruce and I were fascinated by the place but after a little while we realised that Aubrey was no longer with us. We found him later in a pub outside the church, happily drinking beer and chatting up the locals in broken Portuguese.

It was as political correspondent of the *Cape Times* that Aubrey Sussens established himself as a man to be reckoned with. He was a very skilful and resourceful journalist and had the ability to get on with people of all kinds. About 50 years ago, when we were both reporters, we attended a meeting held by the then prime minister, Dr D F Malan, in his constituency, Piketberg, 130 kilometres north of Cape Town. The *Cape Times* was widely regarded by the National Party as being a first cousin of *Pravda* in Moscow, a dangerous communist newspaper. When a photograph was taken of several little old ladies presenting flowers and koeksusters to Mrs Malan, the prime minister's wife, Aubrey asked the elderly women for their names for the caption. He spoke fluent Afrikaans and they liked him, and after a while one of the little old ladies said, '*Meneer, jy is seker van* Die Burger?' ('You're from *The Burger*, aren't you?', *The Burger* being Cape Town's Afrikaans paper). Aubrey replied in the negative: '*Nee, ek is van die* Cape Times.' The little old lady reeled back in horror, whereupon Aubrey gave a boisterous peal of laughter, put a friendly arm around her, almost breaking a couple of ribs in the process, and lifted her right off her feet, eventually setting her down again, plonk.

By this time, everybody was laughing and the *Cape Times* political correspondent had made some new friends for himself and maybe for his paper. Perhaps an early example of his natural flair for public relations.

Aubrey was certainly resourceful. Legend has it (and apparently this is true) that the Speaker of the House of Assembly, on a walk in the parliament grounds in Cape Town one fine morning, came across Aubrey Sussens hanging upside down against an outside wall of parliament, held by his ankles by colleagues at an open second-floor window. Inquiries were made, of course, and it emerged that Aubrey had decided to carry out a little espionage by listening in at the window of the National Party's caucus room, where the governing party's caucus was discussing some very delicate subjects. He escaped without censure. Presumably, the Speaker had a sense of humour.

His resourcefulness often took a comic form. In 1953, when I was living in London, he came over from South Africa on a short visit. He wanted to borrow my car to visit a South African friend, Monty Morris, at Sheffield. I agreed, albeit reluctantly; Aubrey had strange driving habits, and I had misgivings about my nearly new baby Fiat, but I could not say no. He went off and returned early the next morning, having apparently slept for a time in the car on the way home. It was winter and, in those days, the London fogs placed a layer of grime on clothing in a very short time. Aubrey was due to fly to Paris that morning and his luggage was at the airport. Having washed in the basin in my bedroom, he examined his dirty shirt collar and cuffs and said he would give them a quick wash. I pointed out that he had no fresh shirt with him but he wasn't deterred. 'It's quick-dry,' he said cheerfully, using toilet soap to wash the collar and cuffs before immediately putting on the shirt with great satisfaction. My idea of hell is wearing a shirt with a wet collar and wet cuffs, but he was obviously made of sterner stuff.

Resourcefulness of a different kind came into play at one of the many dinners that Aubrey Sussens hosted for the South African Nieman Fellows, journalists who have won a fellowship to Harvard University in the United States (he was the first South African to win such an award). It was 1975, and we were at the game lodge in the famous Chobe game reserve, in northern Botswana. We were having our formal dinner, black tie, in a private area in one of the lodge's public rooms. We were seated in one part of a very large room, with a curved wall reaching about three-quarters of the way to the ceiling separating us from a public bar on the other side, from which we could hear the low murmur of conversation.

Our dinner was graced by a guest from the United States, a very boring speaker who went on and on. Aubrey, the host, was sitting next to him and I next to Aubrey, whose attention was visibly wilting. Eventually, Aubrey whispered an excuse to me and went off quietly, looking like a man who wanted to spend a penny. A couple of minutes, later the low murmur of conversation behind the screening wall rose perceptibly, with much laughter and Aubrey's unmistakable chuckle the loudest of all.

Our American speaker droned on, oblivious to all this, and Aubrey returned after a few minutes, trying hard to look like a man who had just been to the washroom. He sat down, listened with concentration to the speaker, nodded, made approving interjections *sotto voce*, good point, quite correct, and then started to droop again. Whereupon, to my amazement, he whispered to me again, theatrically, and tiptoed out, trying to look like a man who was making his second trip to the loo. And once again the conversation level behind the wall rose, with much merriment. Sussens was an original, if ever there was one.

His ability to laugh was always one of his biggest assets and particularly his ability to laugh in adversity. A minor example occurred long ago, when he offered to cut me some planks to repair a garden bench. He produced some floorboards and I held these over the edge of one of his garden tables while he used a circular electric saw to take off plank after plank. We had been at this some time when there seemed to be a problem; the saw wasn't cutting as quickly as it had. 'Must be a tough knot,' said Aubrey, exerting more pressure on the saw. Eventually, he reached the end of the plank, which fell off, and so did a sizeable part of the garden table underneath. This is the sort of situation that would drive most people to strong language and high blood pressure. Aubrey just collapsed with laughter. I was aghast. 'But what about your garden table?' I said. 'It's lopsided now.' 'Oh, that's no problem,' he replied, and with a quick thrust of the saw took off a piece on the other side of the table. 'There, it's even now.' Resourceful, as usual.

He could also laugh at himself. He had a pacemaker, an electrical device to regulate his heartbeat that had to be checked from time to time. On one such occasion, I went with him to the doctor's rooms and waited in the car while he had it done. His own doctor was away and a locum attended to him. He was a typical Johannesburg doctor, whatever that may be. Aubrey came back to the car laughing helplessly and recounted an amusing tale about how the doctor bade him take off his upper clothing, shirt and vest, and lie on his back on an examination couch. Aubrey was very large at this time of his life. The doctor turned away to wash his hands and plug in his stethoscope, then turned back to the patient and for some time gazed thoughtfully at the imposing form recumbent on the examination table. Eventually he said solemnly, 'Tviggy, you're not.'

Aubrey Sussens was proud of the fact that he had worked on just about every English-language newspaper in South Africa. He had a spell at *The Friend* in Bloemfontein a couple of years before I moved there from Cape Town, and he loved it. He was there for only about eighteen months, but after I arrived I discovered that everybody seemed to know him. His wife, Penny, was a Capetonian, but her grandfather, a man named Gustav Baumann, had been Surveyor General of the Free State early in the twentieth century, a piece of history that Aubrey enjoyed reminding people about.

He was a political writer on *The Star* in Johannesburg, then the country's biggest daily, when he married Penny in 1955. Shortly after the honeymoon, he was paging through the newspaper files on a rack in *The Star's* editorial offices when Horace Flather, the editor, walked past. Flather, originally from England, was one of South Africa's most distinguished editors, and he looked and spoke the part: trim figure, iron-grey hair, immaculate pin-stripe suit, club tie, clipped accent. He was 'Mr Flather' or 'sir' to all but a handful of intimates. He called out to Aubrey Sussens that he would like a brief report the next day on some political development. Aubrey, still in the mists of honeymoon endearments, replied absently, 'Okay, sweetie-pie', a term he often used to Penny. An alarmed Flather leapt back a metre or two. It was no good trying to explain. For some days after that, Horace Flather kept his distance from Aubrey Sussens, eyeing him warily and speculatively from time to time.

It was in the early 1960s that Aubrey Sussens stepped out of journalism into a new career that was to make him the undisputed pioneer of corporate public relations in South Africa. He was at the time an assistant editor of the *Rand Daily Mail* in Johannesburg, where he devised some innovative schemes to further the fortunes of that paper. One was an advertising swop column, another was a big walk for all and sundry, things that are quite common today but were new then. Soon enough, it occurred to him that he could be doing these things for his own benefit as well as the paper's, and doing them for other clients as well. The upshot was that he formed a company called Group Editors, with a staff composed mainly of young journalists, and began persuading big business that they needed to improve their communications with the public and their shareholders, via the media, and via Group Editors.

He was persuasive and clever and confident, and it didn't take long before he was well on his way. He almost invented the in-house journal that a large organisation uses to reach its own staff, and at one stage Group Editors produced between 70 and 80 publications of this kind. He also recognised the news value of information emanating from business and industry, and saw how it could benefit business itself. When I was a young reporter, big corporations held aloof from the press, saying disdainfully that they did not need any cheap publicity. It is a different story today, when the public image is all-important to commerce and industry.

It was typical of Sussens's success that his first client, one of many, was the *Rand Daily Mail*, who paid him a fee well in excess of the salary they had paid him to work for them full-time. In effect, he created a need for businesses to bestir themselves from the complacency of the past, and when he had done so he provided the answers himself, at a handsome price. Simple and brilliant, like most really good ideas.

I have never been a public relations man myself. In about 1970, when I was deputy editor of the *Daily News* in Durban, Aubrey tried to persuade me to join his company at a salary much higher than the newspaper's. I declined. I was much too deeply entrenched in the culture of newspaper journalism. I had been an editor and, in due course, I became an editor again. And the glitter and glamour of Johannesburg's swinging public relations society did not appeal to me.

But Aubrey Sussens and I remained the closest of friends. It was an unusual friendship because we had widely divergent interests. My predominant interest has always been music, whereas Aubrey would never have claimed to be musical. He was an expert in matters technical, like building houses or fixing car engines, and I'm absolutely hopeless at that. The common ground was, I think, a sense of humour, shared experience and the background of newspapers. Aubrey Sussens spent nearly 40 years in public relations and without question he is best remembered in this capacity. But I felt that, at heart, he was always a newspaperman. He loved reminiscing about editors and reporters of old, and he had a phenomenal memory for details of the past.

His career had its ups and downs. At its peak, he lived in a grand house in Craighall Park, Johannesburg, and travelled around in a Rolls Royce car driven by a chauffeur named Firos Malanga, who later opened a dry-cleaning business in a rural area in the Northern Province, having observed how to be an entrepreneur. When he was 55, Aubrey and Penny went to England after he had sold his controlling interest in the Group Editors company, but he returned to South African after two years when he heard that Group Editors was in financial trouble. There were unpleasant scenes in Johannesburg when Aubrey accused his younger colleagues of running his company into the ground.

Withal, he remained unchanged over the years, especially to his friends. I spoke at his 70th birthday party and there was prolonged applause from a very large crowd when I quoted Rudyard Kipling and said that Aubrey could meet with triumph and disaster and treat those two impostors just the same.

After the closure of Group Editors, he started another public relations company, sold his interest in that and retired to a farm near Louis Trichardt, which he had bought 30 years before. He loved this place above all others, and indeed it has great serenity and beauty, being located high in the Soutpansberg mountains in the Northern Province. Over the years, he had built with his own hands a barn-like living room and many rondavels and bathrooms, and at the age of 78 he converted them into accommodation for paying guests. The place became very popular. The brochure for Lokovhela Mountain Lodge, as it is called, was obviously written by Aubrey himself, and it contains his authentic touch in the following passage: 'Please do not expect plastic food designed by interior decorators. The food is nourishing and wholesome: beef, chicken, pork and lamb roasts, casseroles, grills, stews, curries, puddings. Good farm breakfasts. Our vegetables are from the garden, crisp and fresh, un-spoiled by pale chefs in tall hats and quivering egos.'

Aubrey Sussens died on his beloved farm in November 2002, shortly after his 79th birthday. He had been ill for some time. I spoke to him on the phone about ten days before he died and he sounded as chirpy as ever. 'Ah, Michelangelo,' he said, as he had said for the past 50 years; he was not one to let a good joke go because he'd used it before. Over the years, he and I built up a stock of humorous memories and anecdotes that were trotted out frequently and with much enjoyment, so much so that the long-suffering Penny once suggested that to save time we should give our stories numbers, so that one of us would say Number 27 and then we would have a good laugh and then the other could say Number 35, and we would laugh again.

In particular, Aubrey clung faithfully to the nicknames that he gave to a wide circle of friends and acquaintances. Norman Marshall, a close friend of our youth who came from New Zealand and eventually made a fortune in England as a magazine publisher, was always Normanski, this because of his early leftist tendencies (he abandoned them when he became rich). Bill Papas, the artist and cartoonist, was Guillaume. Monty Morris of Johannesburg became Afrikanerised into Moors. Alan Scholefield, who became a novelist, was Scholebeck, after John Steinbeck. My son, Geoffrey, was Jefferson. A difficult landlady was Mrs Trygve Lie, after the Norwegian who was the first secretary-general of the United Nations (I never understood the reasoning behind this, but it seemed appropriate).

A few days after Aubrey died, a memorial was held in Johannesburg. I was the main speaker and had to give some thought to what I said. Aubrey was not a religious man and it was not a religious service. 'He was a total heathen, you know,' somebody said cheerfully to me.

Maybe. Notwithstanding our closeness over a very long period, we never discussed such matters. At the gathering, I quoted Hamlet's words about his father – 'we shall not look upon his like again' – and we drank to his memory. Then his daughter, Vicky, who lives in Munich with her husband and children, showed me a photograph she had taken on the day his ashes had been scattered on his farm. It was of an unusual cloud formation. The cumulus had arranged itself into a kind of halo that looked remarkably like Aubrey's grey hair. And beneath it, wisps of cloud had constructed an uncanny resemblance to his face, with special reference to the eyes that always creased and crinkled when he laughed.

EIGHTEEN

Foreign parts

My son Geoffrey was 26 years old, recently married, having completed his medical degrees, his hospital housemanship and his compulsory military service, when he phoned me from far away. He and his wife, Cathy, also a doctor, were on a holiday trip before settling down and looking for jobs in Cape Town. He told me that they were in New Zealand, had been offered medical posts there, and had decided to stay.

I was aghast. 'New Zealand,' I exclaimed. 'A country full of sheep and rugby players. You must be out of your mind.' He was patient. 'It's really very nice here. We like it, and we've both been offered jobs in a medical practice in a lovely little country town. It seems too good an opportunity to miss.'

That was at the beginning of 1987. I was not mollified, and it took me a long time to get used to the idea. We kept in touch by letter and phone. Their South African possessions – some furniture and a car – were shipped out, and before long they had moved from Patea, a small town, to Auckland, the big town of the North Island. They produced two children, moved to Sydney in Australia for a year for Geoffrey to undertake specialist studies, came back to South Africa on holiday, and went back to build a house in a good part of Auckland. Five years after their initial decision to emigrate, my wife, Heather, and I went out to visit them, the first of several trips we have made to New Zealand.

He was right, of course. It is very nice there. I am not making invidious comparisons with South Africa; still less am I urging South Africans to emigrate to New Zealand or anywhere else. But there is such a fund of misinformation, deliberate or otherwise, about the country that perhaps one should correct some of the wrong impressions.

New Zealand is not a small country. It is bigger than the British Isles: England, Scotland, Wales and Ireland. It does have a small population, about four million people. Most people recognise that this is a virtue, not a fault.

Most of it is not down in the far south. Auckland, the main city in which nearly one-third of the total population live, is roughly the same latitude as Melbourne, Cape Town and Buenos Aires. It is a bit cooler than Cape Town in winter, but the climate is usually described as temperate. Places like Dunedin and Invercargill in the South Island are indeed bitterly cold in winter and more or less unremittingly wet, but they are more than 1 500 kilometres south of Auckland.

Proudly, South African journalists are fond of describing New Zealand as fast asleep, that nothing ever happens there. Well, to some degree, that's correct. You have far less chance of being mugged or hijacked or burgled there than you do in South Africa. Everything works, which I suppose is boring in its own way. But there are things to do apart from tending the sheep and playing rugby. My son, who has become a fairly typical New Zealander, has had holidays skiing, yachting, scuba diving off the South Pacific island of Tonga, three hours' flight away, and free-fall parachuting. Auckland has a top-class symphony orchestra that has made commercial recordings sold internationally, and the city has plenty of exotic restaurants.

New Zealand was the last country in the world to be settled by human beings, Pacific islanders who arrived there in their long canoes about 800 years ago and later became known as the Maoris. It was also the first country in the world to become a full democracy, when it gave women the vote in 1893. It is a much more even society than South Africa, without the blatant extremes of wealth and poverty that so often jar sensitivities here. New Zealand is an affluent country and you will find plenty of big houses and smart cars. On my most recent visit to

Auckland, I noted that one motor dealer advertised fourteen used and new Porsche cars at prices ranging from R500 000 to R1,6-million. But you will not find any beggars on street corners, or car guards, or barbed-wire fences.

Some South African visitors to New Zealand have said afterwards that that they found it pleasant, but that the standard of living was too low for them. The fact, of course, is that the per capita income in New Zealand is much higher than it is in South Africa. I don't want to sound prudish, but there are more things in life than the vulgar display of wealth, especially if the money comes from the taxpayers. Conspicuous consumption is not, I think, a feature of life in New Zealand, but it is a rich country, very much first world rather than third. An economy still based largely on farming, with tourism playing an important role these days, is able to provide well for a relatively small population. Social services such as education and health are good. My son is a specialist in geriatrics, the care of older people, a sector of the medical profession that is very much a luxury of a first world country.

Scenically, New Zealand is one of the two most spectacular countries I have ever visited, the other being Switzerland. There are other similarities with Switzerland, a country I have visited several times, and which I admire, in contrast to the sneering and maybe jealous comments sometimes made about it by people who have never been there. Apart from the scenery, there is the efficiency and the low-profile politics. It seems to me that the Swiss and the New Zealanders are hardworking; moderate in their political, religious and social attitudes; and not overawed by politicians. Very few outsiders could name the political leaders of Switzerland, or for that matter New Zealand, a sure sign of maturity in a country. Generally speaking, the less one sees or hears of politicians, the better for the country as a whole.

About three-quarters of New Zealand's population are white. The Maoris of New Zealand, an eighteen percent minority, have been to some degree a socially disadvantaged community, but problems such as unemployment, poverty and alcohol abuse have affected only a minority of that minority and are gradually easing. Against that, many Maoris have been notably successful in business, sport and the arts. The lot of the Maoris as a whole has not been comparable with that of black Africans during the long years of apartheid in South Africa.

Other significant minorities include Asians (about six percent, mainly from Taiwan, Hong Kong, China and Korea) and Pacific islanders (four percent, from places such as Samoa, the Cook Islands and Tonga). Quite a complicated cultural mixture, but there is hardly a country in the world that would not happily exchange its own racial problems for New Zealand's.

One thing that strikes almost every visitor and commentator is the pleasantness of New Zealanders as a whole, whether their origins are in Scotland or the Polynesian islands. They are not as aggressive as Australians (although, as I have pointed out many times to friends, not all Australians are like their sports commentators). New Zealanders are quieter, softer-accented and have almost old-world habits of courtesy and consideration for others, arising perhaps from their geographically isolated position in the world at large (the country is on exactly the opposite side of the world from Britain, twelve hours ahead of Greenwich Mean Time).

And they are not short of a dry sense of humour. My wife and I took a bus trip in the South Island that started at Christchurch, a city that resembles some of the old towns of England. Our driver/conductor (New Zealanders tend to be versatile in labour matters, probably because there are so few of them) was a young man who looked as if he might be a student doing a vacation job. As the tour got under way, he introduced himself on the loudspeaker system and told us where we would be travelling. Then he added, in the manner of a Kruger Park guide: 'If we're lucky, we might see a few sheep today.' A couple of kilometres further along, we had to stop for about ten minutes while hundreds of sheep were herded across the road. There are 40 million of them in New Zealand.

The scenery of New Zealand is nothing if not varied, from subtropical forest to snow-capped mountains. The sea is always close. No part of New Zealand is more than 130 kilometres from the sea, and the country's coastline is about the same length as that of the United States, thanks to the myriad bays and inlets. For example, Auckland stands on an isthmus that is, at its narrowest, only about seven kilometres wide and is bounded on both sides by the Pacific Ocean. It calls itself the City of Sails, and with justification. The proportion of boat owners among its inhabitants is the highest of any city in the world.

I tend to judge the real economic size of a city by the thickness of its phone book. Auckland's telephone directory is fatter than Cape Town's or Durban's, even though its population (1.3 million) is much smaller than those of the two South African cities. The reason is, of course, that Auckland's people are nearly all economically active. Unemployment and poverty are not major problems in New Zealand.

An international survey of cities conducted by a London firm specialising in such matters places Auckland among the ten most desirable cities in the world. The others are Zurich, Geneva and Bern (Switzerland), Vancouver (Canada), Vienna (Austria), Sydney (Australia), Copenhagen (Denmark), Amsterdam (Holland) and Frankfurt (Germany). No cities in South Africa, alas, or for that matter on the African continent. The criteria for the survey included prosperity, environment, health, education, transport and safety. The capital city of New Zealand, Wellington, is placed fifteenth.

New Zealand's North Island has many fine beaches and the South Island has fjords that are similar to those of Norway. The most famous of these is Milford Sound, a breathtakingly beautiful stretch of deep water surrounded by mountains, one of which, Mitre Peak (so named because it looks like a bishop's mitre), rises 1 700 metres sheer from the water. Not far from it is Mount Cook, New Zealand's highest mountain (3 764 metres), named after the British explorer Captain James Cook, who sailed around New Zealand three times in the eighteenth century and landed at various points.

The South Island is cold in the winter, but its mountain, sea and lake scenery is memorable and unspoiled by large-scale development. This is why it was chosen for the filming of J R R Tolkien's *Lord of the Rings* series, films that ended up winning many Hollywood Oscars. Of the small urban concentrations, my favourite is a place called Queenstown, at the edge of the calm waters of Lake Wakatipu, with mountains on all sides. In atmosphere and appearance, this is rather like a Swiss lake town.

Another exceptionally attractive small town is Napier, a port in the middle of North Island. It was named after Sir Charles Napier

(1782–1853), a British soldier and colonial administrator. South Africa has its own Napier, about 200 kilometres east of Cape Town, but that one is named after Sir George Napier, a nineteenth century governor of the Cape.

Napier in New Zealand is in the Hawke's Bay area, which is well known for its moderate climate and fine wines. In 1931, a severe earthquake destroyed the town centre, killing 256 people. Within two years, the town was rebuilt in the then contemporary style of architecture, a style now called Art Deco. As a result, Napier is an architectural anachronism, with elaborate and ornate public and commercial buildings painted every colour of the rainbow. The effect is brilliant, and Napier is visited by people from many parts of the world who drink coffee and wine in an open-air pedestrian mall and admire the taste and fashion of yesteryear.

In the north of North Island is the Bay of Islands, named long ago by the redoubtable Captain Cook. The weather here is mild to warm, and the bay is dotted with islands, some of them no more than scraps of rock rising above the water. A lovely place for a beach, boating or fishing holiday. Here you can swim with friendly dolphins by dropping over the side of a boat in the bay.

New Zealand does not have a long history, but much of it is encapsulated in a group of buildings at the Waitangi National Reserve, close to the Bay of Islands. This part of the country was the first to be settled by Europeans, who arrived here in the early 1800s, 150 years after Jan van Riebeeck landed at the Cape, to trade with the Maori people. Inevitably there was conflict, but in 1840 Maori leaders met British officials at Waitangi and debated the question of accepting the sovereignty of the British Crown. The upshot was that more than 500 Maoris put their names to a document acknowledging Queen Victoria's authority, as British subjects, and she in turn guaranteed them the possession of their lands, forests, fisheries and other property. That was not the end of the story, of course; conflict continued intermittently until 1870, but peace eventually came. The Maoris still have some grievances, hinging mainly on land rights, but I think it fair to say that New Zealand is a remarkably placid country compared with many others with a history of cultural clashes.

At Waitangi there are some old European colonial houses, a huge Maori meeting house that formed the centre of Maori culture and society, and, most interesting of all, a 35-metre Maori canoe. Carved from three massive kauri trees that were felled nearby, this boat is of the same design as the somewhat smaller canoes that carried Maoris on long voyages in the South Pacific for hundreds of years. How they did it defies belief: manpower alone for propulsion, no shelter, no compass, no maps. The canoe at Waitangi is launched once a year and paddled by 80 Maoris to commemorate the signing of the Waitangi Treaty in 1840.

For me, much of the charm of New Zealand lies in its calm sense of security and wellbeing. You drive on the left, and the national speed limit is 100 kilometres an hour. Most of the roads are fairly narrow and winding, and on a long trip you are doing quite well if you cover 80 kilometres in an hour. Very different from pounding across the Karoo at 150kph. And it is a country where you do not want to drive too fast. There is too much to see: glassy blue lakes that are fed by the snows and glaciers of snowy mountains; palm-fringed beaches in the north; the Canterbury Plains of the South Island, wide sheep pasturages that look like parts of what some New Zealanders still call the old country; geysers sending plumes of hot water upward; comfortable and safe-looking villages and towns with beautiful gardens. One former South African newspaper editor who has settled with his wife near Christchurch in the South Island wrote and told me it was like living in paradise.

One of the advertisements in South African newspapers for emigration possibilities has a picture of a deserted beach and the caption, 'Rush hour in New Zealand.' That is true to a degree. There is also an apt description in a recent article in a London newspaper that described New Zealand as a 'gigantic adult playground'. That is also true. But of course the people who live there have to work, and they do work hard. It is very much a do-it-yourself society. Domestic service is virtually unknown, except on a limited part-time basis. Furthermore, New Zealand is not big-time territory for the entrepreneurial classes. Australia, nearly 2 000 kilometres away at its closest point and very different in many respects, is more the place to make a fortune.

Many South Africans have, of course, opted for this type of life, in which making money and spending it is not top priority. Most of them are well-qualified people. Some years ago, my wife and I arrived in New

Zealand on Christmas Eve for a short holiday. The next day, my son and his wife had a lunch party at home for about twenty people. They were all doctors, with their husbands and wives – medical people tend to stick together – and with two exceptions, they were all former South Africans.

I suppose this is the brain drain that politicians sometimes complain about, but it does seem to me that if you believe in human rights, one of the most basic of them all is surely the right to live where you wish (assuming you can get there).

I don't think South Africa is in danger of losing large numbers of its trained people to New Zealand. Our own country has plenty to offer, not least the weather and the physical amenities of beach and berg, game reserve and rugby field. I know one young man who lived in London for three years and was very pleased to return to South Africa because he was tired of going to work in the dark and going home in the dark for much of the year. The weather is not a trivial consideration. It is a profound factor in determining the quality of life.

So most of us in South Africa will stay right where we are, living in a difficult but hopeful society where at least the elementary principles of justice and fair play now apply to all. And perhaps New Zealand is 'a bit too perfect', to quote that London travel writer again. But if you want a holiday taste of something quite different, well you could try flying eastward to that other Eden, demi-paradise.

NINETEEN

Freebies

I was about eighteen years old and the most junior reporter on the *Cape Argus* when G P Canitz walked into the office one day and said he wanted to see the editor about the wine-drinking habits of Capetonians. He conveyed this request at the reception desk to the head messenger, Mr Mitchell, a grave and dignified man who had had long experience of people who wanted to see the editor. He said he would tell the news editor, the man in charge of the reporters. The news editor's interest in the visitor was zero. He looked around the corner of his cubicle, spotted me at my desk, and shouted, 'Green, see this man please.'

I found the visitor, of whom I had never heard, a beguiling character. He was an animated man of about 70, wore a beret, looked vaguely arty, and explained that he was an artist and also a wine farmer. In fact, the German-born Georg Paul Canitz had achieved renown in both departments. By the time he died in 1959, he had become one of South Africa's better-known painters, producing landscapes with a gentle but sure touch; and his wine farm, *Muratie* at Stellenbosch, was and is widely known for its own charms – it stands at the side of a picturesque, tree-lined lane – and those of its wines.

Muratie, which was established in 1685, is one of the oldest wine farms in South Africa. The name comes from the Dutch murasie, meaning ruins, and indeed the place was almost derelict when G P Canitz bought it in 1925. Over the years he transformed it, and he was one of the first people at the Cape to make red wine from the pinot noir grape, the cultivar that is the basis of the great wines of Burgundy.

Canitz had a slightly bohemian air. He lived on his farm but he also had a studio in a warehouse building in Bree Street in Cape Town where he held regular, merry wine parties at weekends. He was a man ahead of his time. He told me in our interview that licensed drinking hours should be extended, that more restaurants should have liquor licences, and that pavement cafes should be established on the streets of Cape Town. All this was quite strong stuff at a time when the sombre shadow of the three Dutch Reformed churches loomed over simple enjoyments such as these. I wrote a report after our interview and sent it to the subeditors in the usual way, wondering whether it would ever see the light of day. It caught somebody's fancy and ended up on the front page of the paper a couple of days later.

I was delighted, and so was G P Canitz, who phoned me and thanked me warmly for arranging for the report to appear on the front page. As a token of his appreciation, he said, he was sending me a dozen bottles of his wine. The case of wine was delivered to me at the office a few days later with a note saying that six bottles were for me and six for the editor. I adopted what I thought was the best course and took the box of wine, with Mr Canitz's note, to my boss, the news editor. 'Leave it here,' he said, 'I'll speak to the editor.'

About ten minutes later, he called me back into his office. 'The editor doesn't want any wine,' he said. (It struck me later that he had almost certainly not spoken to the editor at all.) 'But,' he added kindly, 'when this sort of thing comes along we share it out. I'll have these three bottles. Here,' he said to his deputy, 'you have these two, and then one for Jackson, one for Johnson, a couple for Van der Merwe, who's out at the moment.' Then he picked up the last two bottles and said, 'You have these.'

This sad little story was my first experience of the freebie, an ugly but apt name for something that is provided free, usually by way of a quid pro quo. People used to refer to perks, short for perquisites, defined in the Oxford dictionary as profits, allowances or privileges given in addition to wages or salary. The word freebie has a more disreputable sound, and rightly so, for it refers these days to a vast range of benefits available to various people, especially journalists, usually in return for favours, direct or indirect.

Very substantial free benefits are available to journalists, most of them involving travel. 'Free trips' is a phrase often used by those in the media. Faced with these temptations, journalists react in different ways. At one extreme, you have the cheerful vagabonds of magazine journalism who make no bones about accepting trips and gifts in exchange for publicity and often acknowledge that they have done so. Indeed, in these publications it is often difficult to determine which is advertising and which is editorial. At the other end of the scale, you have the sea-green incorruptibles, to use Thomas Carlyle's famous description of the French revolutionary, Robespierre. These are the people who don't visit a country if they don't like the government, or touch a product if they don't like the company. Predictably enough, most of them stay at home.

One of the bizarre stories of South African journalistic folklore concerns an imposing and high-principled editor who was so incensed when a public relations man called at his office to deliver two dozen cans of free beer that he chased the visitor down the corridor, pelting him with beer cans and shouting abuse. Ah, the characters of yesteryear.

The object of the freebie philosophy is plain enough. Editorial coverage in the media, print or broadcasting, is more valuable than paid-for advertising because it has a higher credibility. Subconsciously, readers and listeners tend to accept information more readily if it comes from the newspaper or magazine or radio or television station, rather than from the mouth and pen of the advertiser himself. It is difficult to put a valuation on this higher credibility, but an American survey done many years ago suggested that editorial publicity was worth eight to ten times the cost of straight advertising. It is little wonder that many businesspeople are alert to the possibilities of free publicity in exchange for a relatively modest outlay on freebies, relatively modest compared with the high cost of ordinary advertising.

I myself was involved briefly in the public relations industry after my retirement from newspaper journalism. For a short time, I was a director of a company owned by my old friend, Aubrey Sussens, but I did not work for them, received no payment, was not comfortable in the board-room seat, and eased out after about a year. As I have observed earlier, I don't really fit well into the world of public relations.

The freebie kings of newspapers are, I think, travel, motoring and entertainment writers. And, I suppose, the editors, some of whom accept very little and others who take virtually everything. Motoring writers are often invited to launches of new cars, locally and abroad, with travel and hotel facilities on a generally lavish scale. One such writer told me years ago that, world-weary, he had decided not to accept more than three free trips overseas a year. I don't know how this affects their assessments of the cars they test-drive. I do know that very rarely is there any kind of harsh criticism of a car (the publication's reliance on advertising from the motor industry is probably a factor here as well).

About twenty years ago my daughter was planning to buy a car and sought my advice. I obtained from her a list of possible purchases and sent it to a motoring correspondent friend asking for his opinions. He took this very seriously and sent me a written report on each car men-tioned. One was a delectable European vehicle that he had praised to the skies in his newspaper column not long before. 'A lovely little car,' he wrote in his note to me, 'but, oh, what a bundle of trouble.'

Specialist travel writers are among the most envied people in the media because of their extensive freebie opportunities. Some newspaper journalists leave interesting and secure jobs to become freelance or mag-azine travel writers because they cannot resist the lure of free travel to exotic destinations several times a year. Some of them have later regret-ted this decision. Freebies do not bring pensions and medical benefits.

Entertainment writers have a less spectacular but nevertheless satisfy-ingly steady flow of freebies. Apart from free tickets for films, concerts, plays and so forth, there are the free meals, and sometimes weekend accommodation, from a restaurant industry that has proliferated enormously in South Africa's major cities in recent years. Some young journalists I have known have forsworn better long-term newspaper opportunities because they did not want to risk losing their freebie pitch-es. One seasoned restaurant critic, now long dead, used to phone a restaurant, say that he would like to write a review of their fare, and add that he would be bringing a party of six for a complimentary meal. Shameless, really. And there are some moderate establishments that receive an inordinate amount of favourable press publicity because they have followed a deliberate policy of providing plenty of free meals.

On a broader and more important scale, senior journalists are often invited to visit other countries on 'information' trips as guests of governments or corporations. What the sponsor is hoping for is the creation of a generally favourable impression in the mind of the recipient, rather than a direct, immediate reward by way of good publicity. Very few South African editors, if any, have not travelled overseas at someone else's expense. I visited Britain, Germany, Greece, Canada and Taiwan as a guest of the governments of those countries, and I did not feel compromised. Taiwan, with its continuing battle to retain its independence of mainland China, has a controversial history, but I don't think my visit there prevented me from seeing both sides of the story. That said, I should declare an opinion. I think that Taiwan has had a raw deal from many governments (including South Africa's) that do not recognise it for cynical reasons of perceived self-interest.

If you take the sponsorship argument to the bitter end, I suppose you could suggest that education benefits such as the Rhodes Scholarships at Oxford University and the Nieman Fellowships at Harvard University are attempts to persuade the recipients to take a favourable view of the host countries and of their traditions and special merits. It is not a persuasive argument. Cecil John Rhodes was the quintessential imperialist, but he was careful to state in his will a hundred years ago that race and religion should not be factors in choosing young people to receive his wonderful scholarships.

It is true that at least one South African, a distinguished Afrikaner of long ago, refused a Rhodes Scholarship because he did not want to be educated in England. But I doubt whether any recipient of scholarships such as these feels obliged at any time to refrain from criticism of the country or the university or any other institution. Certainly many South African Nieman Fellows who studied at Harvard have, as newspaper editors, been highly critical (as is their right) of United States policy in the Middle East.

To return to a more mundane level of freebies, I don't know of any South African journalist who has actually accepted money – cash – in return for editorial favours. Which is not to say that money has not been offered. When I was a young reporter in the Cape Town Magistrate's Court, some sad souls, simple people in trouble, would tell me that they wanted the case kept out of the paper, adding that they understood there was a scale of charges to accomplish this. I had to disillusion them. On the same note, my older colleague, Scott Haigh of the *Cape Argus*, used to say drily that he didn't mind being offered bribes, it was just that the bribes were so insultingly small.

But I imagine that serious transgressions may occur from time to time. I once had a reporter come to me with a letter from a financial firm about whom he had written a favourable report. The letter thanked him and said they were transferring R20 000 worth of unit trusts into his name as an expression of their appreciation, and were looking forward to continued co-operation in the future. Was this all right, my colleague asked nervously, adding that he was planning to sell the unit trusts and go overseas on holiday on the proceeds, but thought he had better check with me first. I told him sympathetically that it was a simple choice between keeping the money or keeping his job. He saw the point and departed sadly, to return the gift and defer his overseas holiday.

And how do you yourself stand in all this, my readers may well ask. I have already mentioned trips paid for by the 'information' departments of foreign governments (I also made several trips abroad at the expense of my employer, the Argus Company). Over the years, I visited Mauritius three or four times as a guest of a hotel group, and wrote what I believe were newsworthy articles about the island. I wrote a wine column for my newspaper for nearly twenty years and had maybe two brief trips to the Cape winelands every year as a guest of various wineries. It is a list of freebies, but not an imposing list by comparison with many others.

In the end, I think, common sense should apply. The world of freebies is dangerous when journalists become trapped in it, living a life of obligation to sponsors and payers. Another peculiar hazard is a loss of perspective, an extraordinary conceit that seems to envelop some freebie experts who become snobbish about the things they have not paid for, be they expensive cars or restaurant dinners. People who do not pay should not really look down their noses at people who do, even if the latter drive smaller cars and eat fish and chips instead of caviar.

But the ruthless exploiters of freebies are a small minority. Ordinary journalists know very well that it is okay to accept a bottle of wine from a contact at Christmas time but not okay to accept a television set or computer. It is the question of obligation that is the acid test.

As for myself, I have travelled abroad more in retirement than I ever did when I was working – and I have paid for my own tickets.

TWENTY

Life in KwaZulu-Natal

Not long after I began work as deputy editor of the *Daily News* in Durban in 1968, the then editor of *The Star* in Johannesburg, John Jordi, asked me to write a fortnightly column called 'Life in Natal'. I accepted with alacrity and enjoyed writing the column, which ran for several years. I felt that I was seeing KwaZulu-Natal with the eyes of a newcomer fresh from Bloemfontein, and I was enthusiastic about some things that the locals probably took for granted.

Many aspects of Natal are familiar to holidaymakers, some of whom return year after year to the same hotel, same restaurants, same stretch of beach with sand so hot that you can hardly walk on it and seawater that sometimes resembles a tepid bath. I thought all those years ago, and I still think, that the KwaZulu-Natal coast's true glory is its vegetation, with flowers and trees that bloom and are in leaf throughout the year. I am not an expert gardener, but in my garden at home there flourish, almost untended, bougainvillea, scarlet clerodendrum, yellow and pink hibiscus, multicoloured impatiens, purple azaleas, orange and lemon trees, a huge mango tree, palms and ferns. And this is entirely typical of the Berea, where I live, an old suburb on the low ridge of hills overlooking the city.

People tend to believe that their own particular surroundings are the best. I knew many people in the Free State who said yes, Durban is nice, but it is even better to have seasons and a real winter with brown grass and leafless trees. And the ultimate in rationalisation came from a young reporter on *The Friend* named Hugh Roberton, who represented the paper in Welkom and later became a distinguished political correspondent in Cape Town. Welkom, 160 kilometres from Bloemfontein, is a modern, rather featureless town that owes its existence solely to the presence of gold mines, but *The Friend* sold plenty of papers there and occasionally we would publish an advertising-supported supplement on the attractions of the place. At certain times of the year, Welkom suffers unpleasant dust storms caused by the wind blowing off ploughed farmland nearby. Hugh Roberton, loyal to the core, wrote in the supplement: 'People complain, but without the dust storms we wouldn't have such lovely sunsets.'

Durban is very different. The summers are hot and humid, but that is alleviated by air conditioning at work or at home, for those who can afford it. And the winters are warm and fine, a benign contrast to the rainy, cold Cape and the dry cold of the Highveld. And there is that wonderful vegetation.

When I joined the *Daily News*, the newly appointed editor was John O'Malley, an experienced and exceptionally able man who had previously been editor of the *Sunday Chronicle*, an upmarket Johannesburg-based paper that had been closed because of lack of support from readers.

The *Daily News* was the dominant paper in Durban, with daily sales about 30 percent bigger than that of its morning rival, *The Mercury* (formerly the *Natal Mercury*). It was not always so. Founded in 1878, the afternoon paper was called the *Natal Advertiser* and it gradually lapsed into a melancholy indifference. The top paper was, without question, the long-established *The Mercury*, and nobody took the 'Tiser, as it was derisively nicknamed, very seriously. A gifted editor who took the helm in 1936 changed all that. His name was Horace Flather. He brightened the paper, changed the name to the *Natal Daily News* (the word Natal was dropped in 1962), coaxed more money out of its owner, the Argus Company, and, most important of all, consistently beat the ponderous and complacent *The Mercury* in news coverage. In the 1940s, its daily circulation overtook that of *The Mercury* and it did not look back for the next 50 years. This has not been the case in recent times, a sad story I shall relate elsewhere.

Every city has its own highly individual characteristics, and the success of a newspaper depends largely on its ability to reflect the interests of its readers. In Bloemfontein, the important events were the annual agricultural show and the speech day at Grey College. When somebody said the weather was promising, he meant it was about to pour with rain. Cricket at the historic Ramblers ground attracted a reasonable crowd, but one not to be compared with the boisterous mob watching rugby at the Free State Stadium. And, of course, the town was strongly Afrikaans in atmosphere. In Bloemfontein, I learned, by force of circumstance, to speak tolerable Afrikaans, sometimes emboldened by the recognition that no matter how indifferent my Afrikaans might be it was better than the other man's English. And I am not referring to the white people alone. The African people, through association, also spoke a good deal of Afrikaans.

Durban, in contrast, was very English, and it remains so to this day, in spite of the fact that the majority of its citizens are Zulu. The African National Congress may hold sway in the city council, but the dignified 1910 City Hall remains an elegant Edwardian witness to civic splendour. The customers at the central post office are almost entirely black, but the pedimented portico and tall pillars remain, as do the plaques on the steps stating that that the building was erected in 1885 and that the National Convention that led to the Union of South Africa met here in 1908. Winston Churchill spoke on these steps after escaping from the Boers in 1899.

In the Durban of my earlier days, the 1960s, '70s and '80s, among the popular topics of conversation were cricket and the old school tie, curry restaurants, weddings and funerals (especially among the large Indian population), and, above all, horseracing. The latter was a compulsive interest across the entire population spectrum, a tradition dating back to the first race meeting in Durban in 1852. It has faded a little in recent years, thanks to the opening of gambling casinos, but racing still has a big following.

I had never been in the least interested in horses, but it was a major concern of the newspapers, and I became quite enthusiastic about the whole business, especially after I became editor of the paper in 1977 and became a frequent guest of racing stewards in their comfortable quarters at the racecourses. Racing was good for newspapers and you ignored it at your peril. Every year, the *Daily News* reached its highest circulation figures in the week before the Durban July. One year, Dirk de Villiers, an old friend of mine from London, was visiting us in July. I came home with the paper, which had a huge page-one headline that said: 'Aron is coughing.' 'Who is Aron?' inquired Dirk. I told him Aron was a horse. His face was a study.

The *Daily News* had a highly efficient young news editor named Chris Smith. His writing was functional rather than stylish and his approach to news gathering was rough and ready, but it worked. He was like a vacuum cleaner, sucking up all the news in Durban. You got a certain amount of dross, but you found the pearls as well. Chris Smith was a local man, a convivial bachelor with excellent contacts. And he was an expert on horseracing, so expert indeed that he eventually left journalism to become a professional buyer on commission of highly bred racehorses, especially from New Zealand. One day, at our morning news conference, the name of a Durban July favourite was mentioned. 'It's tragic,' said Chris Smith heavily. Had the horse died, we wondered. 'Yes, it's tragic,' he continued. 'He keeps running across the rest of the field [of horses] and losing ground.'

The *Daily News* had many distinguished and interesting people on its editorial staff during the 24 years I worked for the paper. Foremost among them was the cartoonist Jock Leyden, who was almost certainly the best-known newspaper journalist in KwaZulu-Natal. He served the *Daily News* for more than 60 years, and his cartoons appeared not only in that paper but throughout South Africa and further abroad. He was an immigrant from Grangemouth, Scotland, arriving in Durban in 1925 at the age of seventeen, and to the day he died in 2000 he never lost his Scottish accent.

Like all good cartoonists, he had an eye for the comic in any situation, and he was an expert in gently deflating the pompous. He was mild in manner and in his drawings, and his satire was bantering rather than bludgeoning. On one rare occasion, a reader wrote alleging that a cartoon was cruel and vindictive. I sent the letter to Jock for his comments. He brought it back to me with a bewildered expression. 'I'm never cruel,' he said indignantly, 'or vindictive.' Which was no more than the truth.

His masterpiece, in detail anyway, was a drawing he made in 1980 of *Daily News* personae over the previous 53 years. It was commissioned by Charles Barry, editor of the Argus Company's house magazine, *Argus News*, and himself an old *Daily News* man, and it contains sketches of 76 individuals from the paper's editorial, management, and printing departments, all of them recognisable. Jock presented me with the original drawing after it had been published in *Argus News*, with the comment that he now knew how Michelangelo must have felt after painting the ceiling of the Sistine Chapel. I knew, at one stage or another, 58 of the people in that cartoon. Eighteen of them became Argus Company editors and another eleven became business managers of papers. Jock knew them all, including, of course, the eight editors with whom he worked in Durban.

Leyden, as he always signed himself, was an intensely professional artist and he never presented a slipshod or inaccurate drawing. He could turn his hand to almost anything. He liked sport, and his drawings of the Kingsmead cricket grounds were always adorned with two mynah birds hopping insolently in a corner of the picture, as they do in reality.

His drawings of theatrical events and personalities were so valued that a selection was hung permanently in the Jock Leyden Gallery of the University of Natal's Sneddon Theatre, one of the city's main cultural venues. He was given Durban civic honours, a Papal award and a lot of other honours. And he was that rare bird, a newspaper journalist who did not drink or smoke. He was also a religious man, a quiet but devout Roman Catholic. Maybe it all added up to a long and happy life. He drew his cartoons until he was in late eighties and died at the age of 91.

Ronnie Tungay, the news editor for as long as anybody could remember, was a volatile and irresistible kind of man, bubbling with enthusiasm and energy. He pursued news like a tracker dog on an eternal hot trail, and he refused to be desk-bound; he often went into the field with his reporters. One of the stories was that, tipped off by one of his many contacts about a bad explosion in the city, Tungay arrived at the scene and was interviewing survivors before the police arrived. He was virtually the founder of the celebrated Drakensberg Boys' Choir School, having established it in the mountains with his wife, Gwen. And he was a fervent

Glenwood High School old boy, working so hard for their club's various sports and social activities that their very substantial sports grounds at Durban North were named Tungay Park. He wore a Glenwood Old Boys' tie to work every day of his life and Reg Sweet, the sports editor, believed that Ronnie used it at night to keep his pyjama pants up.

Withal he was the kindest of men. Harvey Tyson, a *Daily News* reporter who later became editor of *The Star* in Johannesburg, has a story about a young reporter who was sent out on what should have been a quick job and was away for hours. Tungay was fuming in his excitable way. 'When he comes back, I'm going to fire him,' he told those near him in the office. 'Just fire him. Straight away. Can't put up with this kind of behaviour.' At that moment, he turned around and saw that the miscreant had just walked in. Ronnie Tungay put an affectionate arm around the young fellow and said gently, 'Where have you been, Wally, my boy?'

(The American poet and critic Dorothy Parker was working one day in a New York newspaper office when a new reporter returned several hours after having been sent out on an assignment that should have taken 30 minutes. 'Where have you been?' raged the news editor. The young fellow was a man of mettle. 'I've been f***ing busy,' he replied heatedly. Without looking up from her typewriter, Dorothy Parker said: 'Or vice versa.')

Reg Sweet, the long-serving sports editor of the *Daily News*, was well known as a rugby writer, having covered several Springbok tours and Test series. He wore in his lapel a little caterpillar badge signifying that he was one of those who had to parachute for their lives from disabled aircraft in the second World War. Reg's moment of truth and good fortune came somewhere over the Mediterranean. The parachute opened and he was taken out of the sea by an Allied boat.

Reg's air force service left him with an entertaining turn of phrase that was almost anachronistic, something one hadn't heard for fifty years. If you asked him to do something he'd say, 'Roger', airman's wireless language for 'okay'. If you asked what time the match would begin, he'd say, 'Eleven ack emma.' Where do you find people who speak like that today?

The *Daily News* was strong on the arts, and for most of my term as editor the arts editor was Sjoerd Meijer, a burly former Hollander who was an excellent film and theatre critic and whose wife, Marianne, is a well-known painter. At one time, our art critic was Andrew Verster, one of South Africa's most prominent artists.

Our coverage of classical music was extensive but we had an eccentric music critic named George Nisbet, who had a full-time job as one of our subeditors. Nisbet, a Scot of faintly comical appearance, short and round, was as mild as milk in his conversation and behaviour but when let loose at a typewriter he could, on occasion, become an aggressive Alsatian. His music reviews went to extremes; things were either wonderful or terrible. His worst characteristic was omniscience. No matter how abstruse or obscure a composition might be, George wrote about it as if he'd heard it a hundred times. Inevitably, he came unstuck. Beethoven wrote ten sonatas for violin and piano and two of them, widely different works, are in the key of G major. Writing in his usual lofty fashion, Nisbet savaged two unfortunate performers, with plenty of advice on how this G major sonata should be played. But it was painfully clear to anybody who knew the music that he was writing about the wrong piece, the other G major.

His moment of untruth came when I received a letter from *The Gramophone,* a famous and long-standing British magazine, pointing out that long sections of its erudite music reviews had appeared frequently, word for word and unacknowledged, in Nisbet's reviews in the *Daily News.* Not a few words; half a dozen long paragraphs at a time. *The Gramophone* threatened to sue the *Daily News* for breach of copyright. I was livid and asked Sjoerd Meijer to speak to Nisbet, mentioning that if I spoke to him myself I might strangle him with my bare hands. Sjoerd came back and reported that Nisbet said yes, he read *The Gramophone* regularly and some of the contents might have been at the back of his mind. I wrote a humble letter of apology to T*he Gramophone,* promising that it would not happen again. Our critic was close to retirement, and we soon found another.

About fifteen years later, I was amused to read that a fashionable young South African magazine writer had written a book that, it turned out, contained large unacknowledged chunks of the writings of Bill Bryson, well known internationally for his wryly humorous books about travel and people. Again, the culprit said that he had indeed read Bryson and something must have stuck in his mind. A feeble and totally unconvincing excuse for blatant plagiarism, which is about the worst crime a writer can commit.

A celebrated *Daily News* staff member who worked on the paper before my time was Laurens van der Post, author and friend of Prince Charles. Van der Post was deputy editor of the paper just twenty years before I took over that job, but he didn't stay long; he had greater ambitions than newspaper work in Durban and he realised them, becoming a best-selling writer.

In the 1980s, he visited Durban, where his nephew, Tommy Bedford, lived. Bedford was an architect, a Springbok rugby player and an old friend of mine. One of our reporters had an unproductive interview with Van der Post, and I sent word that if he were agreeable I would host a lunch for him, in the *Daily News* executive dining room, to which various prominent and interesting local people would be invited. The invitation met with a curt refusal, and I formed the impression that he didn't want anyone to be reminded of his past connection with the paper. Understandably, I was not heartbroken when, after his death in 1996 at the age of 90, Van der Post was exposed by a biographer as having fibbed and exaggerated on a grand scale, always with a view to self-aggrandisement.

The life of an English-language newspaper editor was difficult and rather dangerous under the Nationalist Party government, as my old friend and colleague Harvey Tyson has testified in his well-documented book, *Editors Under Fire*. We lived with the constant threat of prosecution in terms of the hundred or so laws that directly affected freedom of speech. We were accused by politicians of being unSouth African or downright traitors. Our phones were tapped (a side benefit in my case was that, whenever my phone went out of order, it was fixed in record time). And it was not only the politicians who made our lives unpleasant. Like most of my colleagues elsewhere, I encountered a good deal of hostility from English-speaking business people who thought I was a troublemaker, people who changed horses with the agility of circus riders when a new government came into power in 1994.

I think the guiding light of us all was the desire, indeed the instinct, to publish the facts as fully as possible. One of the many states of emergency visited upon us by the government included a long list of dreadful prohibitions on publication of this and that. An attorney I knew was truly alarmed and told me he thought he should address the entire editorial staff. They packed into my office and listened to a long, doleful list of things they couldn't do, lest they be severely punished by the law. A heavy sense of depression hung over the proceedings. When my lawyer friend had finished, I decided to say my own piece. I told my colleagues that the policy of the paper was to publish as much as it possibly could, to strain against the law if necessary, to risk prosecution, to apply the laws of common sense and fairness rather than the laws of the government. As I spoke, I could feel the atmosphere becoming more cheerful, and they left in much better mood. Afterwards, I received several notes from staff members saying that they all felt much encouraged by what I had said.

The desire, nay the duty, to publish simple facts often brought an editor into conflict with the police. One of the states of emergency imposed in the 1980s included a prohibition on all reports relating to police activity unless the information had been confirmed by the police themselves, and there were heavy penalties for infringing this law. Needless to say, the police used this clause to conceal anything that reflected adversely on them. The newspapers pushed and shoved against the law as best they could.

On one occasion, a well-known Durban political activist, a member of the city's Indian community, was detained without trial, a common enough experience in those days. His case was different, however; he became ill and spent some time in hospital undergoing treatment, under police guard. *The Daily News* was aware of this, and indeed two of our reporters who knew the detained man had seen him at a window of the hospital and had waved to him. According to the emergency law, we could not publish this information without confirmation from the police, and the police doggedly declined to make any comment at all.

We notified the detainee's wife – who had known nothing about her husband's illness – and eventually she obtained a reluctant statement from the local police chief that her husband was in hospital, that he was not seriously ill, and that she could not see him. She passed this information on to us and it was published in the *Daily News* and, a few days later, in the *Sunday Tribune*. About a week later, two members of the security police came to see me, a smooth-talking major and a taciturn captain who looked like a heavy, to use today's jargon, the type of person who is a natural bully. They accused me of breaking the law. I explained that we had obtained the information from the detained man's wife, who herself had received confirmation from the chief of police. 'Ah, yes,' said the smooth major, 'but did he confirm it to you yourself? That's what the law says.' They departed with the promise that I would be hearing from them again.

There was an amusing sequel. Before they left my office, they asked where they could find the editor of the *Sunday Tribune*, Ian Wyllie. As I directed them to Ian's office I felt, illogically, slightly better. If the boat is sinking it's more comforting if there are two of you rather than one. Later, I checked with Ian. He told them exactly the same story and received exactly the same response. Ian Wyllie was short and rotund, mostly bald with some grey hair. As the interview came to an end the smooth police major said: 'Thank you for your help. Sorry to have worried you, but it's our job.' 'Worry me?' said Ian. 'Worry me? If I allowed this kind of thing to worry me, I'd be bald, fat and grey.' The two policemen shot each other looks and hurried out of the office. Ian heard them laughing outside the door. In those days, it was always gratifying to score a point off the security police. We heard no more officially, but the *Daily News* police reporter told me the police had decided to drop the matter. Perhaps they realised that a court case would make them look silly.

The detained man, who recovered soon and was released from detention not much later, was Pravin Gordhan, later well known as the Commissioner of Revenue Services.

The strong arm of the law sometimes had its funny side. One of the many restrictions introduced by the Nationalist government was the Key Points Act, which prohibited unauthorised publication of strategically important 'key points'. The government of the day was nothing if not paranoid, seeing enemies around every corner. Maybe some of the key points needed to be kept secret, but, as usual, the law was all-embracing and threatened dire penalties for transgressors, which of course were most likely to be newspapers. There was one little snag. They didn't tell you what the key points were, so you never knew if you were breaking the law or not.

The *Sunday Tribune* published an entirely harmless supplement about the commercial growth of Richards Bay, the port 150 kilometres north of Durban, and included a fine aerial photograph of the Richards Bay harbour. The police descended and warned the editor that the paper faced prosecution because Richards Bay was a key point. The threatened prosecution was dropped when it was pointed out that the photograph came from the Richards Bay Publicity Bureau and that it had appeared on the cover of the Natal North Coast phone book.

It was sometimes necessary to help individual staff members who had run foul of the police or the government. At one point, our representative in the 'independent' Transkei, a reporter named Peter Honey, was threatened with immediate arrest under that territory's own emergency laws, and the *Daily News* had to move swiftly to get him back to the relative safety of South Africa. On another occasion, Carmel Rickard, a reporter who has subsequently become well known for her coverage of legal matters, came to me in some alarm, saying that two policemen had arrived to interrogate her. I invited the policemen into my office and sat Carmel Rickard down next to me, and together we tried to reply to their questions. After they had left, Carmel wrote me a note of thanks, saying that it had been very important to her psychologically that I put her on my side of the desk and the policemen on the other side, us versus them. Of course, one acts like that without thinking about it.

There were not many black newspaper editors around during my working career – they have proliferated since 1994 – but some of them had a much tougher time than the white editors. The late Percy Qoboza, editor of the successful Johannesburg newspaper *The World*, was detained in prison without trial for several months, and repeated protests by the press here and abroad made no difference. The government of the day was all-powerful. He was eventually released without ever being charged with any kind of offence. Other black editors suffered a similar fate.

Another old friend of mine, Obed Kunene, editor of the biweekly Zulu paper, *Ilanga*, ran into trouble of a different kind. Following publication of a controversial article in *Ilanga*, he and his family had to flee from their home in Umlazi, the township near Durban, after an angry section of the community threatened to burn the place down. I happened to be dining with John Featherstone, business manager of the *Daily News* and *Ilanga*, when Obed phoned to tell him what had happened. Featherstone and I offered to accommodate him and his family at our homes until the trouble blew over, but he declined with thanks. He said he would lose all credibility in the black community if he were perceived to be taking refuge in a white suburb. He and his family stayed with friends in the neighbourhood until passions had subsided.

I don't think, quite honestly, that the newspapers had strong support among the white inhabitants of Natal as the press battled against a domineering and racist government. White Natalians had a well-deserved reputation for political conservatism, and it took a long time to persuade them to change their minds, which I think they have done now. *The Mercury* was the clear voice of this section of the community. Both the *Daily News* and *Sunday Tribune* had a much more liberal approach to racial matters in particular. Readership surveys indicated that the *Daily News* had many more Indian readers than did *The Mercury*.

During my fifteen-year editorship, it was reckoned that about half our readers were Indian, and in some ways that simplified the job of running the paper. The interests of white and Indian readers overlapped at many points and I always felt that, basically, they were interested in the same kind of news. At a personal level, I had the most cordial relationship with members of the Indian community, and even now after more than ten years of retirement I am greeted by many of them in the street and in offices and homes.

The large and growing Zulu population were not typically readers of the *Daily News*, still less of *The Mercury*. For many there was a language problem, and in any case they had in *Ilanga* a good biweekly Zulu paper. But I have no reason to think that the Zulu people were in any way hostile to the *Daily News*. They knew that we were not on the side of a government that pushed them around. I had a friendly relationship with Dr

Mangosuthu Buthelezi, head of the Inkatha Freedom Party, and I remember him sending me a message of congratulation when the *Daily News* urged the electorate (as many other English papers did) to vote against P W Botha's ill-conceived tricameral parliament of 1983.

The conservatism of white Natal was demonstrated by the province's dogged retention of the United Party, later the New Republic Party, when it was being discarded elsewhere in favour of the Progressive Party and its successors. Natal did not have a Prog in parliament until 1976, when Harry Pitman, a clever and personable lawyer and farmer, won the Durban North seat. I was to take over the editorship of the *Daily News* the following year and my accession to that post had already been announced, but John O'Malley was still very much in charge. On the parliamentary by-election there was no difference of opinion between us. The *Daily News* mounted a massive campaign in favour of Pitman, who won the seat against the odds. Later, the defeated United Party candidate lodged an official complaint with the South African Press Council saying that the *Daily News* had treated him unfairly in that it had given one-sided coverage to the election. I wrote a formal response, pointing out that a newspaper was perfectly entitled to be partisan in politics and citing the extreme example of some Afrikaans newspapers that, come election time, did not even mention the names of opponents of the Nats. The complaint was rejected.

From time to time there were errors of judgment on my part. Who can go through life without making mistakes? One such occurred with the formation of the Congress of South African Trade Unions at a rally in Durban in 1985. I underestimated its importance and the event was covered, but not given sufficient prominence in the paper. As a result, two reporters and a photographer resigned in protest, activated, I think, by one of their number who was politically very aware. I regretted this at the time, but as they did not seek to discuss the matter with me there was not much I could do about it. Two of them have disappeared from the press scene. The third has done very well indeed, becoming an editor himself. I hope he has forgiven me my error of judgment. After that, the *Daily News* gave fair and adequate coverage to Cosatu.

Two significant anniversaries during my editorship were the centenary of the *Daily News* in 1978 and that of the Anglo-Zulu War in 1979. We celebrated the first with a banquet in Durban at which the main speaker was Natal's foremost businessman, Chris Saunders of the Tongaat-Hulett sugar company. The second was commemorated, among various ways, with another large dinner attended by quite a strong contingent of old soldiers from Britain. Those who had medals of ancestors involved in the war were asked to wear them on the right side of the chest, not the normal left. My old friend, Ian Player, the celebrated conservationist, has, like me, a grandfather who fought in the war of 1879, and he insisted that we should wear these old medals.

An elegant and courteous British general with a big white moustache proposed a toast to the gallant Zulu dead, and Dr Buthelezi responded with a toast to the gallant British dead. He himself is a descendant of a Zulu prince who participated in the war. After all the festivities, the descendants were presented with a commemorative tie, showing assegais and a shield above the stripe of the British campaign medal's ribbon. I was a little careful about wearing it in case it be viewed as faintly racist, but I was reassured when I saw Mangosuthu Buthelezi wearing the tie. The next time I thought I might see him at a function, I wore it. He came across the room, beaming, and said: 'I see you are very well dressed tonight.' He has his critics, but he is a man of great charm.

Justice Alexander, who worked on the *Daily News* for about 40 years, told me that because of my 1879 grandfather I had the longest connection with Natal of any editor of the paper except the first, a wry thought considering that I was 38 years old when I joined the staff. Justice, a great character, was fascinated by military history. With his trim grey moustache and aristocratic mien, he looked rather like a retired general but in fact he advanced to corporal in World War II. He was most interested in my grandfather's Anglo-Zulu War campaign medal, a chunk of solid silver inscribed with his name, but he complained that it had no ribbon. 'Looks rather undressed,' he said. I said that the ribbon had disappeared long before I inherited the medal from my father, and I didn't even know at that stage what it looked like. Justice produced from his office desk a little book with colour pictures of the ribbons of all British medals over the past 300 years or so. 'There it is,' he said triumphantly. 'I'm going over to London soon and I'll get you a ribbon from a good military tailor I know there.'

A few weeks later, there was an envelope on my desk with the ribbon in it. I thanked Justice, who had returned to work the day before. He said I owed him nothing. His military tailor had turned out to be not so good after all. 'The blighter tried to fob me off with an Ashanti War ribbon, but I had my little book with me and showed him it was the wrong one.' He then traipsed across London to a military museum, tracked down the right medal in a glass case, and spoke to the curator. After a brief search, the latter found a length of the ribbon and cut off a piece with a pair of scissors. Simple.

In 1989, Ian Wyllie retired and I was asked by the Argus Company to assume responsibility for the *Sunday Tribune* as well as the *Daily News*. I was called editor-in-chief of both papers and had a large and good staff of about 130 journalists. The change was not welcomed by the *Tribune* people, who thought that their paper's individual identity might be affected. In the end I was able, I think, to reassure them. They had their own editor, my deputy, Jonathan Hobday, and I sat in the background as a kind of wicketkeeper, fielding any loose balls and keeping gentle control of policy decisions.

Journalists are talented and sometimes temperamental people and they have to be handled with care. Every month I wrote a lengthy bulletin for the editorial staff, trying to keep them informed about the fortunes of the papers, complimenting them (by name) on good work and criticising them (anonymously) for shortcomings. It was hard work because it involved keeping a hefty cuttings file, but it was worthwhile. And the success stories were most rewarding of all. Nine of my colleagues became newspaper editors within a few years of my retirement. Meanwhile, the sales of both the *Daily News* and the *Sunday Tribune* were burgeoning, with the daily comfortably over the 100 000 mark and the Sunday paper selling about 125 000. *The Mercury* circulation at this stage, in 1992, was about 68 000.

The *Daily News* and *Tribune* had been Argus papers for as long as anyone could remember, but *The Mercury* had always been independent and operated in offices some distance away. In 1985, it sold out to Argus and moved into our building. Naturally, the editor of *The Mercury*, James Macmillan, had misgivings, but he was allowed to exercise independent control and seemed to accept philosophically what had become economically inevitable. He retired at the end of 1990 and then a big change came: the first appointment of an authentic Argus man to the editorship of *The Mercury*. This was John Patten, whom I had known for years and whose father, Jack Patten, was editor of *The Star* in Johannesburg during my time at *The Friend* in Bloemfontein.

Patten introduced a new, more liberal tone to *The Mercury's* editorial comment and news presentation, and he tried to gain access to the extensive and expensive overseas news services that were provided for other Argus papers, including the *Daily News*. I resisted this strenuously and, in the end, the Argus head office upheld my view that the historical competition between the two papers would obviously be diminished if they both had the same news and feature services. I had nothing against John Patten or *The Mercury*, but the first duty of an editor is to protect his own paper, and the people who work on it.

My relationship with my old friend was cordial but guarded, and he seemed to understand. When I retired, John Patten wrote a generous and gracious editorial in *The Mercury* that said, inter alia: 'We have long known Michael Green as a professional, and therefore formidable, competitor of *The Mercury* in his capacity as editor-in-chief of Durban's other daily newspaper. But even from our adversarial position, it is only right to acknowledge publicly at the moment of his retirement the outstanding part he has played in helping defend a free press in South Africa and in upholding the best traditions of a free press over many years.'

TWENTY-ONE

A crucial role

When, in 1994, the Argus Company ended more than a hundred years of newspaper publishing in South Africa by selling its interests to Independent Newspapers of Ireland, a young South African magazine journalist wrote a foolish article saying that now that 'Auntie Argus' was disappearing from the scene, we would get brighter and better newspapers. 'Auntie Argus' was the patronising and mildly abusive term invented by journalists on non-Argus papers who envied the financial and circulation strength of their competitors.

For about half a century, Argus afternoon newspapers in Johannesburg, Durban and Cape Town had consistently outsold their non-Argus morning rivals, English and Afrikaans, and had made far greater profits. Taking second place is more comfortable if you can argue that the winner is in some way morally inferior, and that is what the morning newspapers did when sourly surveying the success of their Argus afternoon counterparts. And there were many bruised egos and furrowed brows when the Argus, some years before it sold out to Independent, took over the commercially failing morning newspapers. The most prominent among them, the *Rand Daily Mail*, had already died because of the losses it incurred.

As far as I know, the sneer about better newspapers after the Auntie Argus era was not answered publicly by any former Argus executives. It was not necessary to do so. The readers gave their answer. Within eight years of the purchase by Independent Newspapers, the sales of many of its papers had dropped by nearly half. For the first time, the Cape Town Afrikaans paper *Die Burger* pulled well ahead of the *Cape Argus* and miles ahead of the *Cape Times*. In Durban, sales of the *Daily News* (afternoon) and *The Mercury* (morning), both now in the same stable, dropped dramatically. In Johannesburg, *The Star* dropped from a 1990 peak of about 230 000 copies a day to a mere 164 000.

That high point of 230 000 was reached when Nelson Mandela was released from prison in 1990 after 27 years of incarceration. The country was agog at the human and political implications, and newspapers enjoyed record sales. I well remember a conversation I had at the time with Harvey Tyson, then editor of *The Star*, and Peter McLean, then general manager of the Argus Company. Between us, we had clocked up about 120 years of newspaper work, and we agreed that things had never been better for our industry. We all knew that you could not sustain indefinitely a high pitch achieved because of immensely strong news values, but history had shown that when the interest had subsided, a residual newspaper buying habit remained. You lost some of the temporary new readers, but not all. We agreed that newspaper circulations in South Africa should remain buoyant for at least ten years.

We were very wrong. Of course, we were all close to retirement – we would not be looking after newspapers for the next ten years – and we did not know that the Argus Company would cease to exist. The sale to Independent came quite suddenly and the motivating force was the Anglo American Corporation, the mining and industrial giant that was, through a subsidiary company, the principal shareholder in the Argus Company. Anglo was worried about the political and business hazards of running newspapers in the uncharted territory of the new South Africa, and took the opportunity of selling its newspaper interests to the rapidly expanding Independent Newspapers group, which was based in Ireland and looking for new worlds to conquer. So the deed was done, and Auntie Argus passed into history.

It may have been coincidental that circulation losses began soon after Independent Newspapers had taken control of most of the English-language newspapers. They certainly did not occur because the newspapers were better than they were in the days of Auntie Argus. Many reasons have been advanced for the decline: big increases in the cover prices of newspapers; the changing patterns of our entire society; the quest for new readers across a broader spectrum, or alternatively the quest for a focused readership; the failure of old-fashioned readers to adapt to political and social change (one editor went so far as to blame his readers for his loss of circulation); competition from television (which after all has been with us since 1976); a shortage of disposable income; and so forth.

One possible reason has been the apparent attempt by the newspapers to broaden their readership base by adopting a more popular approach to the choice and presentation of news, along the lines of British and European tabloids. The theory seems to be that large headlines and eye-catching (but sometimes trivial) news will attract new readers. It does not seem to have worked. The new readers have been few, and many old readers have been lost because the newspapers no longer contain much of interest to them.

I retired before Independent Newspapers took over a large part of our daily and weekly press and I have no direct knowledge of their modus operandi. It does seem, however, that editors are under direct or implied instructions to tap, at all costs, the vast potential market of black readers. Not an easy job, considering the divisions of the past and the fact that a number of well-produced and cannily edited 'black' newspapers already serve this market.

It also seems that editors have less individual freedom as policy-makers than they did in the old days. One of them, Peter Davis, former editor of the *Sunday Tribune*, went on record as saying that the business manager of his paper was the man he reported to. That would not have been said in the Argus days. Editors were appointed by the chairman of the company's board of directors and were answerable to him alone. The responsibilities of managers and editors at the various newspapers were clearly divided, the manager being responsible for the money and the editor for the content of his paper. Obviously their lines often crossed, and equally obviously there were occasional disputes about matters like the proportion of advertising space in a paper (taken to extremes, the argument is that editors would like to have no advertising and managers would like to have only advertising). But these disputes were almost invariably settled amiably with the application of some common sense. The last resort was to refer them to the executive chairman of the Argus Company and I can never remember this happening.

Nor, for that matter, can I recall in twenty years of editorship receiving an instruction from the chairman or any other manager on how I should conduct the editorial affairs of my newspaper. You were given the responsibility and left to get on with it, knowing that if you were a complete flop or an irresponsible fool you could lose your job. Argus Company editors and senior journalists were experienced, well trained, independent-minded and well attuned to the needs and interests of their readers. Typically it took 25 to 30 years for a good man to attain a major editorship, and usually he had done many jobs for the company in various places (in my case, ranging from parliamentary reporter to theatre critic in places as diverse as Kimberley and London). The editor was given the freedom to form his own judgment and opinions. Nobody from the head office ever said, 'Please be careful, you understand the risks, we've got a valuable property, etcetera.' You knew this.

I think today's editors have a difficult task as they balance the need for profit with the costs of running good newspapers, and running them with staff members who, by force of circumstance, are largely inexperienced and sometimes do not have English as their home language. Add to that a kind of ethical necessity to abandon the readership patterns of the past and establish new ones in accordance with the new South Africa, and the task becomes even more difficult. It's not a job that I would care to have now, though in one important respect newspaper editorship is much easier than it was in my day: the political and legal pressure is far less. There are many merits to the new South Africa, and paramount among them, in my opinion, is the almost total freedom of speech – a welcome change from the iron-fisted clamp on information in the apartheid days. I have referred elsewhere to some of the sinister and bizarre restrictions on information imposed by the Nationalist government, prohibitions that would be unthinkable today.

Argus Company newspapers fought long, hard and honourably in the battle against the apartheid juggernaut. Many who have served the new ANC-dominated government had earlier enthusiastically endorsed, or at least condoned, the apartheid policies of the National Party. No Argus newspaper did that. One or two conservative-minded editors of 40 years ago tried to reason with the then government, more in sorrow than in anger, but as the excesses of apartheid increased so did the resistance of the English-language press, in which the Argus was a major factor.

The papers run by the Argus Company were characterised by the belief that the news was all important. Comment is free, facts are sacred, C P Scott (1846–1932) wrote in a famous aphorism. Scott, who was editor of the Manchester Guardian for 59 years, pointed out in an editorial written for his paper's centenary in 1921 that the primary purpose of a newspaper to gather news, and it must see that the supply is not tainted.

This was the way my generation of journalists was reared. As young *Cape Argus* reporters, we were repeatedly told that our views were irrelevant and unimportant, the news was the thing. We were ticked off if we wrote that people spoke 'angrily' or 'emotionally' or made a 'fierce' attack on someone. Let the reader decide whether the attack was fierce or not, we were told. One editor, Morris Broughton of the *Daily News* and later the *Cape Argus*, took the dispassionate approach to reporting to such extremes that he didn't like indirect speech, which he feared might give the reporter the opportunity to be selective. He preferred: the mayor said, quote, and in due course, close quotes.

Interestingly enough, Broughton held strong and, at the time, unusual political views. He supported the republican cause at the time of the Republican Referendum in 1960, which eventually led to breaking the historical connection with the British crown and to South Africa's departure from the Commonwealth. Broughton stuck to his position in spite of the fact that most of his readers favoured the monarchy and made that clear in hundreds of letters to the editor. He argued that a republic was inevitable, so you might as well start off on the right foot. At about the same time, Broughton was the first editor to support the newly formed Progressive Party when it broke away from the United Party, another stance that brought forth criticism from many *Cape Argus* readers. But

Broughton never allowed his views, well aired in editorials, to influence his reporting of events, political or otherwise. And this was the practice, by and large, of most English-language editors (the Afrikaans papers were official organs of the National Party and they made no bones about their partisanship at every level, to the point of ignoring speeches made by their political opponents).

In contrast, today's newspapers are peppered with chatty columns, giving the writers' views on everything from traffic jams to barking dogs. I wrote a weekly column myself for nearly twenty years, but in it I tried to give background news and information that, for one reason or another, might not get into the paper in the usual way. I have the impression that some of today's writers are much more interested in themselves than in their readers, an impression confirmed by an old friend, the widow of a distinguished colleague of mine, who said: 'They're always writing about themselves.'

It has been said that, in the past, most South African newspapers concentrated on white readers and neglected the interests of black people. That is partly true, but the reality is that newspapers, like all individuals and organisations engaged in commerce, have to recognise and serve markets. *The Times* in London does not aim at people who prefer *The Sun*, and the *Sowetan* is not trying to beguile the housewives of Houghton.

What the English-language newspapers did, and what in the end helped shape the future of the country, was to keep their readers constantly alert to the injustice, immorality and folly of apartheid. When I was a young journalist on the *Cape Argus*, I investigated and reported the story of a black man who had repeatedly tried to resume married life with his wife, who was legally employed in Cape Town. The husband was constantly sent back to the Transkei in terms of the influx control laws. In the end, he hanged himself in despair, another victim of a truly ugly system.

Nearly 40 years later, as editor of the *Daily News* I was trying, in the face of menacing warnings of prosecution from the police, to publish the facts about police brutality in one of the Durban townships. The police threatened the paper and me with several of the restrictive laws that existed then. In the end, I persuaded a member of parliament, the late Harry Pitman, to raise the matter in the House of Assembly, so that we could report the facts under the protection of parliamentary privilege. Nat MPs promptly complained that this was an abuse of parliamentary privilege!

The battle against apartheid was long and bitter, and my experiences were no more than typical of those of hundreds of brave journalists and dozens of brave editors who were determined that the public should be given the facts, no matter how risky that was. Steve Biko's death in police custody, a turning point in many ways, might have been hushed up if the English-language newspapers had not revealed the facts in the face of official resistance. Likewise, the Department of Information scandal of the late 1970s, which was fully exposed by a judicial inquiry but only after it was uncovered by a persistently inquiring and dogged press.

The occasional references these days to 'white' newspapers of the past really don't hold water. These papers were promoting black journalists to senior positions long before affirmative action became the flavour of the month. Many of those journalists are now editors themselves, having reached that status in a much shorter time than that taken by their white colleagues of an earlier era. They did not make such rapid progress because they were more brilliant than their predecessors but because they were black, and the newspaper proprietors felt an urgent need to have black editors.

Nearly all the so-called 'white' newspapers have for decades had a substantial number of readers who were not white: black people in the case of *The Star* in Johannesburg, which used to publish what was delicately called an Africa Edition; Coloured people (or, if you like, so-called Coloured people) in the case of the *Cape Argus*, Cape Town; Indian people in the case of the *Daily News*, Durban. Today, long after the advent of the new democratic South Africa, the success of the Cape Town-based *Die Burger* rests largely on Coloured people, reading in their home language, Afrikaans. This is ironic, considering that *Die Burger*, as the faithful voice of the National Party, spent 40 years kicking the Coloured people in the teeth with vigorous support of policies such as forced removals, job reservation, racial separation on buses and trains and the infamous Immorality Act. *Die Burger* has, of course, changed its tune today.

When I became editor of the *Daily News* the readership was about half white, half Indian. The Zulu component in the local population was served mainly by the biweekly *Ilanga*, published in Zulu. We did not publish special 'Indian pages' or an 'Indian section' in the *Daily News*. We believed that the interests and lifestyles of our various groups of readers overlapped to such a degree that no distinction was necessary, and I think we were proved correct. The paper prospered commercially because all our readers were interested in buying the cars, television sets, do-it-yourself kits and corn flakes that were advertised in our pages. And we steadily gained circulation because the news in our pages interested all of them some of the time and some of them all the time.

For many years, the morning paper in Durban, *The Mercury* (formerly the *Natal Mercury*) took a different position, aiming to be the paper for upper-income white readers. This led to its near collapse; its private owners sold the paper to the Argus Company when it was on the verge of financial breakdown. Under Independent Newspapers there seems to have been a renewed attempt to give *The Mercury* (and the *Cape Times* in Cape Town) an upmarket focus, to use a term much loved by market researchers and other sundry guessers. Perhaps it will work. There is much to do. The circulations of both papers have dropped by about 40 percent since 1994.

Newspapers give plenty of publicity to their readership figures, less to their circulation figures. Perhaps I should explain the difference. Circulation figures are audited and are factual, reflecting the average number of papers sold per day, or per week in the case of a weekly, over a six-month period. Only sold papers can be included. You can't boost your circulation by giving away papers or dumping them in the veld, as has occurred a few times, according to rumour.

Readership is a different game altogether. Normally each copy of a newspaper or magazine has several readers: the members of a family, for example, or the patients in a doctor's waiting room. Market-survey people try to establish the number of readers per copy. Multiply that by the circulation figure and you have a lovely big readership figure, which more or less ignores the fact that some of those 'readers' may merely glance at the paper for a minute or two. In my working days, I was never very impressed by readership figures, which I regarded as a vague and optimistic guess, and I see no reason to change my mind now when I see the extravagant claims periodically made by the newspapers.

It is difficult to prove or disprove the accuracy of readership figures, but they did come under scrutiny a long time ago when the *Reader's Digest* raised some interesting questions. This is an international magazine that sells in many countries, and the paper's head office in the United States noted with interest that each copy of the *Reader's Digest* sold in South Africa was read by a much larger number of people than was the case anywhere else in the world. What was happening, of course, was that the definition of a reader was much looser and more flattering to the readership figures here, in South Africa, than it was anywhere else. Subsequent inquiries showed that a suburban train passenger who read the main sports headline on the back page of a paper held by another passenger sitting opposite him was classified as a reader. Thank you, I prefer the facts.

Unquestionably, one of the factors behind the decline in circulations has been the big rise in cover prices, cover price being the industry term for the actual price of the newspaper. Paradoxically enough, falling sales do not necessarily mean falling profits; not initially, anyway. The cost structure of the newspaper industry is such that it can be more profitable, in the short term at least, to sell fewer papers at a higher price. There can be a huge saving on newsprint, the actual paper used, which normally accounts for about one-third of total production costs. Distribution costs will be lower. If you can link this to a strong volume of advertising revenue, plus a higher cover price, you will make more money.

Today's editors walk a very difficult path. With one party dominating the political scene, and that moreover a party of the masses who have historically been the underdogs, it is easy to descend to a one-party state, the benevolent dictatorship, with control of the media as a prime imperative. One has only to look north to the government-controlled newspapers and broadcasting services of Zimbabwe to see the danger.

In this situation, the role of the newspaper editor is crucial and fraught with hazard. He wants to maintain an independent line but he must take cognisance of political realities. So he treads warily. Readers are denied full information on matters like crime and AIDS for fear of upsetting group sensibilities. There is a muted response to the hardship caused by affirmative action. There are pious statements that, on the international scene, terrorism does not pay. This is rubbish. It paid in Palestine, in southeast Asia, in Ireland, in various parts of Africa, in south and central America. Many of these acts were committed in what were eventually accepted as good causes, but that did not change the nature of the strategy. There are equally pious assertions that crime does not pay when it obviously pays very well. There are references to 'another pointless killing' when some unfortunate is shot at the wheel of his car. There is nothing pointless about it at all. Dead men tell no tales, and they cannot identify their assailants. So, protected from the death penalty themselves, the killers adopt the perfectly logical policy of permanently removing possible witnesses.

Be that as it may, the political change that came to South Africa in the 1990s was inevitable, logical and desirable. But the role of the newspaper journalist has not been made much easier. I retired in 1992, feeling that I was ridiculously young and that I could have gone on editing newspapers for another ten years. I don't feel that way now.

I would have been vexed by the linguistic errors that occur every day in our English papers, errors that are perhaps inevitable when one considers that we now have eleven official languages. Throughout my working life, I believed that one of the main responsibilities of the English press was to maintain a good standard of English. I used to nag reporters and subeditors about the difference between imply (to suggest) and infer (to deduce), between flaunt (to show off) and flout (to defy). I tried to persuade them that media was a plural word (the singular being medium). I battled vainly for the now almost defunct gerundive form: I object to Jack's going to town, rather than I object to Jack going to town (the objection is to the going, not to Jack).

Alas, the subtleties of the richest of all languages are now largely ignored in the media, the reason being, I suppose, that only a minority of our people have English as their home language. There are many comical errors made by people interviewed on the radio, where accents don't bother me but the standard of English does. I heard a news report in which a police officer said he had been 'defamated'. The word is defamed. Defamated sounds rude. 'Defamated on.' And, in another broadcast, an official was asked how he felt about South Africa's success in some arena of international sport. He replied: 'I'm delightful.' To be fair, these pleasant blunders were the fault of the interviewees, not the radio service.

More worrying are the occasional absurd inaccuracies and exaggerations. A financial report in one of our major newspapers was headed: 'Anglo makes huge profits out of black buyers.' This referred to the sale of Johnnic shares to the National Empowerment Consortium. The headline and the initial thrust of the report suggested that the white sellers, Anglo, had made money, probably unfairly, from the black buyers. Further down, the report revealed that Anglo American had bought the shares in 1960 and that the price charged in 1996 to the Empowerment Consortium was much higher ('huge profits'). What did the reporter expect, after 36 years? In fact, the price charged for those shares was lower than the ruling price on the Johannesburg Stock Exchange. Was the newspaper report mischievous, or ignorant, or both? I don't know.

The propensity to commit errors is sometimes matched by an equal propensity not to admit to them. A twenty-centimetre headline on the front page of the business section of several of our newspapers said: 'Old Mutual to pay dividend despite loss.' The next day, the papers published the information that the Old Mutual had actually made a profit of some R4,7-billion. The correction of this minor error appeared under a two-centimetre headline that said 'For the record'. In my day, a correction was published under a headline that said, 'Correction', and for an error of this magnitude there would have been an apology as well.

Some journalists will go through painful contortions in refusing to admit to error. I used to tell my colleagues that mistakes were bound to occur from time to time and that when they did it was best to admit the error openly and correct it. Long experience taught me that most angry critics and complainants are disarmed if you say, 'Sorry, we made a mistake, we correct it and we apologise.'

At the same time, the quest for accuracy must be endless. I have cited here some serious and comical examples of inaccurate statements, but it seems to me that a newspaper should try to be accurate in the small things as well. I remember checking a *Daily News* report that urged people to support a charity film show, saying that only a few tickets were still available. In response to my inquiry, the journalist concerned said that only a handful of tickets had been sold and that many hundreds were available. By creating a sense of shortage, she hoped to urge people on and help the charity. I told her that in my view any ticket buyer who looked at the rows of empty seats in the cinema would conclude, correctly, that the *Daily News* had misled him, and as a result the paper would suffer a small loss of credibility. A detail, but multiply that a hundredfold and there would be a big loss of credibility.

She was, of course, unimpressed.

Having uttered a few words of gentle concern about the problems of the press, let me add that there is a huge counterbalance. The media, and the newspapers in particular, are freer now than they have been at any time in the past 50 years. The intricate network of laws devised by successive Nationalist governments to silence critics and suppress facts has been removed. The constitution guarantees freedom of speech, and so far that guarantee has been honoured. The public seem at last to have recognised that press freedom belongs to them, not to the press as such. The media act as their agents or proxies, exercising their rights to be present in public affairs, from the galleries of parliament to a political meeting in Pofadder. In spite of the excesses of some excitable politicians, there is also evidence of a better appreciation of the role of the press as a watchdog, sniffing out the whiff of corruption and self-indulgence and wrongdoing.

Newspapers face an uphill road. They have lost many old readers and have not yet found many new ones. They will rectify that if they stick to the old formula of reporting the facts, including the unpalatable ones, and keeping the needs and interests of their readers in mind. Much hinges on their success or failure. The political health and reputation of South Africa will depend to a great degree on whether its newspapers will be able to maintain in the future their long tradition of publishing the news without fear or favour.

Index

Page numbers in italics relate to picture inset, pp 114–125.